International Social Attitudes

the
10th BSA
report

International Social Attitudes

the

10th BSA

report

Edited by
Roger Jowell
Lindsay Brook
& Lizanne Dowds
with Daphne Ahrendt

Published by
Dartmouth Publishing Company Limited
Gower House
Croft Road
Aldershot
Hants GU11 3HR
England

Dartmouth Publishing Company Limited
Old Post Road
Brookfield
Vermont 05036
USA

British Library Cataloguing in Publication Data

International Social Attitudes: 10th BSA Report
    I. Jowell, Roger II. Brook, Lindsay III. Dowds, Lizanne
    IV. Ahrendt, Daphne
    303.380941

ISSN 0267 6869
ISBN 1 85521 471 7 (Hbk)
ISBN 1 85521 480 6 (Pbk)

Printed in Great Britain at the University Press, Cambridge

Contents

CHAPTER 3. RELIGION, MORALITY AND POLITICS
by Anthony Heath, Bridget Taylor and Gabor Toka

CHAPTER 4. WHAT CITIZENS WANT FROM THE STATE
by Peter Taylor-Gooby

CHAPTER 5. SATISFYING WORK - IF YOU CAN GET IT
by John Curtice

Foreword

by Howard Newby*

This is the tenth annual report on British social attitudes, a decade of achievement which should not pass without receiving the recognition it deserves. The series began in 1984 and has now become a well-established fixture on the social science calendar. It has been a magnificent achievement based on foresight, professionalism and sound management. But above all, as those involved would surely acknowledge, it has been based on commitment and sheer stamina: success of this kind is only achieved through meticulous attention to detail allied to an astute sense of what is important as well as timely.

In many respects the *British Social Attitudes* (BSA) series has been in the best traditions of British social science. Translated into a modern idiom it echoes the great Victorian tradition of social enquiry and even today provides an essential complement to the Government's own *Social Trends* as a commentary on the social condition of modern Britain. Through ten years of the *British Social Attitudes* series we have come to know more about ourselves - an essential component of an open and democratic society.

Over this period the *British Social Attitudes* series has itself evolved and developed. Fascinating though the individual snapshots of attitudes undoubtedly are, the real value accumulates as changes can be tracked through time. Ten years on the information gained from the *British Social Attitudes* series has become recognisably cumulative and its value continues to be enhanced as a result. There is always a balance to be

* Chairman, Economic and Social Research Council

struck between replication and novelty and the *British Social Attitudes* series has achieved this remarkably well, allowing a secure finger to be held to the pulse of social change in Britain.

Value has also been added by linking the British study to a network of comparable studies in other countries - as this volume demonstrates all too clearly. The International Social Survey Programme (ISSP), as this network is called, now draws upon participants in 21 countries. We therefore not only have available comparisons over time, but across different cultures and nations.

In one other respect the conduct of the *British Social Attitudes* series has been exemplary. The proper dissemination of results has always been regarded as an integral part of the research process - dissemination not only to a specialist academic audience but to the wider public *via* the mass media. The data and accompanying documentation are deposited in the ESRC Data Archive at the University of Essex, where they can be accessed remotely and are available for detailed secondary analysis. The *British Social Attitudes* series therefore provides not only factual information but an important research resource.

The ESRC's involvement in the *British Social Attitudes* series has been mainly limited to funding the methodological development work and the international comparisons. The funding of the surveys themselves has come from elsewhere - most notably the Sainsbury Family Charitable Trusts. It is largely through their far-sightedness and continued support that we now possess this unique national asset. Long may it continue.

Introduction

SCPR's *British Social Attitudes* (BSA) survey series is about to enter its twelfth year. As always, we owe a debt of gratitude to the Sainsbury Family Charitable Trusts for their core-funding (since 1984) that has allowed the series not just to survive but to expand in ways that neither we nor they could have envisaged nearly a decade ago.

One of the main offshoots of the BSA series has been its participation in the *International Social Survey Programme* (ISSP). Indeed SCPR, together with US, West German and Australian colleagues, was one of the *Programme's* four founder members. Now the ISSP is a voluntary grouping of 21 study teams throughout the world, each of which undertakes to field an annual questionnaire module on an agreed topic among a nationwide, probability-based sample of adults (for further details, see Davis and Jowell, 1989, and Appendix I of this book). Current members are research centres in the following countries:

Australia	Hungary	Norway
Austria	Irish Republic	The Philippines
Britain	Israel	Poland
Bulgaria	Italy	Russia
Canada	Japan	Slovenia
Czech Republic	The Netherlands	Sweden
Germany	New Zealand	USA

Each annual questionnaire is designed by a working group representing a nominated team from several countries and is finalised at a plenary session in which all the national teams participate. New applications for ISSP membership are also decided by the whole membership, as is the programme and timetable for future modules. A list of topics fielded so far, and planned for the future, is shown below:

1985	Role of Government
1986	Family Networks and Support Systems
1987	Social Inequality
1988	Family and Changing Sex Roles
1989	Work Orientations
1990	Role of Government II (part-replication)
1991	Religion
1992	Social Inequality II (part-replication)
1993	Environment
1994	Family and Changing Gender Roles II (part-replication)
1995	National Identity
1996	Role of Government III (part-replication)

In 1989 we produced a *Special International Report,* the 6th in the annual series of *British Social Attitudes* reports, in which we presented and discussed preliminary findings from the first four ISSP modules (1985-1988). In this 10th Report, contributors have been invited not only to explore and present findings of more recent modules (up to 1991), but also to return to earlier ones to look at the results in more depth or from a different perspective. Only now do the data at last offer us a chance not only to look at between-country differences (or similarities) but also at differences *over time*. It was always the intention of the ISSP to repeat modules at (suitable) intervals[*]: for instance, as shown above, the *Role of Government* module, first asked in 1985, was asked again in 1990; the 1987 *Social Inequality* module was repeated in 1992; and the *Family and Changing Sex Roles* module is scheduled for repetition in 1994. These replications help us to investigate whether and in what respects certain social attitudes, values and beliefs change over time, but also - because we have a wealth of *other* information about each ISSP member nation - why it seems that the speed and direction of attitude change varies between countries. As some of the chapters in this volume show, there have, even over a fairly short time-span, already been some quite marked shifts in the way people in different countries see the world and themselves. But it is still too early to talk confidently of decisive trends.

---

[*] Or, at least, part-replicate modules. Despite pretesting, some items fail to work as well as hoped and are replaced, and new items are introduced to reflect fresh concerns.

This volume of *International Social Attitudes,* like its predecessor *The 6th Report,* could not have appeared without the participation, help and co-operation of our ISSP colleagues, especially the ISSP's archivists at the German *Zentralarchiv* (ZA) in Cologne. We have all come to rely heavily on the annual datatapes, as well as the codebooks that the ZA produces to document each dataset, and have an abiding admiration for the thoroughness and professionalism with which they impose order on an inherently complicated and messy set of results. British (and Northern Irish) ISSP data are also deposited each year with the rest of the BSA and NISA datasets at the ESRC Data Archive at the University of Essex.

SCPR's special thanks go to the Economic and Social Research Council (ESRC) for their contributions (since 1989) to the funding of British membership of the ISSP. This long-term funding commitment has enabled us to contribute fully to a coherent programme of cross-national scientific research. It is channelled through the *Joint Unit for the Study of Social Trends* (JUSST), an ESRC Research Centre linking SCPR and Nuffield College, Oxford. Funding for a further five years has recently been awarded to JUSST in order to develop and expand its programme of research. This new award means that British participation in the ISSP is assured until almost the end of the century, and it also includes provision for a six-monthly panel survey of voters to look at changing values and party allegiance in Britain. Thus, the productive collaboration between the long-running *British General Election Study* series and the *British Social Attitudes* survey series is to continue until at least the next general election.

Results of the latest BSA survey (1993) will soon be available, and a selection will be presented and interpreted in *The 11th Report,* which is to appear in autumn 1994. Meanwhile, the design of the 1994 survey - to be administered in all probability by interviewers using lap-top computers[*] - is now underway. As one of the pioneers of CAPI (Computer Assisted Personal Interviewing) in Britain, SCPR was fortunate enough to receive ESRC funding to mount split-run experiments (see Martin and O'Muircheartaigh, 1991), which led us to introduce this innovation into several other surveys, including the BSA series.

Participation in the ISSP is not the only way in which the *British Social Attitudes* series has become less 'insular'. Between 1989 and 1991, the Central Community Relations Unit (CCRU) in Belfast and the Nuffield Foundation provided funds to extend BSA to Northern Ireland.[**] Now all the Northern Ireland Departments have decided to support this

---

[*] In 1993, as an experiment we conducted a random half of the interviews using laptop computers.

[**] Fieldwork in Northern Ireland is conducted by interviewers from the Policy Planning and Research Unit (PPRU) in Belfast. The Nuffield Foundation also generously funded the initial meetings to plan the formation of the ISSP.

initiative for a further three years (1993-95), giving us the unique opportunity to compare attitudes regularly and systematically (*via* the ISSP) in Britain, Northern Ireland and the Republic of Ireland (see, for instance, Greeley, 1992). More recently, SCPR and social research organisations in four other countries (Germany, the Irish Republic, Italy and the Netherlands) have formed the European Consortium for Comparative Social Surveys (COMPASS), which has obtained EC funding to carry out a major cross-national study on environmental attitudes and behaviour within the EC. The data, expanding on the 1993 ISSP module on environmental issues, will be available soon.

All surveys have their perils, none more so than cross-national ventures such as the ISSP (see Davis and Jowell, 1993, pp. 4-6), and many problems in collecting comparable data have yet to be overcome. In particular, important classificatory variables (for example social class, industrial sector, educational qualifications) are minefields. Nonetheless, these problems *are* being tackled, and the ISSP datasets are now widely and productively used by social scientists throughout the world. An ever-growing list of books, articles and papers based on the seven datasets archived so far attests to the need for such data and - dare we say it - to the confidence that scholars place in them. As more countries come to deposit data, and as repeat readings multiply, the datasets become richer and more valuable. Already many tens of thousands of respondents in countries as far apart as Poland and the Philippines, Norway and Japan, have agreed to take part in ISSP surveys. Our grateful thanks, and those of our colleagues in 20 nations, go to them all.

RMJ
LLB
LD
DA

References

Davis, J. and Jowell, R. (1989), 'Measuring National Differences', in Jowell, R., Witherspoon, S. and Brook, L. (eds.), *British Social Attitudes: special international report,* Aldershot: Gower.

Greeley, A. (1992), 'Religion in Britain, Ireland and the USA', in Jowell, R., Brook, L., Prior, G. and Taylor, B. (eds.), *British Social Attitudes: the 9th Report,* Aldershot: Dartmouth.

Martin, J. and O'Muircheartaigh, C. (1991), *Evaluation of Computer Assisted Survey Systems. Report 1: Introduction to Computer Assisted Systems,* JCSM Working Paper Series No. 4, London: SCPR.

1 Disengaging from democracy

*Michael Johnston**

A democratic state is often defined as one in which only minimal governmental restraint is exercised over the political and economic choices of individuals and groups. During the euphoria that existed at the fall of communist regimes in Eastern Europe - when newly-installed governments announced early elections, guarantees for civil liberties, and plans for market economies - hopes for an orderly transition to recognisably democratic politics ran high. No one seriously believed that the transition would be easy or immediate, or that 'democracy' could be put in place merely through institutional changes. Still, it was tempting to believe that the recognition of private rights and the easing of state restrictions were at the centre of the changes taking place.

Recent events have painted a much starker picture of the potential for fundamental changes of this sort. The splitting up of Czechoslovakia, Russia's political and economic tightwire act, and even racist violence in parts of Germany remind us that, where basic democratic values and traditions have been absent, political and economic liberalisation may in the first instance lead to disorder. Civil war in the former Yugoslavia is grim proof that the aftermath of (or alternative to?) central control may be seemingly irreconcilable conflicts over land and identity in which individual rights within a civil society figure hardly at all. Although nobody these days disputes that personal liberties and choices are good

---

* Professor and Chair, Department of Political Science, Colgate University, Hamilton, New York.

things in themselves, it is increasingly apparent that they are not enough in the real world to override other considerations.

Partly in response to these events and problems, political analysts have recently directed their attention to politics as a social process, and have begun to reconsider the relationship between state and society.[1] At the heart of the issue are questions about trust in the political process, the strength and vitality of 'civil society', the legitimacy that people accord to the state (as well as to the government of the day), and popular respect for the rights of others. In a sense this is a return to classic questions and arguments raised over 150 years ago by writers such as de Tocqueville,[2] and more recently by the analysts of political culture.[3] Once again, a key question is whether, and by what mechanisms, societies can open up their politics - and their markets - while still maintaining order, and to what extent social attitudes and values will ease or obstruct the process. This chapter considers only a small part of that larger issue, focusing upon popular perceptions of the state, of politics, and of fellow-citizens in ten democratic or democratising nations. (Limited data from eastern Germany will be included as an eleventh 'nation' for purposes of comparison.) It will examine the extent to which government is (or is not) regarded as overly powerful, as well as popular interest in politics more generally, and the ways in which these factors interrelate. It will look at the extent to which government is seen to play an appropriate role in society, and at how people seek to influence it through the sanctioned political process, trusting others to do the same.

The power of government

How concerned are people about the power accorded to government? In 1990 respondents were asked to rate the power of government on a five-point scale ranging from 'far too little', through 'about right', to 'far too much'. For purposes of comparison, we asked parallel questions about the power of trade unions and business. The next figure compares the percentages in each nation saying each of the three had 'too much' or 'far too much' power:

Power of unions, business and government

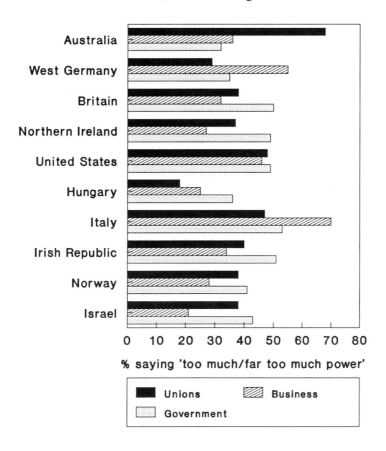

% saying 'too much/far too much power'

Unions   Business
Government

Government power appears excessive to at least a third of the adult population in every nation surveyed. In Italy (53 per cent), the Irish Republic (51 per cent), and Britain[4] (50 per cent), outright majorities voiced concern over governmental power, though the Italian result must be judged against the 70 per cent voicing concern about business power (which recent scandals seem to justify). In Australia, where the smallest percentage (32 per cent) is concerned about government power, trade unions seem to be a much greater cause for concern: around two thirds of Australians see unions as having too much or far too much power, in contrast to around a third who feel the same about government. In West Germany (this question was not asked in the former East Germany), perceptions of excessive business, union and government power exist in much the same *relative* relationship as in Italy, but the overall levels of concern are markedly lower.

In the USA, government, union, and business power are *all* significant issues. Americans seem to be apprehensive about concentrated power wherever they perceive it - perhaps not surprising in a nation with fragmented institutions, whose citizens are accustomed to witnessing ostentatious access to the political process at all levels by a great variety of interests. Hungarians, in contrast, emerging from forty years of one-party rule and confronting rapid economic and political change, are much less likely to see government nowadays as too powerful, and even fewer see business and unions as threatening. It is likely, of course, that Hungarians are judging the more liberal present especially favourably in comparison with the power of the former communist regime. Even so, Hungarians are also the most inclined among the eleven nations to say that government has too *little* power, reflecting perhaps the state of flux in a country where no single group seems yet to have gained the ascendancy.

Concern over the power of government might, of course, partly reflect distaste for the policies of the party in power. But the results resist such a straightforward interpretation. No patterns across countries with similar objective circumstances could be found, suggesting that some real 'cultural' or value differences are at work. In western Germany, for instance, where a centre-right coalition has governed for around a decade, apprehensions over business power significantly exceed concern over that of government, while Britain, after an even longer period of Conservative rule, shows the opposite pattern. Israel's results, after a dozen years of centre-right coalition politics, are not strikingly different from those found in Norway, where social democratic governments have predominated. Moreover, after ten years of being warned by Republican presidents that government power was excessive and that market-driven values should be reasserted, Americans' perceptions of government power do not differ greatly from their perceptions of business and union power.

In most democracies, then, the amount of power that should be accorded to governments appears to be a matter of mild interest and debate rather than of fierce or fundamental dispute. In seven of the ten nations, at least 40 per cent saw government power as about right, with results ranging from 43 per cent in the Irish Republic and 46 per cent in Britain up to 61 per cent in western Germany.

The economic balance

Public perceptions of government power may reflect, among other things, the extent to which political decisions and actions are seen to depend on 'clout' by one interest or another. No government is neutral, and still less likely to be seen as such. But does people's concern over the power of government depend on the extent to which they see government as too closely linked to powerful private interests? The table below shows whether perceptions of government power are also associated with perceptions of power in business or unions. Large positive correlations suggest that high levels of concern about one institution are linked with high levels of concern about the other, and large negative correlations suggest that high levels of concern about one institution are linked with *low* levels of concern about the other. A zero (or close to zero) correlation indicates no relationship at all.

Correlations between perceptions of government,
business, and trade union power

	Union and government power	Business and government power	Union and business power
Australia	.26 *	-.03	-.07 *
Britain	-.22 *	.15 *	-.08 *
Germany	-.06 *	.30 *	-.11 *
Hungary	.18 *	.31 *	.40 *
Irish Republic	.04	.15 *	.12 *
Israel	.07 *	.12 *	.10 *
Italy	.06	.06	.02
Northern Ireland	-.14 *	.17 *	.05
Norway	.13 *	-.14 *	-.19 *
USA	.06	.18 *	.02

* = statistically significant at the .05 level

These statistics have their limitations, since an association, however large, cannot tell us anything about cause and effect, or anything about an individual's reasons for responding as he or she did. Moreover, the terms themselves ('government power', 'business power' and 'trade union power') may well carry different connotations for different people in different countries.

Nonetheless, the results do reveal diverse perceptions of the state and its relationship with major economic interests. For instance, in Australia, where only a relatively small percentage of respondents rated government power as excessive, those who did also tended to rate union power as excessive. In Germany, there is an even stronger correlation between perceptions of government and business power - a reflection, perhaps, not only of a long period of centre-right government, but also of the extensive interconnections between government and business in Germany's 'social market economy'. For Norway, perceptions of government and union power are positively related and there is a marked *negative* correlation between perceptions of business and union power: thus, people who think that business has too much power tend to think that the unions have too little.

In Britain, perceptions of government and business power are positively correlated, and there is an even stronger tendency for those who regard government as too powerful to see unions as not powerful enough. Popular fears of union power were widely believed to have played a part in Mrs. Thatcher's first election victory in 1979. In 1985, an impressive three out of five British people still saw unions as excessively powerful. In 1990, however, by which time trade union power and influence had been severely curbed by successive Thatcher administrations, this concern had significantly abated (see below).

In contrast, although Americans in 1990 were more likely than the British still to judge union power as excessive, their concern over unions was not linked to perceptions of government power, perhaps because American unions had not been as politically strong as their British counterparts to begin with and because Republican Party policy had focused more on taxes and deregulation than upon anti-union action as such.[5] The perceived linkage between government and business power, noted among the British, was, however, evident among Americans too.

But perhaps the most striking American result, in terms of a balance of economic power, is the lack of a correlation between perceptions of business and union power. The two concerns seem to exist largely as separate issues, perhaps reflecting the fragmentation of American government and parties, the state's relatively limited role in the national economy, and the less acute class divisions in American politics than in Britain. In the USA, concern over government power seems to be related to issues other than the classic struggle between workers and employers.

The most intriguing results are found in Hungary and Italy. In Hungary, as we noted earlier, concern over the power of government, unions and business is not great. But the correlations above tell us that feelings about all three institutions are closely and positively associated (when we might expect the associations to be negative). Indeed, the strongest direct correlation in the entire table is between perceptions of business and union power in Hungary. This reinforces the commonsense notion that the fall of communism in Hungary was followed by a scramble for advantage in which an orderly balance among interests would take some time to emerge. The Italian findings, looked at in terms of that sort of balance, are surprising indeed. Although, as we have noted, Italians in 1990 were concerned about the power of all three institutions, uniquely among the 10 nations there was no systematic relationship between them.

A moderate pace of change

General perceptions of the power balances in society are probably more deeply-rooted and slower to change than are sentiments about current leaders and policy issues. Yet they are by no means immutable features of each nation's political culture. As influential interest groups contend over policies and access to decision makers, and as governments pursue new initiatives or withdraw old ones, perceived power relationships do demonstrably change. Since both the 1985 and the 1990 ISSP surveys included these three 'power' questions, we can compare results between 1985 and 1990 for five out of the 10 nations.

% saying 'too much' or 'far too much' power	1985	1990
Australia		
Unions	78	68
Business	35	36
Government	37	32
Britain		
Unions	59	38
Business	26	32
Government	52	50
West Germany		
Unions	36	29
Business	51	55
Government	30	35
Italy		
Unions	59	47
Business	71	70
Government	41	53
United States		
Unions	64	48
Business	49	46
Government	58	49

Although the picture is broadly one of stability rather than change, there are some noticeable shifts, even over the fairly short span of five years. The most striking change is a general decline across all countries in fears about excessive union power. In Britain, the percentage saying unions had 'too much' or 'far too much' power dropped by a third, no doubt because of the Thatcher governments' successful efforts to weaken them. (Although the 1985 data were gathered in the wake of the bitter year-long miners' strike, much the same conclusion may be drawn by comparing the results with BSA data from 1983 and 1984.) In the United States, where national policy was similarly (if less aggressively) anti-union, concern over union power dropped by about a quarter; and substantial declines were also seen in Italy and Australia.

Assessments of business power were, in contrast, less volatile, the largest absolute increases being in western Germany and Britain, while in Italy concern over the power of business remained at a high level. Concerns about excessive *government* power changed in more diverse ways, increasing in some countries, declining in others, and remaining essentially unchanged in Britain. Overall, the data reveal no fundamental reassessment of the appropriateness of government power in the five years within the five countries that were surveyed both in 1985 and 1990. They do, however, suggest a reassessment of union power, which is reassuring given the objective changes in circumstances between the two readings.

Links to the political process

While democratic politics often appear to be disorderly and riven with controversy at any given time, their virtue in the longer term is that they have a cohesive influence on society. Thus, where politics is seen as irrelevant, remote or corrupt, or where the system is seen to be breaking down in other ways, important connections between the state and its citizens tend to be weakened.

Levels of political disengagement

We asked citizens in the various countries how interested they were in politics, and found considerable variations:

Personal interest in politics

		Not at all	Not very	Somewhat	Fairly	Very
Australia	%	3	14	31	37	15
East Germany	%	6	14	39	25	16
West Germany	%	5	16	41	24	14
Britain	%	8	26	26	31	10
Northern Ireland	%	20	30	21	24	6
United States	%	7	17	36	28	13
Hungary	%	17	26	19	27	11
Italy	%	19	32	18	28	4
Irish Republic	%	16	22	28	26	8
Norway	%	3	14	42	35	7
Israel	%	15	19	25	27	14

As can be seen from the table, in none of the nations is the population utterly alienated from the political process; in six of the eleven, at least 40 per cent say they are 'fairly' or 'very' interested in politics, with Australians topping the table. But in several nations, large proportions admit to very little interest in the political process: some 51 per cent of Italians, and 50 per cent of Northern Irish, say they are 'not very' or 'not at all' interested; and in Hungary and the Irish Republic more people are uninterested than interested. Also noteworthy is the extent to which the results for eastern Germany so closely resemble those from western Germany.

Such estrangement from politics in nations which are, after all, democratic or democratising is striking and worrying. Those nations with the largest percentages of people uninterested in politics have had their troubles in recent years. Italy, for instance, has been wrestling with violence, corruption, regional divisions and frequent changes of government; the Irish Republic and Northern Ireland are caught up, in differing ways, in a long-standing struggle over religion, territory and identity; and for Hungarians 'politics', until recently, was the province of a one-party authoritarian regime. Such political changes as there have been in these countries (and there have been many on the surface at least) may have demonstrated merely that political changes *per se* have conspicuously failed to produce solutions to the pressing political and social problems, at least in the short term. Political disillusionment may therefore be a precursor or concomitant of political apathy.

Had we found the highest levels of political disengagement in western Germany, Britain, Australia or the United States, we might perhaps have interpreted them as signs of complacency, or as indications that politics was simply too commonplace in mass-media cultures to engage interest or excitement. But to find that interest is lowest in the nations that have been the most troubled is more ominous. It suggests that in these countries, where the political process ought to be offering opportunities to change things, it may instead be seen by many people as failing them and as a distant or even futile process.

The possible causal connections are complex and run in at least two directions: on the one hand, remote or ineffective governments and politicians may alienate people from politics; on the other hand, a politically-disengaged citizenry may not give politicians the support and legitimacy they require to be effective and responsive. In any event, low levels of political interest raise questions about the extent and reliability of support upon which governments can draw when (or if) they seek to establish national goals or defend established rights. While all democracies live in conditions of greater or lesser disorder and manage to fulfil their citizens' wishes only imperfectly at best, it is striking that in the three or four nations in our study which could clearly benefit most from close and reliable political links between state and citizenry, popular disengagement from the political process runs deep.

There is a fascinating contrast between Hungary and eastern Germany. Both experienced the collapse of one-party communist regimes in the late 1980s, with the former DDR, thought by many to be one of the least likely candidates for change, collapsing much more abruptly than the old Hungarian order. Both are enduring the shock of re-immersion in the world economy. Yet the eastern Germans report levels of political interest much higher than those of the Hungarians, and indeed roughly equal to those of their fellow-citizens in the west. Is this because in 1990 the East Germans were being assimilated into an established political and party system with which many had already become familiar, *via* travel and West German television, in the preceding decade? Politics in the *Bundesrepublik* is open and accessible: and in the run-up to unification, the parties and leading politicians of the Federal Republic virtually took over mass politics in the east. This is not to minimise the dislocations and resentments which that process may have created; among the early casualties were the nascent social movements, such as *Neues Forum*, which had done so much to organise support for change in the east but which were then overwhelmed by the established western parties. Nor can we be certain that German data from 1993 would produce the same results. (The ISSP is not due to repeat these questions until 1996.) Nonetheless, the former East German citizens who found themselves in a Germany with established parties and leaders stand in sharp contrast to Hungarians who had gone through a similar upheaval 'on their own'. There, a political system which had at least been predictable was suddenly filled with new parties, slogans and unfamiliar procedures. Hungarians could be forgiven for viewing that new opportunist political atmosphere with considerable scepticism.

To be sure, democratic politics works best when there is some 'slack' in the system - that is, when there is a core of politically uncommitted people, groups, and political resources whose presence can moderate most conflicts and encourage negotiation and compromise (Dahl, 1961). But too much disengagement from the mainstream political process is not a healthy sign. People who do not care about politics are by no means necessarily apathetic about social issues or public affairs. Indeed, they may care intensely about these things. But when those issues become most pressing, they may be less likely to express themselves through legitimate political means, or to make their choices from among alternatives enjoying broad social support, or (as we shall see) less inclined strongly to support the rights of others.

Sources of political disengagement

As with perceptions of government power, popular disengagement from politics could have many causes. Not surprisingly, perhaps, the data reveal no strong links between level of interest in politics and people's stance on various policy issues (redistributive taxation, government responsibilities for social welfare, regulation of business, and so on). After all, those who tend to be uninterested in politics are probably less likely than others to have any systematic outlook on the main political issues of the day, and *vice versa*. Low levels of political interest seem instead to be a function of marginal status within (or a history of exclusion from) mainstream politics; for instance, as the next table shows, women in *all* the countries for which we have data are considerably less interested in politics than are men:

% 'not very' or 'not at all' interested in politics	Women	Men
Australia	20	13
Britain	40	25
East Germany	23	18
West Germany	28	14
Hungary	52	32
Irish Republic	45	32
Israel	39	28
Italy	61	40
Northern Ireland	55	45
Norway	20	14
United States	27	20

So in Italy, Hungary, Northern Ireland and the Irish Republic - where there are relatively high levels of political disengagement generally - this is particularly the case among women. But in Australia and Norway - where the opposite is true - women's interest in politics *still* lags behind that of men. Indeed, the tendency is for the 'gender gap' to be the greatest where general disengagement is the most widespread. Doubtless there are variations in the political status of women across the eleven nations, but it still seems to be the case that women, who have almost universally been accorded a secondary role in politics, are (as a result, perhaps?) less interested in the process as a whole. The same is true of manual workers, often despite being well-represented in bargaining with government.

Once again, comparisons between eastern and western Germany are of interest. In both regions, women are apparently more distanced from politics than are men, but in eastern Germany the gap was significantly lower than in the west. Despite the many faults of the old DDR, women there were accorded a variety of protections and entitlements that they are not given in the Federal Republic, such as extensive day care provisions for children, job guarantees, and a liberal abortion policy (Ardagh, 1991). Perhaps these benefits, or the prospect of losing them, caused women there to be relatively less estranged from politics.

In any event, these results suggest that low levels of political interest are not just reactions to the government of the day but have historical and structural roots. They are associated crucially with the estrangement of traditionally marginal constituencies - a condition that probably thrives on lower levels of income among these groups, linked to prejudice and barriers which block their access to influence and office. We will return to this theme later in this chapter.

The democratic balance, the policy process and civil liberties

So far we have found strong evidence that the eleven democratic or democratising societies represented in this survey vary considerably in terms of popular perceptions of governmental power, and in terms of interest in politics generally. We have suggested that, in some of those nations at least, such findings may be reason for concern about the vitality of the relationships between state and citizenry. Weak relationships of this kind tend to create problems for orderly policy debates, to erode support for civil liberties and to diminish trust in the political process. In this section we explore these aspects of the balance between state and society.

The policy debate

It might be argued that survey results showing widespread concern about the power of government simply reflect the fact that some governments *are* actually more powerful than others. If this were the case, arguments about political estrangement, based on these data, would be at best premature.

Many factors can affect perceptions of government power. Do officials and institutions appear to be remote and insensitive rather than approachable and respectful of the values and customs of the population? Do ethnic or regional divisions specific to a given country make generalisations about the nation as a whole misleading?

However, as our earlier findings show, concern over government power does not seem to be a direct function of political circumstances, or of social provision, or even of citizens' assessments of the health of the national economy. The correlations shown earlier suggest instead that perceptions of government power are associated more with political balance, that is with the access and influence that the system offers to various interests in society. So assessments of excessive government power seem to depend not so much (or not only) on what governments do, as on broader questions of accessibility and responsiveness. This point will become clearer from an examination of how public perceptions of government power relate to views on major issues of public policy.

Modern nations have a number of policy problems in common which help to define the terms of the debate over the role of the state: do people favour an aggressive, interventionist government, or do they see its appropriate role as considerably more limited? At what point does government overstep those expectations? Chapter 4 in this volume contains details about cross-national attitudes towards government intervention in the economy. But a few general comparisons are useful here to reveal connections between opinions on policy and perceptions of the state.

The next table presents results for five questions[6] covering attitudes to taxation, spending, the regulation of business and job-creation - basic functions that help define the extent of power that government can legitimately have and use. To facilitate comparisons, countries are rank-ordered according to the percentages saying that government had too much or far too much power in each respect.

		Tax the rich	Cut spending	Less regulation	Spend for jobs	Provide jobs for all
% favouring each item[*]	(%**)					
Italy	(53)	84	70	43	90	85
Ireland	(51)	83	(na)	(na)	(na)	71
Britain	(50)	85	42	43	83	63
USA	(49)	62	78	41	70	44
N. Ireland	(49)	86	43	45	87	76
Israel	(43)	77	91	60	88	88
Norway	(41)	75	71	53	84	84
Hungary	(36)	85	82	73	77	89
W. Germany	(35)	87	76	37	73	74
Australia	(32)	66	75	53	70	42

*   The table shows percentages favouring a 'much larger' or 'larger' tax burden for the wealthy; 'strongly in favour'/'in favour' of spending cuts, less regulation, and government spending for jobs; and saying government 'definitely' or 'probably' should provide jobs for all who want them.
**   % rating government power excessive.

It is immediately apparent from the table that the rank-ordering in terms of concern over government power does not reflect an underlying ordering in economic terms. Neither the relatively successful nor the troubled economies cluster together, nor do countries in which the government is generally interventionist or *laissez-faire.* More to the point, there seems to be little connection between perceptions of excessive government power and preferences on these five major policy issues. (Indeed, on the item that comes closest to a systematic pattern - whether government should spend money to create jobs - some of the countries in which government power is most widely seen as excessive are also ones in which more people *favour* government action - though even this connection is weak.) Of course, these issues scarcely exhaust the range of important policy options, and the objective variation in policy on nearly all these items is different in each country. Nonetheless, if judgements of government power were indeed highly related to opinions about policy options, we would have expected *some* relationship between the two on a number of issues.

But before jumping to the conclusion that it is government power itself - not what government does with its power - that is the overriding issue, we must consider the possibility that the relationships between perceptions of government and policy issues are qualitatively different in differing political settings. Thus, where people see politics and the issues it tackles as relevant to their concerns (and so worthy of their attention), we might expect them to judge government power according to the sorts of things they think government ought or ought not to be involved with. But where large numbers of people are estranged from the process, then the issues debated and promises made in the formal political arena may come to seem irrelevant. In these cases, competition for power and the use politicians make of it may seem to be more a matter of personal concern to politicians, remote (or even hidden) from the public. Under those conditions, the links between perceptions of government power and policy issues might weaken or break down.

We examined this possibility, again using correlation statistics, to look at associations between responses to the five policy items above and ratings of government's power. And the results are generally consistent with the argument above. The countries in which larger than average proportions of the population show an interest in politics are indeed the ones where perceptions of government power are more closely linked to policy issues. Those in which people tend to be less interested are the ones where the relationships become weaker and less consistent: in those societies - notably Italy, Northern Ireland and Hungary - the perception that government is too powerful seems to transcend policy preferences. Since it is likely that people in these societies are also less informed about those issues or distracted by deeper problems, this is bound to further weaken the links between policy preferences and perceptions of state power, and also discourage openly competitive policy debates.

So the data certainly lend support to our interpretation that the 'power-of-government' items do indeed tap relationships between state and the citizenry, rather than simply pass judgement on the activities of the government of the day. They also add force to the argument that a healthy balance between state and society involves more than just limiting the power of government. If people are to work out their differences in an open and orderly way, they must first reach some consensus on the issues of moment, believe that the options are genuine, and regard the political process as worth the time and energy it requires. Otherwise, key democratic linkages between state and the citizenry are bound to come under considerable stress.

Civil liberties

The idea of a democratic balance also extends to relationships within society. The sort of open politics described above requires mutual tolerance and support for the rights of others to express differing views. Questions on civil liberties, therefore, are important not simply as indicators of the depth of commitment to democratic values in themselves, but also for what they may suggest about levels of trust among citizens and about the general state of politics as a social process.

The next table shows the percentages of people in each nation who say they would 'definitely allow' people to take part in three forms of protest activity - protest meetings, publications, and demonstrations - "against a government action they strongly oppose". The figures are broken down by levels of interest in politics. The pattern is strong and clear: those who say they are interested in politics are most likely to tolerate various protest activities, while those who are disengaged from the process give much weaker support. National contrasts can still be seen: for instance, even among British respondents who are 'not very' or 'not at all' interested in politics, around three in five would still 'definitely' allow participation in protest meetings - results roughly equal to those among the *most* politically-interested in the Irish Republic and Northern Ireland. Within nations too the pattern is strong and consistent,[7] and this linkage between political interest and tolerance of protest is replicated (with varying degrees of strength) for a number of other civil-liberties items not shown here.

Those who are interested in politics are, of course,the most likely to be familiar with the contrasting views and interests of their fellow-citizens, and perhaps to have some sense of the processes of debate and interchange involved in reaching mutually acceptable decisions. Given that the politically-interested are also likely to be among those with the strongest political preferences, it is salutary that they are nonetheless the most supportive - in all the countries surveyed - of the right of others to disagree publicly and, if necessary, to protest actively against government actions and policies.

Tolerance of the right to protest

% saying they would 'definitely allow'	Level of interest in politics				
	Very	Fairly	Somewhat	Not very	Not at all
Australia					
meetings	72	55	48	40	46
publications	64	47	39	30	38
demonstrations	48	33	28	25	35
Britain					
meetings	79	67	64	57	62
publications	73	57	56	45	49
demonstrations	65	46	37	31	33
East Germany					
meetings	72	62	51	44	42
publications	42	32	21	19	14
demonstrations	59	55	42	37	35
West Germany					
meetings	67	62	51	44	42
publications	54	48	32	19	24
demonstrations	59	54	37	23	26
Hungary					
meetings	68	57	42	42	33
publications	43	38	24	24	23
demonstrations	54	46	29	28	18
Irish Republic					
meetings	61	59	53	46	42
publications	59	53	43	37	38
demonstrations	45	47	39	32	29
Israel					
meetings	80	74	66	58	54
publications	71	64	57	49	45
demonstrations	74	69	60	52	50
Northern Ireland					
meetings	61	57	56	48	37
publications	61	47	45	35	36
demonstrations	46	35	33	28	17
Norway					
meetings	90	82	73	66	61
publications	83	76	63	61	57
demonstrations	73	68	57	47	50
United States					
meetings	67	58	41	34	42
publications	58	50	35	30	34
demonstrations	57	48	29	25	29

N.B. Questions on tolerance of protest activities were not asked in Italy.

We also asked whether people should obey the law without exception, or whether following one's conscience on occasion was acceptable, "even if it means breaking the law". In most nations the respondents who were less interested in politics were more likely than their politically-engaged counterparts to say that the law should always be obeyed. This connection is not as strong as that in respect of the right to protest, nor as consistent across nations. But where it is clearest - in the two Germanies, the two Irelands, Hungary and the United States - it lends added support to the notion that those who are most estranged from the political process are the least likely to trust, or to be trusted by, their fellow citizens.

Restrictive or censorious attitudes towards civil liberties may have many origins, ranging from personality or cultural factors (such as a low tolerance for disorder or uncertainty), to ignorance (unfamiliarity with the existence of other viewpoints or with the powers of the state), to value orientations (a credo which holds that certain protest actions are, *per se,* an abuse of a free society), to simple faith which persuades them that, however bad governments might be, protesters are always likely to be worse. Nonetheless, it appears to be very important to the bulk of citizens in the societies surveyed (and to an even greater proportion of the politically aware) that although most important procedures of democratic politics should be guaranteed by government itself, citizens too should be allowed to be vigilant on their own behalf, even when they are saying or doing things against the mainstream. Notably, however, even the politically-interested in Hungary and eastern Germany are still relatively ambivalent about protecting freedom to publish. Could it be, perhaps, that the more politically-interested in those two countries tend to be those who were formerly more active in the communist party, and who are still coming to terms with the startling changes in their countries?

Conclusion

We have found that people who regard government as too powerful tend to have a lower than average interest in politics. This is not unlike the thesis by Galbraith (1992), which argues that the 'contented' are the most likely to participate in a democracy. What then can these two measures of 'estrangement' from the political process tell us about the state of health of democratic politics in the nations under study?

The next figure offers a tentative look at this question. Nations are plotted in terms of the percentages claiming not to be interested in politics ('not very' or 'not at all'), and those saying that government is 'far too powerful':

Perceived power of government in relation to interest in politics

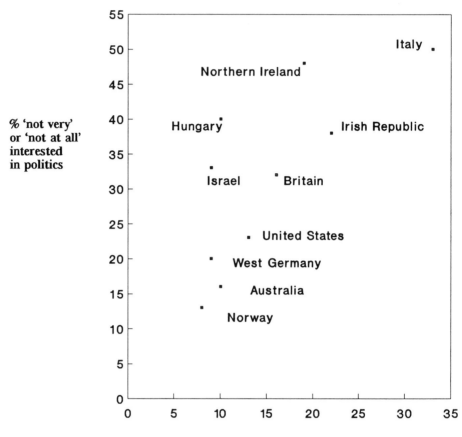

% saying government has 'far too much power'

In theory we might have expected a connection between apprehensiveness about government power and *high* levels of political interest in countries such as these where citizens concerned about government power are free to try to do something about it. But the trend is strongly the reverse: high levels of concern over governmental power are associated with high levels of political apathy or estrangement, and the association becomes stronger the greater the concern about government power.[8] In contrast, where government is widely seen as having about the right amount of power, people are generally more interested in the established political process. In sum, one kind of political estrangement apparently begets another.

Which comes first? Survey data can never answer that sort of question, but (speculatively) one type of disengagement almost certainly feeds off the other. Thus, those who believe that governments are all-powerful might well begin to regard politics as an exercise in futility. Similarly, those who have little interest in politics may well come to regard government itself as the tool of a few powerful individuals or interests, or as a remote embodiment of power itself.

The cross-national contrasts apparent in the figure are not particularly surprising. Italy, for instance, has been witnessing mounting evidence of exceptional corruption at the highest levels of politics and business. Although the most recent events postdate our survey, suspicion of politicians and of political institutions is certainly long-standing there. Germany, in contrast, has also had an unsettled public life in recent years, as euphoria over unification has given way to economic stress and outbreaks of anti-immigrant violence. But there popular responses, as seen at the polls and in the 'candlelight marches' against racism, have tended to be much more supportive of the established order.

The three societies that diverge furthest from the overall pattern - that is, those with significantly higher levels of political disengagement than we would expect on the basis of perceptions of government alone - are Israel, Northern Ireland, and Hungary. In the first two, where national life has been marked by high levels of violence and direct threats to society, it is no wonder perhaps that people should express low interest in 'politics-as-usual'. Rather, they are more likely to be concerned in the short term about bullets rather than ballots. In Hungary, of course, decades of no political change gave way suddenly to a period in which virtually everything has changed. People there need to relocate their expectations and judgements in an atmosphere in which belief itself is probably still suspended. In that atmosphere too, a question about interest in politics is hardly apposite.

It is tempting to select two or three nations from those surveyed and to describe their condition as one of political crisis. But such a conclusion would be uncalled for on the basis of these data. First, we are looking at only a few of the many aspects of government-citizenry relationships, and even so on very limited evidence. Second, when considering the health of a democratic system, it is not always clear just what is the good news and what is the bad. For instance, is it a healthy or unhealthy sign in Italy that people are deeply sceptical of a system which has apparently countenanced corruption on a large scale? Is the presence of the United States in the lower left-hand quadrant of the figure a solid indicator of healthy politics, or do we also need to remember that, given the opportunity to choose the most powerful elected official in the world, only about half the adult population can apparently be bothered to vote?

Democratic societies, with their rough-and-tumble competition among private interests and their determination that they can be both effectively governed and essentially free, are to do with disorder as well as order - indeed, they derive great vitality from disorder. Perhaps the essence of a vital democracy is that it is always just a few steps away from a crisis.

On the other hand, discontent with one part of the political system apparently spreads to other parts as well, with the result that some of the nations in the study face much bigger challenges in reconciling government with their people than do others. Further, while no one would dispute the idea that material well-being has much to do with political opinions (see, for instance, Inglehart, 1990), the data presented here do not support any attempt to link perceptions of the nation's political health with perceptions of its economic health. True, some of the most affluent of the nations are concentrated in the lower-left corner of the figure; but Australia has endured significant economic difficulties during the past decade, while Italy (in the top right corner) has grown (albeit unevenly, in regional terms) into the world's fifth-largest industrial power. Beyond 'pocketbook politics' lies a complex realm of perceptions and expectations, commitments and estrangement that help define the relationships between government and citizens.

However comforting the thought, it is therefore highly improbable that the newly-democratising states of central Europe and the former USSR have only(!) to revive their economies for a revitalised democracy to begin to emerge. On the contrary, economic change of any sort, growth included, tends to lead to renewed debate over the role of the state, over the distribution of wealth, and over political structures as a means of addressing both questions. Without a widely shared set of political values and perceptions, economic growth can produce further disorder. This may have implications for the West's policies on aid - in particular that it should be supplemented by efforts to encourage the growth of the intermediate institutions of civil society. It is also doubtless critical to appreciate that the way in which benefits are *seen* to be allocated, and how decisions are *seen* to be reached, is probably at least as important as the outcomes themselves. As for the more established democracies, these results provide little room for self-congratulation, even in the post cold-war era. There too democracy is a delicate social and institutional balancing act - not so much a permanent achievement as a continuing experiment.

Notes

1. For example (Cohen and Arato, 1992; Devine, 1991; Huntington, 1991; Perez Diaz, 1993; Rau, 1991; Rothchild and Chazan, 1988; Sartori, 1991; Seligman, 1992; Shils, 1991; Walzer, 1991).
2. See the translated edition; de Tocqueville, A. (1969), *Democracy in America,* (J. Mayer, ed.; G. Lawrence, trans.), New York: Harper and Row.
3. For example (Almond, 1963; Almond and Verba, 1980; Brint, 1991; Chilton, 1991; Inglehart, 1977; 1990; Nevitte and Gibbins, 1990).
4. 'Britain' as used in this chapter refers to Great Britain only, and not the United Kingdom, since data are reported separately for Northern Ireland. References to Britain and Northern Ireland as two out of ten 'nations' are made here only for the sake of brevity, and are not intended to imply an argument about Northern Ireland's place within the United Kingdom.
5. While the Reagan administration did pursue a number of anti-union measures, such as changes in picketing laws and seeking to deny food stamps to strikers, its most visible anti-union move - the dismissal of unionised air traffic controllers - occurred

in the first months of President Reagan's first term. Even so, for most of the rest of the 1980s, American labour unions were politically very much on the defensive.

6. "Here are some things the government might do for the economy. Please show which actions you are in favour of and which you are against."

"Cuts in government spending?"
"Government financing of projects to create new jobs?"
"Less government regulation of business?"

(The response categories were: Strongly in favour of, In favour of, Neither in favour of nor against, Against, Strongly against.)

"Some people think those with high incomes should pay a larger proportion (percentage) of their earnings than those who earn low incomes. Other people think that those with high incomes and those with low incomes should pay the same proportion (percentage) of their earnings in taxes. Do you think those with **high** incomes should...

...pay a **much larger** proportion
pay a **larger** proportion
pay the **same** proportion as those who earn low incomes
pay a **smaller** proportion
pay a **much smaller** proportion?"

"On the whole, do you think it should or should not be the government's responsibility to...provide a job for everyone who wants one?"

(The response categories were: Definitely should be, Probably should be, Probably should not be, Definitely should not be.)

7. For all percentage breakdowns in the table, except for the tolerance of protest publications in Northern Ireland, the associations between support for civil liberties and political interest, and the linear nature of that association, are statistically significant at the .01 level; for protest publications in Northern Ireland, the significance statistics are still quite strong at .015 and .03 respectively.

8. This figure presents nation-by-nation aggregate results, but the pattern was discernible at the individual level as well.

References

Almond, G. (1963), *The Civic Culture: Political Attitudes and Democracy in Five Nations*, Princeton, New Jersey: Princeton University Press.

Almond, G. and Verba, S. (eds.) (1980), *The Civic Culture Revisited: An Analytic Study*, Boston: Little, Brown.

Ardagh, J. (1991), *Germany and the Germans*, London: Penguin.

Brint, M. (1991), *A Genealogy of Political Culture*, Boulder, Colorado: Westview Press.

Chilton, S. (1991), *Grounding Political Development*, Boulder, Colorado: Lynne Rienner.

Cohen, J. and Arato, A. (1992), *Civil Society and Political Theory*, Cambridge, Massachusetts: MIT Press.

Dahl, R. (1961), *Who Governs?*, NewHaven: Yale University Press.

Devine, P. (1991), 'Economy, State and Civil Society', *Economy and Society*, 20.

Galbraith, J. K. (1992), *The Culture of Contentment*, Boston: Houghton Mifflin.

Huntington, S. (1991), *The Third Wave: Democratization in the Late Twentieth Century*, Norman, Oklahoma: University of Oklahoma Press.

Inglehart, R. (1977), *The Silent Revolution: Changing Values and Political Styles among Western Publics*, Princeton, New Jersey: Princeton University Press.

Inglehart, R. (1990), *Culture Shift in Advanced Industrial Society*, Princeton, New Jersey: Princeton University Press.

Nevitte, N. and Gibbins, R. (1990), *New Elites in Old States: Ideologies in the Anglo-American Democracies*, Oxford: Oxford University Press.

Perez Diaz, V. (1993), *The Return of Civil Society: the Emergence of Democratic Spain*, Cambridge, Massachusetts: Harvard University Press.

Rau, Z. (ed.) (1991), *The Reemergence of Civil Society in Eastern Europe and the Soviet Union*, Boulder, Colorado: Westview Press.

Rothchild, D. and Chazan, N. (eds.) (1988), *The Precarious Balance: State and Society in Africa*, Boulder, Colorado: Westview Press.

Sartori, G. (1991), 'Rethinking Democracy: Bad Polity and Bad Politics', *International Social Science Journal*, XLIII.

Seligman, A. (1992), *The Idea of Civil Society*, New York: Free Press.

Shils, E. (1991), 'The Virtue of Civil Society', *Government and Opposition*, 26.

Walzer, M. (1991), 'The Idea of Civil Society', *Dissent*, 38, Spring, 1991.

2 The family way

Jacqueline Scott, Michael Braun and Duane Alwin*

It is almost a cliché nowadays that the traditional nuclear family is becoming a somewhat endangered species. Some refer to the changing family, others to its decline. One thing is certain: people today feel they have more choice than before: for instance, whether to cohabit before marrying or to marry at all; whether and when to have children, and how many; whether to stay in an unhappy marriage or to separate or divorce. In practice, of course, people's choices are still heavily constrained by economic and social circumstances. Nonetheless, the range of acceptable and feasible family options seems to have expanded enormously, with fewer and fewer seeming to be beyond the pale.

In this chapter we explore international differences in family options using comparable data from the questionnaire module on Family and Changing Gender Roles, which was fielded in 1988 as part of the *International Social Survey Programme* (ISSP). The exact wording of questions is given in Appendix III. We pay particular attention to British attitudes and compare them with their European and American counterparts.

As we shall see, it would be premature to mourn the loss of traditional family values in Britain, or, for that matter, in Europe or the USA. For

---

* Jacqueline Scott is Director of Research at the ESRC Centre for Micro-social Change in Britain, University of Essex; Michael Braun is Director of the German General Social Survey at Zentrum für Umfragen, Methoden und Analysen, Mannheim, Germany; and Duane F. Alwin is Professor of Sociology and Program Director at the Survey Research Center, University of Michigan, Ann Arbor, USA.

instance, most people in all the countries surveyed regard children as an important, if not essential, part of a marriage. Yet there are some signs of strain. Women, in particular, are not at all certain that marriage is a recipe for happiness, and are more likely than men to favour divorce if the marriage goes wrong. And there are also signs of change. Support for traditional gender roles is eroding: for instance, although there is a widespread belief that mothers should stay at home when they have *young* children, there is also an acceptance that they should work both to maintain their independence and as a matter of economic necessity for the family.

So traditional family values now co-exist with values of individual autonomy and gender equality, allowing people's options to become more and more a matter of choice rather than expectation.

In this chapter, we compare our findings in Britain with those in the Irish Republic, West Germany and the United States.[1] We look first at the institution of marriage, then at the decision to marry and have children, then at the dual role of women at home and work, and lastly at the more contentious issues of divorce, single parenting and homosexual marriage.

Decline of the nuclear family?

There are profound objective changes in the structure, composition and functioning of the family throughout Europe and North America. Birth rates, for instance, have reached an all-time low and, with the exception of Ireland, fertility rates in most European countries have dropped below population replacement level. This trend towards smaller families is accompanied by an increase in non-traditional family forms at the expense of the traditional nuclear family. So more and more people are living alone, or living together outside marriage. Divorce rates have reached an all time high in Britain, and there has been a dramatic increase in the number of single-parent families, mainly because of marital dissolution but also because of births out of wedlock. Taken together, despite the fact that many of the family's basic socialisation functions with respect to children have remained intact, these other changes amount to a dramatic shift in the social organisation of the family.

The growth of feminism may have contributed to many of these trends. Yet, while changes in family forms have occurred, many of the traditional gender-roles have remained steadfast. For instance, around 90 per cent or more of single-parent families tend to be headed by women, with men remaining relatively distant, or even absent, from the daily demands of child-rearing activities (Furstenberg and Cherlin, 1991). This does not mean that 'modern men', who take their share of household chores and childcare tasks, do not exist. In fact there is some evidence that men *have* increased the time spent on routine domestic tasks and childcare, but only by a small amount (Gershuny and Robinson, 1988). It does mean, however, that the 'traditional man' is far from an endangered species. In many instances the increase in the number of households headed by women reflects other more basic social changes affecting the family, notably the unprecedentedly high levels of divorce and remarriage nowadays (Björnberg, 1992). Ireland, with its strong Catholic tradition (Greeley, 1992) and where divorce is still illegal, offers a stark exception.* In Europe, trends towards secularisation have helped undermine the once sacred marital vows that imply chastity before, and fidelity within, marriage. In addition, the contraceptive pill, the women's movements, and the growing economic independence of women, have doubtless helped to make the traditional marriage contract somewhat less durable than in the past. Moreover, people's first marriages tend to be later in life than they used to be, partly because of the extension of higher education, and partly because cohabitation has become a viable, socially acceptable alternative in many European countries and in the United States.

But perhaps the most potent force that has undermined traditional family arrangements in western Europe and the USA has been the steady rise in the proportion of women in paid work, especially those with young children (Björnberg, 1992). Naturally, for many women work is simply an economic imperative (Braun, Scott and Alwin, forthcoming). But for many it also stems from a desire for independence which challenges the traditional gender roles of the man as breadwinner and the woman as responsible for the family and children.

None of these factors are, of course, likely to overturn traditional gender role behaviour and attitudes overnight. It remains true that in most western countries large majorities still favour a primary familial role for women, especially when there are young children in the family. Moreover many women opt for employment arrangements that accommodate family life as much as possible (Scott and Duncombe, 1991), stopping work altogether when the children are very young and then working only part-time: in Britain in the mid 1980s, for instance, 45 per cent of all women employees worked less than 30 hours per week (Eurostat, 1991). Even so, the increase in maternal employment does raise a number of contentious issues in respect of child-rearing and childcare, and strong cross-national differences in attitudes towards such issues are bound to exist alongside marked differences in family policy and in the availability of childcare services (Kamerman, 1991).

There are undoubtedly more changes in the pipeline. For instance, children in some countries are already beginning to flex their legal muscle by taking their parents to court. As gay rights movements increase their momentum, marriage between homosexuals may become a political issue

---

* In 1989, however, the law was changed to allow 'no-fault' judicial separation which, while allowing the couple to live apart, does not permit remarriage.

in Europe and North America, as may the right of gay and lesbian couples to adopt children.

We focus in this chapter on the likely direction, nature and sources of social change in the family, examining whether there is any supporting evidence for Popenoe's (1988) claim that people increasingly favour individualism and self-fulfilment above family commitment. In pursuing this question we examine international differences on topics such as the desirability of marriage and attitudes towards cohabitation; whether the purpose of marriage is viewed more in terms of companionship than procreation or financial support; how much value is placed on children; and the acceptability of divorce and lone parent families.

In our preliminary analysis of these issues, described in *The 7th Report* (Scott, 1990), we suggested that women were in the vanguard of change. In this chapter, we examine whether British women's decreasingly traditional and more egalitarian views hold true across different countries and cultures. We will also examine how far there is a generation gap in family values throughout Europe and North America, and whether younger cohorts are disturbing, or even destroying, long-standing family values.

Cohabitation and marriage

We asked respondents what advice they would give - first to a young woman, then to a young man - as to whether to live alone, live with a steady partner without marrying, live together and then marry, or marry without living together first. There is little or no evidence of a double standard in the advice given, as the recommendations for both a young man and a young women are substantially the same. Moreover both male and female respondents give very similar advice.

Advice would give to a young woman[*]

	Britain	Irish Republic	USA	West Germany
	%	%	%	%
Live alone without a steady partner	4	3	9	5
Live with steady partner, without marrying	4	1	3	11
Live with steady partner and then marry	43	32	26	50
Marry without living together first	37	59	46	19

[*] advice for a young man is substantially the same

As the table shows, the majority of the British, Irish, Americans and Germans advise a young person ultimately to marry, with or without prior cohabitation, though the Germans are clearly the most suspicious of marriage. Not surprisingly the Irish, with their strong Catholic tradition, adopt the most traditional view, the majority of them urging young people to marry without living together first. The Americans and the British fall in between, with the British a little closer to the Germans and the Americans a lot closer to the Irish.

Only a few decades ago living together was definitely something shocking. Now cohabitation without marriage is commonplace and a vast majority of young people regard sex before marriage as perfectly acceptable (Kiernan, 1992). It seemed to us likely, however, that older generations who grew up in an era of stricter sexual morality, would be far less likely to endorse cohabitation than would the young. Older women, in particular, might adopt the role of protector of traditional family values and urge marriage, while younger men might be the most favourable to cohabitation without commitment.

% advising marriage without living together first (by birth cohorts)

	Total	Men born in ...			Women born in ...		
		1950-1970	1930-1949	Pre-1930	1950-1970	1930-1949	Pre-1930
Britain	37	17	41	64	17	46	61
Irish Republic	59	38	68	86	44	69	86
USA	46	32	46	65	36	49	65
West Germany	19	6	18	39	8	22	40

In fact, older people in all four countries *are* much more likely than younger cohorts to recommend that a young person should marry without first cohabiting, but older women are no different from older men in supporting traditional family values. In Britain and Germany, both young men and women overwhelmingly reject the option of marriage without living together first, although (as we have seen) a clear majority still recommends eventual marriage. Given the overwhelming endorsement of marriage by the Irish and the relative suspicion of it by Germans, we anticipated that these same national differences would be apparent in more general beliefs about marriage, such as whether married people are generally happier than unmarried people.

% agreeing that married people are generally happier than unmarried people

	Total	Men born in ...			Women born in ...		
		1950-1970	1930-1949	Pre-1930	1950-1970	1930-1949	Pre-1930
Britain	33	19	40	59	15	33	56
Irish Republic	46	40	61	64	30	43	61
USA	51	43	59	71	36	48	67
West Germany	38	23	49	59	21	40	54

Indeed it is the British and Germans who are least convinced that married people are any happier than the unmarried, while Americans appear to have a touching faith that marriage is a recipe for happiness. Ironically, the United States has gone further than any European country, except Sweden, in making marriages easy to end. Perhaps, therefore, the term 'happy marriage' is becoming a tautology to Americans, since only happy couples stay married!

The marital experience is, of course, quite different for men and for women. It is now two decades since the American sociologist and feminist writer Jessie Bernard (1973) suggested that there are two marriages, the wife's and the husband's. Since both historically and in contemporary society men have derived more (objective) benefits from marriage than have women, it is hardly surprising that men and women should have different outlooks. Things are changing. We have already noted that the time men spend on household chores is increasing, if only by a small amount. Far more significantly, perhaps, women nowadays spend a much smaller proportion of their time than they used to on routine domestic tasks (Gershuny and Robinson, 1988). Yet, although domestic work might be more evenly shared by couples than in the past, it is still true that women, even when in full-time employment, bear the brunt of the 'double shift', and remain primarily responsible for both childcare and chores in the home (Witherspoon and Prior, 1991).

Marriage and happiness

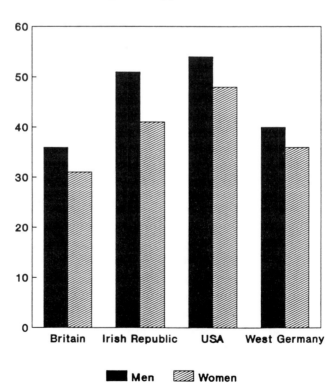

% agreeing married people are happier than unmarried people

So it is not surprising that in all four countries, for the time being at any rate, women are consistently less convinced than men that marriage brings happiness, with the gender gap the greatest in the Irish Republic where family values are the most traditional.

Women's greater scepticism about marital happiness may help explain why they are (as we shall see) more favourable than men towards the escape route of divorce. However, it is important not to exaggerate this gender gap since, as the next table shows, men and women have very similar views about the purposes of marriage. The table also shows that men and women alike overwhelmingly reject the notion that a bad marriage is better than no marriage at all.

Although men and women share the same attitudes in each country, there are some interesting country differences in these answers. Once again, it comes as little surprise that Ireland is the most likely of the four countries to endorse the view that the main purpose of marriage is to have children. Americans are relatively unlikely to support any notion that marriage has an instrumental main purpose - whether it be children or financial security - presumably because they tend to see marriage more as an end in itself. Marrying for financial security does, however, receive high support in Germany, where the existing tax policy clearly favours married couples.

	Britain		Irish Republic		USA		West Germany	
	Men	Women	Men	Women	Men	Women	Men	Women
% agreeing that:								
People who want children ought to get married	72	69	83	81	74	70	73	74
The main purpose of marriage is to have children	21	19	34	30	12	11	27	29
The main advantage of marriage is financial security	18	18	23	22	15	17	30	34
Personal freedom is more important than the companionship of marriage	10	13	16	15	16	14	15	13
It is better to have a bad marriage than no marriage at all	3	2	6	4	6	4	5	4

When we look at attitudes of different birth cohorts to the first statement above ("people who want children ought to get married") we find, as expected, that those in the youngest age-group are once again far less likely than are older cohorts to endorse this view. This is especially true in Britain, where young people are evenly split on whether there is a moral imperative to marry for those who want children.

Children

This tolerance of out-of-wedlock births reflects demographic trends: in the United Kingdom, there has been a dramatic increase in the proportion of births occurring outside marriage, rising from about nine per cent in 1975 to 25 per cent in 1988 (Simons, 1992). Still, the great majority of couples clearly prefer to get married before they become parents. Although, as we have seen, only a small minority agrees that children are the main purpose of a marriage, a considerably higher proportion believes that a marriage without children is "not fully complete" (see table below). Of particular note, however, is the striking difference between cohorts: in Germany, Britain and the United States the oldest age-group is almost twice as likely as the youngest to agree that marriage is incomplete without children.

% agreeing marriage without children is not fully complete

	Total	Men born in ...			Women born in ...		
		1950-1970	1930-1949	Pre-1930	1950-1970	1930-1949	Pre-1930
Britain	45	35	54	73	29	40	63
Irish Republic	48	45	59	55	39	48	54
USA	44	34	46	64	34	46	56
West Germany	37	24	45	54	25	40	51

This question is one of several items tapping the value placed on children. In general, it is clear that children are regarded, on balance, as a joy rather than as a burden, that their virtues outweigh the loss of parental freedom.

In all four nations there is clear support for the first three items in the table below, though Germans are far less convinced than people in other nations that children are worth the parental sacrifice in terms of loss of freedom. By and large, enthusiasm for children reflects the relative fertility rates of the different nations, with Ireland being the most pro-children and Germany the least.

% taking a pro-children stance

	Britain		Irish Republic		USA		West Germany	
	Men	Women	Men	Women	Men	Women	Men	Women
It is better *not* to have children because they are such a heavy burden *(% disagree)*	88	87	92	94	83	83	75	77
Children are more trouble than they are worth *(% disagree)*	86	86	92	91	85	84	72	80
Watching children grow up is one of life's greatest joys *(% agree)*	80	82	85	89	84	86	71	79
Having children interferes too much with the freedom of parents *(% disagree)*	71	73	81	86	73	72	42	45
A marriage without children is not fully complete *(% agree)*	51	41	51	45	44	44	38	36
People who have never had children lead empty lives *(% agree)*	25	22	30	29	15	16	32	35

Interestingly, this pattern of cross-national differences only fails to hold for the last item in the table above, with Americans being the least likely to agree that the childless have empty lives. A further puzzle is that whereas, in the three European countries, it is the youngest cohorts who are most likely to reject the notion that the childless have empty lives, in America the reverse is true: it is the oldest in the US who are least likely to endorse the view that having no children impoverishes life. Perhaps in some nations childlessness is assumed frequently to be intentional, while in others it is usually associated with infertility. On the other hand, it may simply be that elderly Americans have less inter-generational contact than is the case in other nations, and that there is a strong ethos of self-sufficiency which goes against the grain of that item.

As the next table shows, there is for the most part broad agreement between men and women in attitudes to children in a marriage. What influences attitudes more, apparently, is the women's employment status. Working women in all four countries are much more likely than either full-time homemakers or men to reject the notion that children are essential to a marriage.

	Men	Women	Women Employed	Women Homemaker*
% agreeing marriage not complete				
Britain	51	41	29	49
Irish Republic	51	46	34	52
USA	44	44	38	52
West Germany	38	36	27	41
% agreeing childless lead empty lives				
Britain	25	23	15	27
Irish Republic	30	29	17	36
USA	15	16	16	15
West Germany	32	35	26	40

* In West Germany and the Irish Republic this reflects a broader category of those not in the labour force

Women's roles

In comparing gender-role attitudes across nations we must clearly take account of how nations vary in the extent to which married women participate in the labour market. In general, women in Ireland and (to a lesser extent) Germany are much less likely to be in paid work than women in the USA and Britain. In addition, part-time employment among women is substantially higher in Britain and Germany than in either Ireland or the USA. In Britain, opportunities for married women to return to work have increased in recent years, partly because of a reduction in the supply of young (school-leaving age) workers, leaving a gap for married women to fill. In Germany, on the other hand, there was probably less economic pressure (at least in the late 1980s) for women to return to the labour force, so the demand for part-time work tended to exceed the supply. The tendency in the USA is for women who do work to work full-time instead of part-time.

There are also, of course, substantial differences in the availability of child care provision in the different countries, though in none of them is it plentiful. So in all four nations, the lack of affordable and flexible childcare is bound to create conflicts for working parents, which in most instances fall on the mother. That is why the focus of the ISSP questions is mainly upon the role of women and the consequences of *women's* employment for the family; we did not investigate how far work and family conflicts are also perceived as a problem for men.

Included in the module are four items to do with the consequences of women working outside the home, which in *The 7th Report* we labelled as 'role conflict' (Scott, 1990). We reported then that, while British people in general are very aware of the disadvantages of women working (far more, for instance than are Americans), British women are much more likely than British men to take an egalitarian stance, rejecting the notion that work and family life are incompatible.

% taking an 'egalitarian' stance on the consequences of women working

	Britain		Irish Republic		USA		West Germany	
	Men	Women	Men	Women	Men	Women	Men	Women
A working mother can establish just as warm and secure a relationship with her children as a mother who does not work *(% agree)*	51	63	52	56	58	69	64	68
All in all family life suffers when the woman has a full-time job *(% disagree)*	37	43	34	40	47	50	25	25
A pre-school child is likely to suffer if his or her mother works *(% disagree)*	29	40	32	45	37	48	13	17
A woman and her family will all be happier if she goes out to work *(% agree)*	14	22	20	23	16	17	16	20

As the table shows, this gender difference in attitudes exists to a degree in all four countries, though least in Germany. Gender differences apart, Americans are the least traditional in their views and Germans are the most, except on the first item - which may well have been interpreted somewhat differently in the different national contexts; in the Anglo-Saxon countries, where maternal deprivation theories have held sway (for instance Bowlby, 1971), people may have responded in terms of the emotional needs of the child, while in Germany this has been less of an issue and more concern is directed at the practical difficulties of juggling work and family roles.

As the next table shows, British people are clearly the most 'feminist' in their rejection of the notion (in all three guises) that "a woman's place is in the home", while the Irish and Germans are the most traditional. At first glance it might seem surprising that there are no clear gender differences in the responses to the last question, but of course choice for women is very much part of the feminist credo and it follows from this that the homemaker's role is not to be disparaged.

% taking an 'egalitarian' stance on gender-role ideology

	Britain		Irish Republic		USA		West Germany	
	Men	Women	Men	Women	Men	Women	Men	Women
A husband's job is to earn the money; a wife's job is to look after the home and family *(% disagree)*	47	58	40	50	47	52	33	35
A job is all right but what most women really want is a home and children *(% disagree)*	41	51	24	35	34	39	31	35
Being a housewife is just as fulfilling as working for pay *(% disagree)*	33	36	17	24	22	21	29	32

An especially interesting issue is whether women go out to work mainly for self-fulfilment, or mainly because of economic necessity (see Braun *et al*, forthcoming). In many western countries women have had to struggle for their right to work, both in their own family setting and in society at large, sometimes supported but often opposed by men. Although this struggle has largely been concerned with women's rights and opportunities, the issue has often been intrinsically linked to the economic necessity of working. In an attempt to disentangle these issues - double income *versus* women's independence - we can examine responses to two ISSP items that tap the importance of paid work for women, as shown in the next table.

% of respondents taking 'egalitarian' stance on importance of work

	Britain		Irish Republic		USA		West Germany	
	Men	Women	Men	Women	Men	Women	Men	Women
Having a job is the best way for a woman to be an independent person *(% agree)*	59	65	55	60	40	44	62	66
Both the husband and wife should contribute to the household income *(% agree)*	50	56	61	66	46	49	48	46

The British and Germans are more likely than are the Americans and the Irish to come down on the side of independence. Not surprisingly, however, the British and the Irish, with their relatively weaker economies, are more likely than the Americans and Germans to accept the need for two incomes. American's low support for the importance of a woman's job for her independence is certainly puzzling. Could it be that in America independence is more closely associated with *financial* independence than it is in Europe (and most women earn far less than men)? Or are Americans, conscious of the problems faced by many women and children after divorce, simply suspicious of the notion of independence (as opposed to dependency)?

Although women's working lives tend to be distinctive - interrupted while the children are young and then resumed once they are older - the actual pattern of women's work does vary somewhat by nation. So some of the cross-national attitudinal differences we find on these sorts of issues may reflect not only structural differences in the labour market and economic circumstances across national boundaries, but also differences in child-rearing provision and policy.[2] This applies particularly, perhaps, to the items in the next table.

Attitudes towards women's work roles

Should a woman work ...	Britain		Irish Republic		USA		West Germany	
	Men	Women	Men	Women	Men	Women	Men	Women
	%	%	%	%	%	%	%	%
... after marrying and before there are children?								
Yes, work full-time	74	79	72	76	59	71	65	69
Yes, work part-time	14	13	17	17	18	13	19	16
No, stay at home	3	2	7	6	6	4	6	6
... when there is a child under school age?								
Yes, work full-time	2	3	8	10	9	10	2	2
Yes, work part-time	23	29	33	34	25	34	18	22
No, stay at home	67	61	53	52	54	44	70	68
... after the youngest child starts school?								
Yes, work full-time	12	14	18	24	27	33	4	4
Yes, work part-time	65	70	44	54	45	45	40	43
No, stay at home	13	10	31	20	14	9	45	43
... after the children leave home?								
Yes, work full-time	54	59	56	69	58	66	35	38
Yes, work part-time	28	29	25	23	19	15	38	34
No, stay at home	3	2	8	6	6	3	12	12

Men and women in all countries approve of a married women working before she has children, though American men have the most reservations. In other respects, Germans (men and women alike) tend to be the most traditional in their attitudes to women's work, especially when there are children at home. Notably, German women (43 per cent) are more than twice as likely as Irish women and four times as likely as British and American women to believe that a woman should stay at home even when all the children are at school (and similar differences are apparent when comparing German men to men in other nations). In contrast, respondents in the United States and Ireland are the most willing to see toddlers' mothers go out to work (thought majorities are still opposed); and, in accordance with their practice, Americans are the strongest advocates of mothers working *full-time* when their children are in school.

The main difference between the United States, Ireland and Britain is the extent of approval of part-time *versus* full-time work, with the British conspicuous in favouring part-time work for mothers of school-aged children. Note also that while British and Irish people are keen to see young marrieds in full-time jobs, they are much less enthusiastic about women working full-time in later marriage, even *after* the children have left home.   Germans are even less likely to support the full-time employment of women at this later stage.

We have seen that women are more egalitarian than men in respect of gender-role attitudes; so also are they more likely to approve of women working outside the home - except, as noted, in Germany, where men and women share much the same attitudes. In Britain and the United States especially, the gender difference is most apparent where there are young children in the household: men are more likely to want women to stay at home to look after the children. It is on precisely this issue that male support for feminism is likely to flounder. Even in Sweden, with state policies supposedly aimed at reconciling family and work for both women and men (fathers are legally entitled to parental leave), few men actually claim such leave (Lewis and Aström, 1992).

Women who work have a more egalitarian outlook on a range of issues, including the labour-force participation of women (see Davis and Robinson, 1991; Alwin *et al*, 1992). This is also true for men whose wives work (Smith, 1985). However, as the table below shows, it is age (or at any rate the stage in a person's life-cycle) that appears to be the most important predictor of attitudes towards working mothers.

% saying a woman should stay at home when there is a child under school age

	Total	Men born in ...			Women born in ...		
		1950-1970	1930-1949	Pre-1930	1950-1970	1930-1949	Pre-1930
Britain	64	48	76	86	46	70	79
Irish Republic	52	37	62	77	37	63	69
USA	48	48	55	66	34	45	57
West Germany	69	60	76	83	59	71	78

In all nations the youngest cohorts are far less likely than the oldest to think that a woman should stay at home when there is a pre-school child. Again, however, German men and women - even those in the youngest birth cohort - have markedly more traditional attitudes in this respect than young people in the other three nations.

Suitability of childcare

As we have suggested, these national differences in attitudes towards women's employment have to be interpreted in the context of the differences in actual labour force participation, and the degree to which national policies towards the family give practical support to women who wish to combine family and work roles. For instance, differences in the perceived suitability of childcare arrangements in each country may at least partly account for differences in attitudes to women going out to work. And, as the table below shows, people in the four nations do have very different views about the suitability of various childcare arrangements "for a child under three years old whose parents both have full-time jobs".

	Britain	Irish Republic	USA	West Germany
% of respondents saying each form of childcare is very suitable				
State/local authority nursery	29	8	19	16
Private crèche or nursery	30	18	31	14
Childminder or baby-sitter	16	25	26	9
A neighbour or friend	10	34	26	8
Relative	39	56	50	23

The British find their public daycare facilities to be relatively more suitable than do Americans, Germans, or (particularly) the Irish - though in the latter case this may well reflect availability, as public daycare is all but non-existent outside the Dublin area, and the fact that public-funded childcare in Ireland nowadays tends to focus on the disadvantaged and children at risk. Around a third of British and Americans, but fewer than one in five Germans and Irish, see private daycare facilities as suitable. And the remaining forms of childcare - baby-sitters, neighbours/friends, and relatives are all much more popular in Ireland and the United States than in either Germany or Britain.

Of course, people without children have little (current) basis on which to make an informed decision about the suitability of different childcare arrangements, and they may partly have been responding according to whether they felt that both parents of a child under three should go out to work in the first place. Nonetheless these questions are about issues that are central to the way family options are changing. In particular, the paucity of suitable childcare arrangements still severely restricts a family's ability to achieve a harmonious balance between family responsibilities and work. And while in most nations there is an abundance of political rhetoric on the importance of support for the family, there is often relatively little practical assistance.

A further problem facing policymakers nowadays in most of the industrial world is the dramatic increase in separation and divorce, resulting in a growing number of lone parent families. It is to these issues that we now turn.

Divorce

In many countries (Ireland excepted), divorce has become relatively easy to obtain, and divorce rates are rising. Britain's divorce rate is among the highest in Europe, although it has not yet reached the staggeringly high American rate.

Opinion of divorce for couples with and without young children

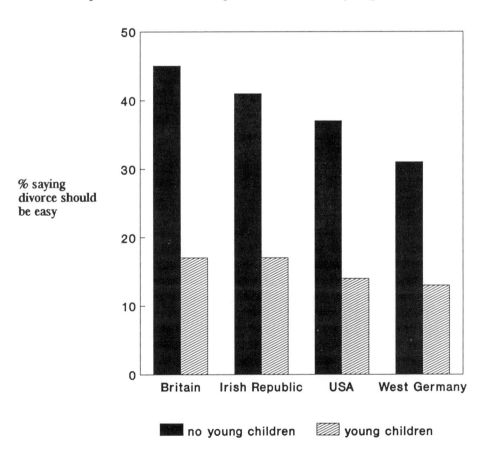

In Britain more than one in three marriages end in divorce within ten years; whereas in America it is estimated that, if current levels persist, three in five first marriages will eventually end in divorce (Kiernan, 1988; Bumpass, 1990). If attitudes towards divorce were to correspond to behaviour, we would therefore expect Ireland to be the most traditional towards, and the USA the most tolerant of, divorce.

Given widespread concerns about the effect of divorce on children, it comes as little surprise that there are clear and consistent differences in attitudes to divorce according to whether or not the couple contemplating it has young children. In all countries, people are markedly less tolerant of divorce if young children are involved. Surprisingly, perhaps, it is the British who are the most sympathetic to the easing of divorce laws for couples with no young children.

If marriage, as some suggest, is a patriarchal institution in which men are the main beneficiaries, then women ought in theory to be more favourable than men to the divorce option - other factors being equal (which, of course, they are not in this case for a variety of reasons which we come to later). In any event, as we see from the table below, in Britain, Ireland and the USA, women *are* far more likely than men to consider that divorce is better than staying together in an unhappy marriage.

% saying much better or better to end an unhappy marriage

	Britain		Irish Republic		USA		West Germany	
	Men	Women	Men	Women	Men	Women	Men	Women
... for children	52	66	45	52	47	60	60	66
... for wife	59	72	52	59	51	60	73	75
... for husband	59	71	51	62	52	61	72	74

* In the Irish Republic a middle alternative "neither better nor worse" was offered and around 14 per cent took it. This undoubtedly deflated positive responses.

As far as country differences are concerned, Germans (both men and women) are the most likely to believe that divorce is preferable to an unhappy marriage. Not surprisingly, respondents tended to be more concerned about the effects of divorce on children than on either the husband or wife. Americans were least likely to make this distinction.

Single parents

Divorce is one of the major causes of the increase in lone-parent families, although, as noted earlier, there has also been a marked increase in the numbers of out-of-wedlock births too. The vast majority of lone-parent families are headed by women, suggesting that biology and traditional gender role ideology may have combined to ensure that children are primarily the mother's responsibility.

% agreeing a single parent can bring up a child as well as a married couple

	Britain		Irish Republic		USA		West Germany	
	Men	Women	Men	Women	Men	Women	Men	Women
A single mother	25	35	42	43	29	42	37	45
A single father	19	28	25	26	26	35	23	28

The table shows the responses to two agree-disagree questions concerning the ability of single mothers and single fathers to bring up children. Not surprisingly, in all four countries a single mother is considered more capable than a single father of bringing up a child, but the distinction is strongest in Germany and Ireland. Yet in all the countries, except Ireland, women are readier than men to believe in the capacity of a single parent (of either sex) to raise a child. Perhaps women are more conscious than men that, even within marriage, child-rearing responsibilities are often left to only one partner anyway.

Homosexual marriage

For most family issues for which time-series data are available, there has been a marked trend, in Britain and other developed countries, towards more liberal attitudes over recent decades. People are more willing nowadays to sanction cohabitation and pre-marital sex; they are more supportive of women going out to work and of egalitarian gender-roles in the home; they are more likely to support child-rearing that encourages autonomy, rather than obedience. The exception, in Britain at least, as successive *British Social Attitudes* Reports have shown, is in public attitudes towards homosexuality (Brook, 1988; Wellings and Wadsworth, 1990; Heath and McMahon, 1992).

The ISSP item we report here is about only one aspect of attitudes to homosexuality - the acceptability of homosexual marriages - and was designed more to tap future changes in attitudes than with any belief that this was yet a current issue of great moment among the general public in any of the four countries.

% agreeing that homosexual couples should have the right to marry

	Britain	Irish Republic	USA	West Germany
Men	12	24	10	14
Women	14	26	12	12

As expected, support for homosexuals' right to marry is low. Yet it is the Irish, by far the most traditional in their views on marriage, for instance, who are the most tolerant of the four nations on this issue, with one in four supporting the right of homosexuals to marry one another. This is around twice the level of support found in the other three countries.

The future of the traditional family

Are family options becoming so much more varied that they are rendering the 'traditional family' obsolete? Are 'traditional family values' being mortally damaged by the assertion and reassertion of the cause of individual self-fulfilment?   Certainly, as far as Britain is concerned, it would be premature to mourn the loss of traditional family values as they are commonly defined.

A recent book exploring the American family poses the question 'New families, no families?' (Goldscheider and Waite, 1991). It defines the 'new family' as more egalitarian and symmetrical, in which both the man and the woman have a paid job and share household duties, including childcare. The 'no family' label is for people, especially the young, who opt for independence instead of marriage and family life. Naturally, these are not, however, the only alternatives. The lone-parent family (though often involuntary) is a third option and, as the vast majority of single parent families are headed by women, such families represent (in one sense) the logical extreme of 'traditional' gender roles: women take almost total responsibility for the direct care of the children, and the father's role, if he is present at all, tends to be severely limited. In addition, there is an increasing number of *couples* who voluntarily decide *not* to have children. In all these versions of modern family life traditional values are far from extinct.

So the most one can say about the so-called demise of the family in Britain is that the *nuclear* family is no longer as common a household type as it used to be. Moreover, as the next figure shows, attitudes in Britain towards various family options vary widely according to the issue.

The figure shows the percentage who:

1. advise a young woman to live with a steady partner, without marrying (COHABITATION);
2. agree that personal freedom is more important than the companionship of marriage (FREEDOM);
3. agree that a single mother can bring up her child as well as a couple (SINGLE MUM);
4. disagree that a husband's job is to earn money while a wife's job is to look after the home and children (WIFE'S JOB NOT HOME);

5. think a women should not work at all when there is a child under school age (WORK AND YOUNG CHILD);
6. disagree that it is better *not* to have children because they are such a heavy burden (CHILDREN NOT BURDEN);
7. agree that having a job is the best way for a woman to be an independent person (JOB INDEPENDENT);
8. agree that both the husband and wife should contribute to the household income (TWO INCOMES).

We use each single item as representative of a broader range of measures in order to construct a picture of British support (or lack of it) for a large number of family choices.

British attitudes on family options: no family or new family?

% in favour of...

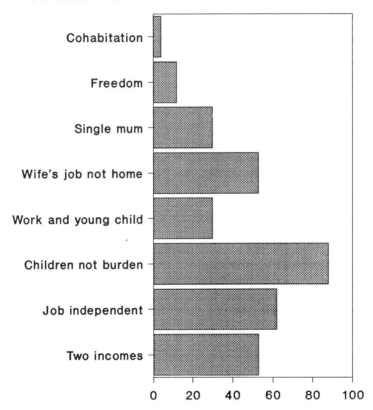

As can be seen, the British public does not appear at all tempted by the option of 'no family'. Only four per cent would advise a young woman to cohabit without eventually marrying, and only 12 per cent believe that personal freedom is preferable to the companionship of marriage. These and other answers suggest firmly that family life still reigns supreme as the desirable state.

But what about attitudes to lone-parent families? As noted, the number of such families has been steadily increasing. And around one in three people in Britain (30 per cent) think that single mothers can bring up children as well as a married couple can. While not a popular choice, single parenthood is clearly not seen as the catastrophe it once was. The 'traditional' asymmetrical family is also not without support among the British public. Although 53 per cent now reject the traditional view that a husband's job is to earn money and a wife's to look after the home and family, this is far from a whole-hearted rejection of the proposition, given the prevalence of women's participation in the labour market. Moreover, traditional family values can hardly be said to be a thing of the past when less than a third of the public (28 per cent) believes that mothers of children under school age should go out to work, even part-time.

Even so, more than half the public nowadays (53 per cent) does believe that both the husband and wife should contribute to the family income, and an even higher proportion (62 per cent) that a job is a good way for women to achieve some level of independence. But it is unclear as to whether support for women going out to paid work is motivated mainly by egalitarianism or by economic necessity; in all likelihood, it has elements of both. Nonetheless, it is certainly clear that support for the two-job, or dual-career, family - once the children are grown-up - is now almost normative.

But, although we have shown that the presence of young children in a family affects people's attitudes to, for instance, divorce, the figure provides no hints that children are perceived as a burden in other respects. The overwhelming majority (88 per cent) rejects this view. Decreasing fertility rates cannot then be attributed to a loss of interest in children; as we have shown, children are still regarded as an important, if not an essential, part of family life. So for the British public, along with most other Europeans and Americans, there is no doubt that families along the lines we have always known them are here to stay.

Conclusions

How do British attitudes compare with those of people in other countries? As always, the answer is not straightforward. The British are more traditional on some issues than the Irish, Germans and Americans, and less traditional on others. For example, the British are the most egalitarian when it comes to gender-role ideology in the home, more willing than even the Americans to challenge the belief that the woman's lot is to look after the house and children. Yet the British back-peddle somewhat when it comes to women's role *outside* the home: along with the Germans, they are more likely to assert that, when there are pre-school children, the woman should not go out to work at all. As we have noted, however, some of these variations across countries may be caused by the perceived (or actual) suitability of childcare arrangements (Alwin *et al,* 1992), or the flexibility of employment practices to accommodate mothers of young children.

The British, who have one of the highest divorce rates in Europe, are indeed the most sceptical among the four countries we examined that married people are generally happier than unmarried ones. That being so, it is not surprising that the British are also the most likely to say that the law should make it easier for couples to divorce, especially when there are no children. British attitudes thus seem highly consistent with their behaviour on this issue, in sharp contrast to the Americans. After all, despite being comfortably the most idealistic (or romantic?) nation of the four with respect to marriage, it also has rates of divorce far higher than any European country. It is possible, of course, that this apparent conflict merely reflects the fact that divorce in the USA represents the best means of making Phoenix rise from the ashes: Americans are increasingly subscribing to the norm of remarriage. The British, with their more jaundiced views of marital happiness, appear to be letting experience triumph over hope.

Although more sceptical than other nations about marital happiness, this scepticism does not extend to the desirability of children. Attitudes towards children, by and large, seem to correspond fairly well to the relative fertility levels of the different countries, with Ireland being the most pro-children and Germany the least. On this, as on most of the family issues, the British are at neither extreme.

Though cross-national differences are clearly apparent on a number of issues, the differences between subgroups *within* a country (such as men and women, and the old and the young) are often much larger. As we noted earlier, Jessie Bernard talked of there being two marriages - the wife's and the husband's; and on the evidence of the ISSP data, women are consistently less likely than men to believe that marriage is associated with happiness. Women are, of course, also consistently more likely than men to take an egalitarian stance on gender role issues. Perhaps surprisingly in view of their frequent vulnerability in divorces, women are also more likely than men to believe that divorce is more in the family's interests than if a couple stays together in an unhappy marriage. On most other issues, however (including cohabitation, the purpose of marriage and the desirability of children), women and men hold very similar views.

There are also clear differences among different groups of women, with employed women far more likely to support egalitarian gender roles than are homemakers. We cannot, of course, be sure which came first - the attitude or the work experience - but having a working spouse is also associated with a greater degree of egalitarianism among men: they (like their working wives or partners) are also much more likely to believe that other women, regardless of their family circumstance, should also go out to work.

On many of these family issues - such as cohabitation, having children outside wedlock, and the necessity of children to make a marriage complete - younger people (born since 1950) have markedly more liberal attitudes than do older people. They are the generation most likely to support the 'no family' option. We raised the question as to whether the younger cohorts are disturbing or even destroying 'traditional family values', and although we cannot answer this question conclusively, it does appear that they are at least more open than older cohorts to various family forms, whether it be 'no families', childless couples, or 'new families'. We cannot yet tell, however, whether their attitudes are merely a function of their relative youth, or whether they will carry these attitudes with them into middle age and beyond, in due course creating a greater tolerance of family diversity in society at large. Evidence from elsewhere (Heath and McMahon, 1991) suggests that, in respect of gender roles at any rate, people do become more traditional with age. If so, change will indeed be slow.

Nonetheless, our interpretation of the data from these four countries is that families will become more diverse and that both the normative acceptability and the practice of different family options is likely to continue to grow. For one thing, women's increased participation in the labour force has shaken the foundations of 'traditional' family life, and it seems unlikely that this process will be reversed. Women who contribute substantially to the household income are doubtless in a far stronger position to seek more equality in the home and more individual autonomy. It may be no bad thing if traditional family values decline in order to accommodate greater egalitarianism.

Notes

1. The other four countries for which ISSP datasets exist (Austria, Italy, Hungary and the Netherlands) are not included in this chapter purely because of space constraints, despite the fact that their findings are valuable for examining family options in a broader European perspective (Braun, Scott and Alwin, 1993).
2. In Ireland compulsory schooling begins at the age of six, but the majority of four and five year olds attend primary schools on a voluntary basis. Public pre-school facilities, however, are minimal and privately-funded childcare services are mainly playgroups where children attend for only a few hours a week (Dunmon, 1991). In Britain, children begin school at the age of five and, apart from school nursery classes, pre-school childcare provision is almost entirely a matter of parents' making (and paying for) their own childcare arrangements. In Germany the situation is hardly better. Although kindergartens are widely available for children over three, their highly restricted hours limit their usefulness. Even when children reach school-age, problems of childcare continue since it is rare for German schools to offer meals and the school day ends very early. In the USA, as in Britain, childcare is mainly arranged privately but, unlike in Britain, tax relief is given on private day-care costs.

References

Alwin, D.F., Braun, M. and Scott, J. (1992), 'The Separation of Work and the Family. Attitudes Toward Women's Labour-Force Participation in Germany, Great Britain, and the United States', *European Sociological Review*, 8, pp. 18-38.

Bernard, J. (1973), *The Future of Marriage*, New York: Bantam.

Björnberg, U. (1992), 'Parenting in Transition: An Introduction and Summary', in Björnberg, U., *European Parents in the 1990s: Contradictions and Comparisons*, New Brunswick and London: Transaction Publishers.

Bowlby, J. (1971), *Attachment and Loss, Volume 1: Attachment*, London: Penguin Books.

Braun, M., Scott, J. and Alwin, D.F. (1993), 'Attitudes Towards Marriage and Divorce in a Comparative Perspective', Paper presented at American Association for Public Opinion Research, St. Charles, Illinois.

Braun, M., Scott, J. and Alwin, D.F. (forthcoming), 'Economic Necessity or Self-actualization? Attitudes Towards Women's Labour-Force Participation in East and West Germany', *European Sociological Review*.

Brook, L. (1988), 'The public's response to AIDS', in Jowell, R., Witherspoon, S. and Brook, L. (eds.), *British Social Attitudes: the 5th Report*, Aldershot: Gower.

Bumpass, L. (1990), 'What's Happening to the Family? Interactions between Demographic and Institutional Change', *Demography*, vol. 27, no. 4, pp. 483-98.

Davis, N.J. and Robinson, R.V. (1991), 'Men's and Women's Consciousness of Gender Inequality: Austria, West Germany, Great Britain and the United States', *American Sociological Review*, 56, pp. 72-84.

Dunmon, W. (ed.) (1991), *Families and Policies: Evolutions and Trend in 1989-90*, Brussels: Commission of the European Communities.

Furstenberg, F.F., Jr. and Cherlin, A.J. (1991), *Divided Families: What Happens to Children When Parents Part*, Cambridge, MA: Harvard University Press.

Gershuny, J. and Robinson, J. (1988), 'Historical Changes in the Household Division of Labor', *Demography*, 25, pp. 537-52.

Goldscheider, F.K. and Waite, L.J. (1991), *New Families, No Families?* Berkeley: University of California Press.

Greeley, A. (1992), 'Religion in Britain, Ireland and the USA,' in Jowell, R., Brook, L., Prior, G. and Taylor, B. (eds.), *British Social Attitudes: the 9th Report*, Aldershot: Dartmouth.

Heath, A. and McMahon, D. (1991), 'Consensus and Dissensus', in Jowell, R., Brook, L. and Taylor, B., with Prior, G. (eds.), *British Social Attitudes: the 8th Report*, Aldershot: Dartmouth.

Heath, A. and McMahon, D. (1992), 'Changes in Values', in Jowell, R., Brook, L., Prior, G. and Taylor, B. (eds.), *British Social Attitudes: the 9th Report*, Aldershot: Dartmouth.

Kamerman, S. (1991), 'Child Care Policies and Programs: An International Overview', *Journal of Social Issues*, 47, pp. 179-196.

Kiernan, K. (1988), 'The British Family: Contemporary Trends and Issues', *Journal of Family Issues*, vol. 9, no. 3, pp. 298-316.

Kiernan, K. (1992), 'Men and Women at Work and at Home', in Jowell, R., Brook, L., Prior, G. and Taylor, B. (eds.), *British Social Attitudes: the 9th Report*, Aldershot: Dartmouth.

Lewis, J. and Aström, G. (1992), 'Equality, Difference and State Welfare: Labour Market and Family Policies in Sweden', *Feminist Studies*, 18, pp. 59-87.

Popenoe, D. (1988), *Disturbing the Nest: Family Change and Decline in Modern Societies*, New York: Aldine de Gruyter.

Scott, J. (1990), 'Women and the Family' in Jowell, R., Witherspoon, S. and Brook, L. with Taylor, B. (eds.), *British Social Attitudes: the 7th Report*, Aldershot: Gower.

Scott, J. and Duncombe, J. (1991), 'Gender-role Attitudes in Britain and the USA', in Arber, S. and Gilbert, N. (eds.), *Women and Working Lives: Divisions and Change*, London: MacMillan.

Simons, J. (1992), 'Europe's Ageing Population - Demographic Trends,' in Bailey, J. (ed.) *Social Europe*, London: Longman.

Smith, T. (1985), 'Working Wives and Women's Rights: The Connection Between the Employment Status of Wives and Feminist Attitudes of Husbands', *Sex Roles*, 12, pp.501-8.

Wellings, K. and Wadsworth, J. (1990), 'AIDS and the Moral Climate', in Jowell, R., Witherspoon, S. and Brook, L. (eds.), *British Social Attitudes: the 7th Report,* Aldershot: Gower.

Witherspoon, S. and Prior, G. (1991), 'Working mothers: free to choose?', in Jowell, R., Brook, L. and Taylor, B. with Prior, G. (eds.), *British Social Attitudes: the 8th Report,* Aldershot: Dartmouth.

Acknowledgements

The support of both the Economic and Social Research Council and the University of Essex is gratefully acknowledged. This work relates to cross-national research on the family that is part of the scientific programme of the ESRC Research Centre on Micro-social Change in Britain. We also acknowledge the support of Zentrum für Umfragen, Methoden und Analysen (ZUMA).

3 Religion, morality and politics

Anthony Heath, Bridget Taylor and Gabor Toka*

The aim of this chapter is to explore the interrelationships between religion, social attitudes and politics in the democratic or democratising nations belonging to the International Social Survey Programme. The British literature on the social bases of politics has largely concerned itself with social class, while in continental Europe, and of course in Northern Ireland, religion has a large impact on people's political affiliations and beliefs (Lenski, 1963; Michelat and Simon, 1977a, 1977b; Lijphart, 1979; Knutsen, 1988; Curtice and Gallagher, 1990). Even in Britain, religion has long been an important factor in politics, although its importance has declined this century (Butler and Stokes, 1974; Wald, 1983; Miller and Raab, 1977). Nonetheless, as we shall see, religion is still as strongly related to social attitudes in Britain as it is elsewhere in Europe.

There are at least three different senses in which religion may be important for politics. First, overtly religious issues may be on the political agenda and involve actual or proposed legislation in parliament; examples in Britain are the requirement for schools to have a daily act of worship and lessons in religious knowledge, and the state funding of church schools. Later in this chapter we introduce a scale of attitudes towards church/state relations.

Secondly, some current political issues, while not overtly religious, are related to the teachings of particular religions or denominations.

---

* All three authors are at Nuffield College, Oxford; Anthony Heath is an Official Fellow; Bridget Taylor is a Research Officer; and Gabor Toka is a Visiting Scholar.

Contemporary examples in Britain, as in several other countries, are divorce and abortion. In the Irish Republic, for example, the Catholic Church campaigned actively during the referendum on abortion, urging its followers to vote in accordance with Church teaching. We later introduce a scale of family values which measures attitudes towards one set of such issues.

Thirdly, even when neither sort of religious issue is on the current political agenda, members of particular religions or denominations may nonetheless continue to identify with and support specific political parties, perhaps as a result of longstanding loyalties or associations (for example the 'freezing' hypothesis as described by Lipset and Rokkan, 1967). In this sense, the persistence of religious cleavages in contemporary political behaviour may be a relic of past political controversies. In Britain, for example, the original division between Tories and Whigs reflected the historic competition between the Church of England and nonconformity (Lipson, 1953). The Tories consistently opposed Whig efforts to remove nonconformist disadvantages, and although these disadvantages have long since been removed, nonconformists are still more likely than Anglicans to support the Liberal Democrats (the modern version of the Whigs).

As societies become more secular, we might expect the role of religion in politics to decline in all three senses, but particularly in the third sense. After all, if secularisation is defined as a weakening of the significance of religion in people's lives (Wilson, 1966), then we would surely expect religious issues in those societies to have a lower priority in voters' minds, and therefore for religious bonds to become less significant in linking people either with one another or with particular political parties.

But we need to bear in mind that, even when the average level of religiosity declines at a particular rate, the importance of religion does not, of course, decline at an equal rate among all members of society. In fact, the variation around the average may well increase if core members of religious groups maintain their beliefs as more peripheral members drift away, leading to new potential conflicts.

In relatively homogeneous religious societies, such as the Irish Republic, we might expect religion to have little potential for conflict. In these societies we would expect to find substantial consensus both on religious issues and on those social and moral values most closely related to religious teachings. Similarly, a homogeneous secular society might also display consensus on these values. But in between (which is where most contemporary societies lie), we might find dissensus and potential for conflict. Thus secularisation in Ireland might lead to a potential for conflict over, say, abortion that would not have been as likely prior to secularisation.

On the other hand, if a relatively heterogeneous religious society becomes more secular, we might expect a decline in denominational conflicts, such as that between Protestants and Catholics in Northern Ireland (insofar as this *is* primarily a religious conflict rather than a political conflict about constitutional issues).

The aim of this chapter, then, is to explore to what extent members of different religious groupings in a range of countries vary in their social attitudes and political affiliations. Of particular interest is the historical legacy of communism in three ISSP member countries we examined - Poland, the former East Germany and Hungary.

Patterns of religious affiliation

The table below shows the patterns of religious denomination and religiosity in 12 ISSP member countries. We distinguish between Catholics, Protestants, 'Others', and people who have no religion; and among the Catholics and Protestants we then distinguish regular church attenders (people who attend church once a month or more frequently) from irregular attenders.[1] This gives us a simple summary of religious affiliation which we can apply to all countries. Throughout this chapter we use the term 'religious affiliation' to refer to this six-category measure. We use the term 'religiosity' to refer to our distinctions between regular attenders, irregular attenders and people who reported that they had no religion.

Religious affiliation

		Regular Catholic	Irregular Catholic	Regular Protestant	Irregular Protestant	Other religion	None
New Zealand	%	6	8	15	38	3	31
USA	%	15	12	34	27	4	7
Irish Republic	%	77	16	2	2	2	2
N. Ireland	%	32	4	35	21	*	9
Britain	%	6	5	14	36	3	36
Norway	%	*	*	9	81	3	6
Netherlands	%	12	10	13	6	4	55
W. Germany	%	17	26	6	38	2	11
E. Germany	%	3	3	3	26	1	64
Italy	%	55	38	*	-	1	6
Hungary	%	21	53	4	17	1	5
Poland	%	78	19	-	-	1	3

* = less than 0.5 per cent

Our schema of religious affiliation leaves out the distinctions between religious groups such as Jews or Muslims which are of considerable interest in their own right, but of whom there are too few in any of these ISSP samples for useful analysis. It also ignores distinctions between the different Protestant groups, which are particularly important in Britain and Northern Ireland, and to which we shall return later. We should also note that some people who placed themselves in the category we have labelled 'no religion' revealed, in answer to other questions, that they did have some religious beliefs (see Greeley, 1992). So this category consists of people who are either irreligious or who did not identify with any of the formal organised churches or religious groupings in their society.

As can be seen from the table, the twelve countries differ enormously in their patterns of religious affiliation. At one extreme are the Irish Republic and Poland, where substantial majorities of the sample report that they are regular church-going Catholics (78 per cent in Poland and 77 per cent in the Irish Republic). At the other extreme is the former East Germany, where 64 per cent reported that they had no religion. In between comes Norway, which might also be regarded as a consensual society in that four out of five Norwegians were Protestants who irregularly went to church. So in none of these four societies would we expect to find much relation between religion and politics: they are likely, according to the arguments above, to be largely consensual societies in respect of religious issues and associated moral values.

The other eight countries, including Britain, are somewhat divided both in denomination and in religiosity (as measured by our church attendance question). There are substantial minorities of regular church-goers in all these countries, both Catholic and Protestant, as well as people with no religion. On this criterion, Northern Ireland and the Netherlands are the most polarised, with rather few *irregular* church-going Catholics or Protestants who might act (so to speak) as a bridge between the one group and another. Indeed, in Northern Ireland only one quarter of the sample fits into this middle category of irregular church-goers. The USA (39 per cent in these middle categories), Britain (41 per cent), New Zealand (46 per cent), West Germany (64 per cent) and Hungary (71 per cent) appear to be less polarised societies, according to this definition. This leaves Italy as the one country which is largely united in terms of denomination but divided in religiosity.

The table below provides a simple summary classification of the twelve countries according to their homogeneity/heterogeneity on these denominational and religiosity criteria.

	Homogeneous in denomination	Heterogeneous in denomination
Homogeneous in religiosity	East Germany Irish Republic Poland Norway	
Heterogeneous in religiosity	Italy	Britain USA West Germany Northern Ireland Netherlands New Zealand Hungary

It is rather striking that eleven of the twelve countries fall into just two of the four cells of the table. It may also be noted that, according to our classification, no common legacy appears among the former communist countries; indeed, they are as varied in their way as are the west European ones. Poland looks very like the Irish Republic in this respect, and Hungary looks like the former West Germany. But the former East Germany stands out on its own, apparently revealing a legacy of atheism which neither Poland nor Hungary shares.

Affiliation and subjective religiosity

A number of caveats must be attached to this first provisional classification. It assumes a common understanding throughout twelve disparate countries of the various categories of religious affiliation. In comparative research of this kind we always have to be aware that the meaning of the categories may vary from country to country. Consider Norway and Britain, for example, which look to be very different in religious affiliation in terms of these figures: 36 per cent of the British say they have no religion, compared with only six per cent in Norway. On the other hand, most of the believers in Norway attend church irregularly, with the proportion attending regularly being no higher than in Britain. We therefore have to ask whether these differences are more apparent than real. Might it not be that a good deal of the religious affiliation expressed in Norway is purely nominal and that the role that religion actually plays in people's lives is much the same as in Britain?

We can never completely resolve these doubts. But we can carry out certain checks - for instance by comparing people's reports of their religious affiliation with their perception of their own religiosity. In all the countries, except Hungary, respondents were asked to classify themselves on a seven-point scale of religiosity:

> *extremely religious*
> *very religious*
> *somewhat religious*
> *neither religious nor non-religious*
> *somewhat non-religious*
> *very non-religious*
> *extremely non-religious*

They were also offered a 'can't choose' option.

We have converted responses into scores (from 1 to 10) so that the higher the score, the more religious respondents perceive themselves to be. 'Can't choose' responses have been added to the midpoint of the scale ('neither religious nor non-religious').

This measure of subjective religious *feeling* turns out to be quite strongly related, at both the individual and the aggregate level, to our earlier measure of religious *affiliation*.[2] The table below shows a pattern that is remarkably similar across the eleven countries.[3]

Subjective religiosity (mean scores)

		Regular Catholic	Irregular Catholic	Regular Protestant	Irregular Protestant	Other religion	None	All
New Zealand	%	7.2	6.0	7.3	5.6	6.3	3.8	5.5
USA	%	7.4	6.2	7.7	6.4	6.1	4.0	6.8
Irish Republic	%	7.0	5.5	†	†	†	†	6.6
N. Ireland	%	6.9	5.3	7.1	5.7	†	4.5	6.5
Britain	%	6.9	6.3	7.1	5.8	6.9	4.1	5.5
Norway	%	†	†	7.9	5.4	7.8	3.8	5.6
Netherlands	%	7.4	6.5	7.7	6.7	7.7	4.4	5.6
W. Germany	%	7.2	5.2	7.4	5.1	6.7	2.9	5.4
E. Germany	%	7.6	4.9	7.6	5.4	†	1.9	3.3
Italy	%	7.1	5.4	†	†	†	2.3	6.2
Poland	%	7.2	6.0	†	†	†	3.8	6.8

† = cells containing fewer than 20 cases

As expected, perhaps, in every case regular church-going Catholics and regular Protestants have the highest mean scores, non-religious respondents have the lowest, and the two groups of irregular attenders lie in between. There are small variations from country to country, but the dominant picture is one of similarity - particularly marked among regular church-going Catholics (their mean scores varying only from 6.9 to 7.6 across the eleven countries). Indeed, regular church-going Catholics are invariably closer on this measure of religious feeling to their equivalents in other countries than to Catholics in their own country who go to church only irregularly.

It is only among the 'others' and among the people with no religion that we find much variation between countries. The 'others' are of course a diverse group (including Jews and Muslims), so national variations are scarcely surprising. But the group with no religion is more interesting, suggesting that in some cultures more than others an absence of religious affiliation by no means implies an absence of religious feeling. On the other hand, these variations could also be due to national differences in interpretation of the word 'religious' by non-religious people, or to national differences in belief in the supernatural (Greeley, 1993).

Affiliation and the nature of religious belief

The ISSP data enable us to look in more detail at differences in the nature of beliefs in the twelve countries. In all countries respondents were asked whether they believed in:

> ...*the Devil?*
> ...*heaven?*
> ...*hell?*
> ...*religious miracles?*

They were offered four possible responses: 'Yes - definitely'; 'yes - probably'; 'no - probably not'; 'no - definitely not'. This was followed by a question about the Bible:

> *Which one of these statements comes closest to describing your feelings about the Bible?*
>
> > *The Bible is the actual word of God and it is to be taken literally, word for word.*
> >
> > *The Bible is the inspired word of God but not everything should be taken literally, word for word.*
> >
> > *The Bible is an ancient book of fables, legends, history and moral teachings recorded by man.*
> >
> > *This does not apply to me.*

For all five questions, as always in ISSP questionnaires, respondents were offered a 'can't choose' option.)

We have constructed an index of religious belief from these five questions (scored from 1 to 10).[4] High scores indicate what might be termed a 'fundamentalist' set of religious beliefs, while low scores indicate more 'secular' beliefs. (For more detailed analysis of the individual items see Greeley, 1992.)

In each country we see the same expected pattern as we did with subjective religiosity - regular church-going Catholics and Protestants are the most 'fundamentalist' in their beliefs, while respondents who said they had no religion are the most secular. And once again, there are no systematic differences between Catholics and Protestants other than those associated with church attendance. (In some of the countries the data allow us to distinguish between the beliefs of different Protestant sects, showing some to be more fundamentalist than others.)

Levels of religious belief (mean scores)

		Regular Catholic	Irregular Catholic	Regular Protestant	Irregular Protestant	Other religion	None	All
New Zealand	%	7.7	6.1	7.8	4.8	7.4	3.2	5.1
USA	%	7.7	6.8	8.6	7.2	4.5	4.4	7.4
Irish Republic	%	7.1	5.2	†	†	†	†	6.6
N. Ireland	%	8.0	7.0	8.0	6.6	†	5.6	7.5
Britain	%	7.5	5.8	6.5	4.5	6.5	3.3	4.7
Norway	%	†	†	8.7	4.0	7.5	2.8	4.4
Netherlands	%	5.0	4.0	7.5	4.9	6.8	2.8	4.0
W. Germany	%	6.6	4.6	6.6	4.3	7.1	2.9	4.8
E. Germany	%	6.8	4.0	6.6	4.1	-	2.5	3.2
Italy	%	7.0	4.8	-	-	-	2.1	5.9
Hungary	%	5.7	2.9	5.9	2.8	-	2.1	3.6
Poland	%	6.5	4.5	-	-	-	2.5	6.0

† = cells containing fewer than 20 cases

However, practising Catholics in different countries seem to differ much more in their beliefs than in their subjective religiosity. For example, practising Catholics in Northern Ireland are much more fundamentalist on our measure (mean score of 8.0) than are Dutch Catholics (mean score of 5.0).

Thus Catholics in two different countries may both describe themselves as 'very religious', may both attend church frequently, but may nonetheless have very different beliefs about heaven, hell and the Bible. Despite the fact that the Catholic Church has a unified worldwide structure of authority, national differences in belief are just as evident among regular church-going Catholics as they are among regular Protestants, with their largely autonomous churches and sects.

Religion, moral attitudes and church/state relations

Moral issues

One common assumption in the study of values is that, while social class is the major basis of economic values (egalitarianism, collectivism and so on), religion is the major basis of moral values (see, for instance, Heath, Evans and Martin, forthcoming).

The ISSP data contain a number of questions on moral issues, notably on sexual relations, abortion (but alas not divorce in this dataset), and on husband's and wife's roles within the family. While people's attitudes towards, for example, abortion do not coincide exactly with their attitudes towards family roles, these different topics do nonetheless go together sufficiently closely to allow us to combine them in a simple index. This index is calculated by summing responses to the following seven questions:

> *How much do you agree or disagree ... a husband's job is to earn the money; a wife's job is to look after the home and family?*
>
> *How much do you agree or disagree ... all in all, family life suffers when the woman has a full-time job?*
>
> *Do you personally think it is wrong or not wrong for a woman to have an abortion ... if there is a strong chance of a serious defect in the baby?*
>
> *Do you personally think it is wrong or not wrong for a woman to have an abortion ... if the family has a very low income and cannot afford any more children?*
>
> *If a man and a woman have sexual relations before marriage, is it always wrong, sometimes wrong,* etc.?
>
> *What about a married person having sexual relations with someone other than his or her husband or wife, is it always wrong, sometimes wrong,* etc.?
>
> *And what about sexual relations between two adults of the same sex, is it always wrong, sometimes wrong,* etc?

The first two each offered five response categories, and the remaining five each offered four response categories.[5] The exact wording of the questions is given in Appendix III. Again we have scored our index so that a high score represents a more 'traditional' or morally prescriptive position, and a low score a more 'egalitarian' or permissive one, the scores running from 1 to 10 as before.[6]

Within each country we find that these values are closely related to religiosity, and there are striking similarities across countries, even including the former East Germany. Thus the most traditional (or morally prescriptive) groups in their family values are the regular church-going Catholics and Protestants, and in this respect these two groups are virtually identical in every country where the two coexist. Next come the irregular church-going Catholics and Protestants. So in every country the people with no religion are the least traditional or prescriptive. (See Michelat and Simon, 1977a, 1977b for similar results in France.)

Family values (mean scores)

		Regular Catholic	Irregular Catholic	Regular Protestant	Irregular Protestant	Other religion	None	All
New Zealand	%	7.2	5.0	6.9	5.1	6.2	3.9	5.1
USA	%	6.2	5.1	6.8	5.6	4.2	4.5	5.9
Irish Republic	%	7.1	5.1	†	†	†	†	6.6
N. Ireland	%	6.8	5.7	6.7	5.7	†	5.4	6.4
Britain	%	6.5	5.1	5.5	5.3	6.2	4.2	5.0
Norway	%	†	†	7.2	4.6	6.8	3.5	4.8
Netherlands	%	5.2	4.0	6.0	4.6	5.9	3.6	4.3
W. Germany	%	6.0	4.5	5.9	4.5	6.0	3.5	4.8
E. Germany	%	5.5	4.6	5.7	4.8	†	4.0	4.4
Italy	%	6.3	5.3	†	†	†	3.8	5.8
Hungary	%	6.6	5.8	6.6	5.9	†	5.0	6.0
Poland	%	6.5	5.5	†	†	†	4.5	6.2

† = cells containing fewer than 20 cases

Clearly then, the position one takes on these issues depends on religiosity, not on denomination or, more surprisingly perhaps, on nationality (at least as far as these twelve countries are concerned). In any event, as the table shows, once we control for church attendance, nowhere are there major differences between Catholics and Protestants in prescriptiveness or permissiveness on these items.

Relations between church and state

We are also able to construct from the ISSP data a scale to measure attitudes towards church/state relations. This scale is made up of the following six items, all offering five response categories including a 'can't choose' option (again see Appendix III for full question wordings).

How much do you agree or disagree with each of the following?

Politicians who do not believe in God are unfit for public office.

Religious leaders should not try to influence how people vote in elections.

It would be better for [Britain] if more people with strong religious beliefs held public office.

Religious leaders should not try to influence government decisions.

In your opinion, should there be daily prayers in all state schools?

Some books or films offend people who have strong religious beliefs. Should books and films that attack religions be prohibited by law or should they be allowed?

As before, we have summed answers to these items, scoring them so that the scale runs from 1 to 10 with high scores indicating support for close involvement of the church(es) in politics and the state.[7]

The next table shows how these attitudes are related to religious affiliation in each country, and it tells almost exactly the same story as the previous one. The highest scores, indicating strong support for church/state involvement, are among regular church-going Catholics and Protestants, but on this issue Protestants tend to be especially firm.

Attitudes to church/state relations (mean scores)

		Regular Catholic	Irregular Catholic	Regular Protestant	Irregular Protestant	Other religion	None	All
New Zealand	%	5.6	4.1	5.8	4.1	5.1	3.1	4.1
USA	%	5.2	4.4	5.9	4.9	3.7	3.6	5.1
Irish Republic	%	5.5	4.0	†	†	†	†	5.1
N. Ireland	%	5.4	4.3	5.8	4.9	4.2	4.1	5.3
Britain	%	5.3	4.5	5.5	4.7	5.9	3.6	4.5
Norway	%	†	†	6.2	3.6	5.2	2.8	3.8
Netherlands	%	4.6	3.8	5.1	3.9	4.3	2.8	3.5
W. Germany	%	5.4	3.6	5.5	3.6	4.8	2.5	3.9
E. Germany	%	5.0	4.2	5.2	4.2	†	3.3	3.7
Italy	%	5.0	3.5	†	†	†	2.3	4.3
Hungary	%	5.3	3.9	6.2	4.0	†	3.0	4.3
Poland	%	4.8	3.6	†	†	†	2.5	4.5

† = cells containing fewer than 20 cases

Once again, at the other extreme, in every country people with no religion have the lowest scores.

Religiosity or nationality?

These rather remarkable results suggest that religiosity has similar effects on family values and attitudes towards church/state relations in each of our twelve countries. Thus Northern Ireland, the Irish Republic and

Poland, which are the three most traditional or morally prescriptive of the twelve societies in their family values, are also the three with the highest degree of religiosity; and this pattern more or less persists. This in turn suggests that overall national differences in family values may be explained more by level of religiosity than by other differences in national culture.

We can check the extent of this statistically with a multiple classification analysis. Using Britain as a baseline, we show in the first column of the table below the extent to which each of the eleven other countries differs from Britain in its family values scores (as calculated above, but allowing for small discrepancies due to rounding). A plus score shows that the country is *more* traditional or prescriptive than Britain, and a minus score that it is *less* so. As we can see clearly from the first column, the Irish Republic, Northern Ireland and Poland are comfortably the most traditional in their family values, and the Netherlands and the former East Germany the least so.

National differences in family values allowing for religiosity

	Gross national differences	Net national differences controlling for religiosity
New Zealand	.05	-.07
USA	.84	.19
Irish Republic	1.58	.38
Northern Ireland	1.34	.43
Britain	.00	.00
Norway	-.25	-.15
Netherlands	-.76	-.80
West Germany	-.26	-.51
East Germany	-.69	-.45
Italy	.75	-.01
Hungary	.91	.77
Poland	1.17	.01

The second column of the table shows the *net* country differences, once we have adjusted for differences in religiosity. In each case, once again, the figures tell us simply how different that country is from Britain after taking account of their respective levels of religiosity; and once again these net differences are in many cases substantially lower than the original gross differences shown in the first column. For Poland, Northern Ireland, the Irish Republic, the USA and Italy, these net differences are dramatically less than the original gross differences. Only in the cases of the Netherlands and New Zealand has the control for religiosity made little or no difference. (We must remember, however, that the figures in the second column represent the differences between each country and Britain. It is certainly the case that the difference between, say, the Netherlands and the USA has been substantially reduced by the control.)

To be sure, this analysis shows that some national differences do, after all, remain. Hungary, Northern Ireland and the Irish Republic become the three most traditional societies once we introduce these controls, and the Germanies and the Netherlands are the least traditional. But these differences are much smaller than those we saw in the first column. And it is possible that even these differences may reflect indirect effects of religiosity: a large core of 'traditionalists' in a country may create cultural norms that influence the expressed attitudes of the more permissive members of that society too.

When we carry out a similar analysis of national differences in attitudes towards relations between church and state, we obtain some intriguing differences (as the next table shows). We begin, as before, by looking in the first column at the gross differences between each country and Britain. Although these differences tend to be smaller than those for family values, the general rank ordering of countries is similar: thus Northern Ireland and the Republic are high in the range, favouring a close involvement of church and state, while the Netherlands and the former East Germany are once again at the bottom.

National differences in attitudes to church/state relations allowing for religiosity

	Gross national differences	Net national differences controlling for religiosity
New Zealand	-.42	-.56
USA	.54	-.14
Irish Republic	.58	-.67
Northern Ireland	.74	-.21
Britain	.00	.00
Norway	-.74	-.66
Netherlands	-1.05	-1.10
West Germany	-.60	-.87
East Germany	-.84	-.60
Italy	-.25	-1.03
Hungary	-.28	-.44
Poland	-.01	-1.22

After controlling for differences in levels of religiosity in the second column, the size of the differences between the countries again falls somewhat but the rank ordering also changes dramatically. It is now Britain that proves to be most favourable to close church/state involvement (all other figures being preceded by minus signs); the Irish Republic and Italy sink down the rank order; and the country which becomes least favourable to involvement of the church in politics is

Poland (which before the controls were added had been indistinguishable from Britain).

These analyses show that national differences in attitudes towards church/state relations, like the differences in family values, can largely be explained by national levels of religiosity but that some important unexplained variations remain.[8] To account for these unexplained variations we need to turn to alternative hypotheses. One possibility is that attitudes towards the church's involvement in politics may vary inversely with the actual level of that involvement. The British may, perhaps, feel safe in looking favourably on church involvement in politics, since they believe the actual participation of the churches in political affairs is so small (or ineffectual). And the opposite may be true of the Poles or Italians.

To mitigate this problem, another ISSP question was asked in all twelve countries on the perceived power of the church:

> *Do you think that churches and religious organisations in this country have too much power or too little power?* (on a five-point scale with 'can't choose' responses recoded to the mid-point)

To be sure, Poland proved to be the country where people were most likely to think that the church had too much power, with Italy next (followed closely by West Germany).

We would need a larger sample of countries to draw any definitive conclusions. But these data certainly suggest that the net national differences we uncovered in attitudes towards church/state relations reflect national differences in perceptions of the power of the church in the first place. And the relationship is inverse: the more power the church is believed to have, the less that people favour church involvement.

Religion and party

We now turn to the relationship between religious affiliation and party preference. Naturally, party systems vary considerably across the twelve countries. At one extreme the Americans usually have a choice of only two major parties in Presidential elections (even though ISSP data on party identification do distinguish a third group - independents - in the USA). And at the other extreme is Poland, with members of the sample having voted for over 20 different parties.

We begin our analysis keeping to country-specific schemes for classifying political parties.[9] For each country we have combined the smallest parties and kept all the main parties distinct. (Full details, and the religious affiliation by party for each country, are given in the tables at the end of the chapter.)

In some countries we have data on vote at the last election; in others (especially those where there had been no recent national elections) we have data on party identification. In general, vote and party identification are closely correlated in Europe, but much less so in America, and we need to bear this limitation in mind. We have excluded non-voters and non-identifiers throughout.

In all twelve countries, there is a significant association between religious affiliation and vote, although the size of the association varies from country to country. Not surprisingly, (see, for instance, Curtice and Gallagher, 1990), the strongest association by far is in Northern Ireland, followed some considerable distance behind by the Netherlands, Norway, Italy and West Germany. (The fact that the secular Netherlands, for instance, is in this group is not surprising, because we are referring here to *associations*, not prevalence.) Moreover, the association takes notably different forms in different countries. One pattern, of which Northern Ireland is the extreme example, is where the biggest differences are between *denominations* voting for different parties. Thus, 58 per cent of Catholics there supported the Social Democratic and Labour Party (SDLP), which favours union with the Republic, while not a single *regular* church-going Protestant in the sample did so. Similarly, 62 per cent of regular Protestants supported the Democratic Unionists or the Official Ulster Unionists, and not a single regular Catholic did so. The 'index of dissimilarity' between regular Protestants and Catholics was an enormous 77 points[10] (that is, 77 per cent of the sample would have had to change political preference for the two distributions to become equal). As the table below shows, differences were almost as great between *irregular* church-going Catholics and irregular Protestants, and followed exactly the same pattern.

Religion and party: index of dissimilarity

	Regular Catholic *v* Regular Protestant	Irregular Catholic *v* Irregular Protestant	Regular Catholic *v* No religion	Regular Protestant *v* No religion
New Zealand	17	23	23	35
USA	7	7	20	25
Northern Ireland	77	67	51	31
Britain	14	12	6	18
Norway	†	†	†	66
Netherlands	20	14	55	48
West Germany	20	6	50	16
East Germany	34	11	51	28
Italy	†	†	50	†
Hungary	40	11	57	51

† = cells containing fewer than 20 cases

In the other countries whose samples yield sizeable numbers of regular church-going Catholics and Protestants, political differences do occur but they are much weaker. Thus in Britain the index of dissimilarity is 14 among the regular churchgoers, with Protestants tending toward the Conservative Party, and Catholics tending toward the Labour Party. Nonconformists in Britain have traditionally leaned toward the Liberal Party and, when we exclude them and focus solely on the distinction between regular church-going Catholics and *Anglicans*, the index of dissimilarity does indeed rise slightly (to 23 points).

New Zealand (with an index of 17 in the first column of the table above), the Netherlands (20) and the former West Germany (20) also display denominational differences, and a division (though smaller) appears to be present in the USA too, with an index of 7 points. (The apparently large differences in the former East Germany and Hungary are based on small numbers of cases and should be treated with caution.) In the United States, as in Britain, we need to distinguish the various Protestant groups; Baptists in the USA - a high proportion of whom are black - are, for instance, disproportionately likely to favour the Democrats. When however we exclude Baptists from the analysis, the regular Catholic/regular Protestant index of dissimilarity hardly changes (rising from 7 to 9 points).

In addition to this denominational cleavage, there is a division between regular church attenders and the non-religious. Perhaps the clearest example of this cleavage is in Italy, where 52 per cent of regular church-going Catholics supported the Christian Democrats, compared with only 10 per cent of the non-religious members of the sample. Conversely, 52 per cent of the non-religious respondents supported the communists, compared with 8 per cent of regular Catholics. The index of dissimilarity in Italy between regular Catholics and the non-religious is 50. Of course, these data were collected in 1991, before the corruption scandals that have so discredited not only the Christian Democrats but other major parties too.

Hints of similar patterns are present in the other two Catholic countries, Poland and the Irish Republic, but the numbers of non-religious respondents in these two countries are too small to sustain statistical analysis. In Norway, the one example in the list of a homogeneous Protestant country, we obtain a very similar result to the Italian one: regular church-going Protestants support the Christian Democrats, and the non-religious support the Socialist Left, giving an index of dissimilarity of 66.

The striking thing about these results, however, is that these cleavages are not confined to societies where religiosity or religious feeling is very widespread, or where there is religious or denominational conflict. In the Netherlands, for instance, the Christian Democrats are relatively strong among both regular church-going Catholics *and* Protestants, but weak among non-religious voters, who tend to favour the more left-wing PvdA. A similar pattern was found in the former West Germany, where regular church-goers (whether Catholic or Protestant) were more likely than non-religious respondents to favour the Christian Democrats, while the non-religious leaned toward the Social Democrats. And a similar tendency exists in Anglo-Saxon countries such as Britain and New Zealand.

What clearly emerges from our analysis is that, among the twelve ISSP countries studied, only in Northern Ireland is the *denominational* cleavage especially strong. In other countries, even those with sizeable minorities of both Catholics and Protestants - such as the Netherlands and the former West Germany - it is the strength of one's religiosity, not the church one belongs to, that is more strongly associated with party preference. Indeed, the only two countries in which we could not detect a link between religiosity and party were the Irish Republic and Poland, both homogeneous Catholic countries in which there were, perhaps, just too few non-religious people in the sample to display any pattern at all.

The link between religiosity and vote is not only more widespread across countries than is the denominational cleavage, but it is also more predictable in direction. For instance, while Catholics in some countries tend to support a 'right-wing' party (such as the Christian Democrats in Germany), in others (such as in Northern Ireland or Britain) they tend to vote for a 'left-wing' party. Non-religious voters, on the other hand, tend in all countries to be more on the left, favouring the Greens, social democrats, socialists or communists.

Such denominational differences in voting as do exist in particular countries are generally explained by identifiable historic circumstances or events in those countries. Thus, in Northern Ireland, they have their roots in constitutional issues related to union with the Irish Republic *versus* the maintenance of the union with Britain (Curtice and Gallagher, 1990). In Britain itself they are partly the legacy of nineteenth-century church/state relations and partly of the 'Irish question' (Wald, 1983). In any event, it would be very unwise to attempt to make any sociological generalisations about the nature of denominational cleavages in politics across countries. The cleavages are certainly not related to our general measures of family values or of church/state relations.

We have to be wary too in generalising about the effect of religiosity on politics. For instance, there are specific historical factors which might help to account for the association between the former communist parties and non-religious voters in eastern Europe; and in any case, it may have been membership of the communist parties in those countries that promoted an abandonment of religion, rather than the other way around. On the other hand, elsewhere in Europe religiosity does appear to have much in common with other familiar dimensions that divide Europeans along political lines, such as the left/right dimension and the materialist/postmaterialist one (Inglehart, 1990). For example, in many countries left-wing parties and the Greens attract votes disproportionately from non-religious voters, while the Christian Democratic parties (which tend, of course, to be right-wing on economic issues) attract the votes of regular church attenders). But the relationship between religion, economic ideology and politics is very complex and difficult (perhaps impossible) to disentangle. As Michelat and Simon have suggested, "Spiritual values, family values, freedom, individuality, and property are ... inseparable" (1977b, p.166). They suggest that there may be a Catholic cultural system which stresses consensus and hierarchy and which, by its nature, is likely to oppose communist political programmes. Similarly, could there be a congruence (even an elective affinity) between certain religious world-views and particular economic ideologies?

Conclusions

Even in Britain, not a noticeably devout society, religion has some association with political behaviour and social attitudes, just as it does in other countries covered by the ISSP.

There is no shared legacy of communism, at least between the three former communist countries studied here - Hungary, Poland and the former East Germany. They are as diverse as the west European countries both in their patterns of religious affiliation and in their relations between religion and politics. Thus Poland looks in some respects quite like the Irish Republic; Hungary resembles the former West Germany; only the former East Germany appears to display a distinctive legacy from its recent communist past.

But in all countries there is - more or less to the same extent - an association between one's attitudes to family life and how religious one is. There are also, to a greater or lesser extent across all countries, political divisions associated with religiosity.

Our hypothesis that the consensual societies would be ones where religion plays a smaller role does not appear at first sight to be false. While religious differences are currently of little importance in the Irish Republic and in Poland, the indices of dissimilarity we calculated for the consensual societies of Norway and the former East Germany are just as large as the indices in the divided societies. Moreover, even in the Irish Republic and in Poland there are hints from the data that non-religious respondents may be as distinctive in their attitudes and politics as are their counterparts in other countries. As yet there are so few of them that their influence is minimal. If these countries were to become more secular, however, so that the proportion of non-religious people increased, both societies would experience uncomfortable conflicts, with divisions over family values being a particularly likely battleground.

Notes

1. Regular attenders are defined as people who reported that they attended 'services or meetings in connection with your religion' once a month or more often. Irregular attenders are people who reported that they were Catholic or Protestant but that they

attended less often than once a month, or never. People who reported that they had no religion are placed in the 'no religion' category even if they attended church sometimes. People who did not answer the religious affiliation question are excluded, even if they answered the attendance question.

2. To test the association at the individual level, we collapsed the six-category religious affiliation measure into three, consisting of regular Protestants and Catholics, irregular Protestants and Catholics, and people with no religion (excluding the 'others'). Eta is the appropriate measure for relating a categorical variable such as this to a continuous variable (like the family values scale). For all countries combined, eta was 0.55.

3. A cognate question on 'closeness to God' showed the same pattern in Hungary too.

4. The reliability of the 5-item beliefs scale in each country was measured by calculating Cronbach's alpha for each country separately: New Zealand (.90), USA (.87), Irish Republic (.80), Northern Ireland (.82), Britain (.85), Norway (.89), Netherlands (.89), West Germany (.84), East Germany (.82), Italy (.88), Poland (.82). The dimensionality of the scale was investigated by carrying out a factor analysis of the five items.

5. All the questions in the ISSP module have a 'can't choose' option. Where there were five response categories, the can't chooses have been added to the mid-point ('neither'). Where there were four response categories, the can't chooses have been recoded to create a mid-point, thus creating effectively a five-point scale.

6. The reliability of the 7-item family values scale in each country was measured by calculating Cronbach's alpha for each country separately: New Zealand (.74), USA (.74), Irish Republic (.77), Northern Ireland (.69), Britain (.69), Norway (.70), Netherlands (.75), West Germany (.73), East Germany (.65), Italy (.63), Poland (.63). The dimensionality of the scale was investigated by carrying out a factor analysis of the seven items for each country. In each case this resulted in a two- or three-factor solution, but since these correspond to the batteries in which the items appeared in the questionnaire, it is possible that a response set was in operation.

7. The reliability of the 6-item church/state scale for each country as measured by Cronbach's alpha was: New Zealand (.75), USA (.65), Irish Republic (.69), Northern Ireland (.64), Britain (.65), Norway (.72), Netherlands (.76), West Germany (.75), East Germany (.64), Italy (.70), Poland (.64). A factor analysis of the six items was carried out for each country to check the dimensionality of the scale. A two-factor solution resulted in each case, but these two factors correspond to the direction of the question wording: items worded in a pro-involvement direction consistently load on a different factor from those worded in an anti-involvement direction (again suggesting a response set).

8. The multiple classification analysis shows that some 15 per cent of the total variance in family values, and around 10 per cent of the variance in attitudes towards church/state relations, are between-country variances. After controlling for differences in church attendance, only around 4 per cent of the between-country variances in family values and in attitudes to church/state relations remain unexplained. In other words, nearly three-quarters of the between-country variation in family values can be explained by church attendance, and three-fifths of the between-country variation in attitudes to towards church/state relations can be so explained.

9. There is an ISSP schema which attempts to classify all parties along the right/left spectrum. Since this yields some nonsensical results for Britain (for example the SNP is classed as a right-wing party), and may do so for the other countries too, we have not attempted to use it.

10. To calculate the index of dissimilarity for any two religious groups we first calculate the percentages of each group supporting the various political parties. We then sum the absolute differences and divide by two. The index tells us what is the minimum proportion of the sample that would have to change political preference for the two distributions to become identical.

References

Butler, D. and Stokes, D. (1974), *Political Change in Britain*, revised edition, London: Macmillan.

Curtice, J. and Gallagher, A. (1990), 'The Northern Irish dimension', in Jowell, R., Witherspoon, S. and Brook, L. (eds.), *British Social Attitudes: the 7th Report*, Aldershot: Dartmouth.

Greeley, A. (1993), *Religion around the World: a preliminary report*, University of Chicago: NORC.

Greeley, A. (1992), 'Religion in Britain, Ireland and the USA', in Jowell, R., Brook, L. Prior, G. and Taylor, B. (eds.), *British Social Attitudes: the 9th Report*, Aldershot: Dartmouth.

Heath, A.F., Evans, G. and Martin, J. (forthcoming), 'The measurement of core beliefs and values: the development of balanced socialist/laissez faire and libertarian/authoritarian scales', *British Journal of Political Science*.

Inglehart, R. (1990), *Culture Shift in Advanced Industrial Society*, Princeton: Princeton University Press.

Knutsen, O. (1988), 'The impact of structural and ideological party cleavages in west European democracies: a comparative empirical analysis', *British Journal of Political Science*, 18, pp. 323-352.

Lenski, G. (1963), *The Religious Factor: A Sociologist's Inquiry*, New York: Doubleday.

Lijphart, A. (1979), 'Religious vs linguistic vs class voting: the "crucial experiment" of comparing Belgium, Canada, South Africa and Switzerland', *American Political Science Review*, 73, pp. 442-458.

Lipset, S. and Rokkan, S. (1967), 'Cleavage structures, party systems and voter alignments', in Lipset, S. and Rokkan, S. (eds.), *Party Systems and Voters Alignments*, New York: The Free Press.

Lipson, L. (1953), 'The two-party system in British politics', *American Political Science Review*, 47, p. 353.

Michelat, G. and Simon, M. (1977a), *Classe, Religion et Comportment Politique*, Paris: La Presse de la Fondation Nationale des Sciences Politiques.

Michelat, G. and Simon, M. (1977b), 'Religion, class and politics', *Comparative Politics*, 10, pp. 159-186.

Miller, W. L. and Raab, G. (1977), 'The religious alignment at English elections between 1918 and 1970', *Political Studies*, 25, pp. 227-251.

Wald, K. D. (1983), *Crosses on the Ballot*, Princeton: Princeton University Press.

Wilson, B. R. (1966), *Religion in Secular Society*, London: Watts.

East Germany: affiliation/attendance by party identification

	Regular Catholic	Infrequent Catholic	Regular Protestant	Infrequent Protestant	Other	None	ALL
	%	%	%	%	*N*	%	%
CDU-CSU	63	42	38	32	*(2)*	15	23
FDP	13	7	19	15	*(1)*	13	14
SPD	10	39	38	39	*(4)*	52	46
Green	13	13	5	12		11	11
PDS	0	0	0	1		9	6
Other parties	0	0	0	1		1	1
Base:	*30*	*31*	*37*	*267*	*7*	*613*	*985*

Source: ISSP 1991 (unweighted)

Full party names are:

CDU-CSU	Christian Democratic/Social Union
FDP	Free Democrats
SPD	Social Democrats
PDS	Left List
DKP	German Communist Party

The following categories are combined in the table: DKP (1) and 'Other party' (5) as 'Other parties'.

The following categories are excluded from the table: 'None/no party' (169) 'Refused' (90), 'Don't know/undecided' (222), 'Not answered' (12).

The party identification question in East Germany asks "If there is a general election next Sunday, which party would you elect with your second vote?".

Great Britain: religious affiliation/attendance by party identification

	Regular Catholic	Infrequent Catholic	Regular Protestant	Infrequent Protestant	Other	None	ALL
	%	%	%	%	%	%	%
Conser-vative	36	40	50	48	13	33	41
SLD/Lib	17	9	15	13	16	18	15
Labour	37	48	31	37	61	43	39
Green	6		2	1	10	3	2
Other parties	3	3	2	2		3	3
Base:	*64*	*53*	*146*	*382*	*31*	*350*	*1026*

Source: ISSP 1991 (weighted)

The following categories are combined in the table: Scottish National Party (23), Plaid Cymru (1) and 'Other party' (2) as 'Other parties'.

The following categories are excluded from the table: 'Other answer' (7) 'None' (84), 'Refused' (30), 'Don't know/undecided' (19), 'Not answered' (2).

The party identification question in Britain asks: "Generally speaking, do you think of yourself as a supporter of any political party? If yes: Which one? Do you think of yourself as a little closer to one political party than the others? If yes: Which one? If there were a general election tomorrow which political party do you think you would be most likely to support?"

Hungary: affiliation/attendance by party identification

	Regular Catholic	Infrequent Catholic	Regular Protestant	Infrequent Protestant	Other	None	ALL
	%	%	%	%	N	%	%
MDF	23	16	10	19	(1)	13	17
KDNP	34	4	9	1			10
FKGP	17	12	46	11	(1)	5	15
SzDSz	6	19	7	23	(1)	17	16
FEDES Z	15	35	13	30		47	30
MSZP	4	7	4	11		3	6
Other parties	1	7	12	7		16	6
Base:	*113*	*277*	*25*	*66*	*3*	*29*	*513*

Source: ISSP 1991 (weighted)

Full party names are not available.

The following categories are combined in the table: Socialist Workers' Party (15) and 'Other' (18) as 'Other parties'.

The following categories are excluded from the table: 'Would not vote' (391), 'Not answered' (89).

The party identification question in Hungary asks "If there is a general election next Sunday, would you go to vote?" If yes: "Which party would you vote for?"

Ireland: religious affiliation/attendance by party identification

	Regular Catholic	Infrequent Catholic	Regular Protestant	Infrequent Protestant	Other	None	ALL
	%	%	N	N	N	N	%
Fine Gael	27	20	(11)	(6)	(6)	(3)	27
Fianna Fail	48	37	(4)	(7)	(1)	(1)	44
Labour	10	16	(2)	(1)	(1)	(4)	11
Green	2	5			(3)	(3)	3
Other parties	13	23	(1)	(1)	(3)	(5)	15
Base:	682	142	18	15	14	16	887

Source: ISSP 1991 (weighted)

The following categories are combined in the table: Workers' Party (34), Progressive Party (42), Sinn Fein (20) and 'Other party' (35) as 'Other parties'.

The following categories are excluded from the table: 'None/would not vote' (36), and 'Not answered' (82).

The party identification question in Ireland asks: "If there were a general election tomorrow which party would you vote for?"

Italy: affiliation/attendance by vote in last election

	Regular Catholic	Infrequent Catholic	Regular Protestant	Infrequent Protestant	Other	None	ALL
	%	%	N		N	%	%
MSI	4	2				2	3
PLI, PRI etc	9	8				10	9
DC	52	22				10	37
PSI	12	16	(1)			7	13
Green	6	13			(3)	11	9
PCI, DP	8	21			(2)	52	16
League	3	9				3	5
Other	7	10			(3)	6	8
Base:	*389*	*276*	*1*	*0*	*7*	*49*	*723*

Source: ISSP 1991 (weighted)

Full party names are not available.

The following categories are combined in the table: PLI (17), PRI (23), PSDI (14), PR (8) as 'PLI, PRI etc'; PCI (107) and DP (7) as 'PCI, DP'.

The following categories are excluded from the table: 'Refused' (98), 'Don't know' (152), 'Did not vote/not eligible' (26).

The vote question in Italy asks "Which party did you vote for in the last election: only one vote?".

Northern Ireland: religious affiliation/attendance
by party identification

	Regular Catholic	Infrequent Catholic	Regular Protestant	Infrequent Protestant	Other	None	ALL
	%	%	%	%	N	%	%
DUP			9	16		10	7
OUP			54	37	(1)	22	30
Conser-vative	6	16	20	27		23	17
NI Alliance	10	5	9	7		13	9
Labour	15	14	3	7		12	9
SDLP	53	39				3	18
Green	4				(1)	2	2
Other parties	13	27	4	6		13	9
Base:	207	21	255	131	2	43	660

Source: ISSP 1991 (weighted)

The following categories are combined in the table: SLD/Liberal/SDP/(mainland) Alliance (9), Sinn Fein (28), Workers' Party (5) and 'Other party' (14) as 'Other parties'.

The following categories are excluded from the table: 'Other answer' (4), 'None' (109), 'Refused' (326) and 'Not answered' (6).

The party identification question in Northern Ireland asks: "Generally speaking, do you think of yourself as a supporter of any political party? If yes: Which one? Do you think of yourself as a little closer to one political party than the others? If yes: Which one? If there were a general election tomorrow which poltical party do you think you would be most likely to support?"

Netherlands: religious affiliation/attendance by pre-election voting intention

	Regular Catholic	Infrequent Catholic	Regular Protestant	Infrequent Protestant	Other	None	ALL
	%	%	%	%	%	%	%
VVD	11	16	6	26	14	21	17
CDA	62	37	55	23	16	6	28
D66	1	4	2	6		8	5
PvdA	25	39	16	42	49	57	43
Other parties	1	5	20	5	22	8	8
Base:	*167*	*207*	*142*	*106*	*37*	*502*	*1161*

Source: Dutch Election Study 1986 (unweighted)

Full party names are:

VVD	People's Party for Freedom and Democracy
CDA	Christian Democratic Appeal
D66	Democratic Party '66
PvdA	Labour Party

Norway: affiliation/attendance by party identification

	Regular Catholic	Infrequent Catholic	Regular Protestant	Infrequent Protestant	Other	None	ALL
	N	*N*	%	%	%	%	%
Conser-vative		*(1)*	12	20		8	18
Progress			1	11		7	10
Centre		*(1)*	9	8	5	1	8
Christian Democrat			58	3	29	3	9
Labour	*(2)*	*(1)*	15	43	52	27	39
Socialist Left		*(1)*	2	10	5	35	11
Other parties			4	5	10	19	6
Base:	2	4	*113*	*838*	*21*	*74*	*1052*

Source: ISSP 1991 (unweighted)

The following categories are combined in the table: Red Electoral Alliance (9), Liberal Party (39) and 'Other party' (10) as 'Other parties'.

The following categories are excluded from the table: 'None/would not vote' (91), 'Don't know' (306) and 'Not answered' (38).

The party identification question in Norway asks: "If there was a parliamentary election *(Stortingsvalg)* tomorrow, which party would you vote on?"

New Zealand: affiliation/attendance by vote in last election

	Regular Catholic	Infrequent Catholic	Regular Protestant	Infrequent Protestant	Other	None	ALL
	%	%	%	%	%	%	%
National	51	37	68	60	44	33	50
Labour	38	44	26	29	32	47	36
New Labour	6	8	2	4		4	4
Green		8		4	16	13	7
Other parties	6	3	4	4	8	4	4
Base:	*53*	*73*	*133*	*325*	*25*	*258*	*867*

Source: ISSP 1991 (unweighted)

The following categories are combined in the table: Democrat (9), Mana Motuhake (6), New Zealand Party (2) and Social Credit (16) as 'Other parties'.

The following categories are excluded from the table: 'Did not vote' (90), 'Other' (1) and 'Not answered' (48).

The vote question in New Zealand asks "At the 1990 General Election, which political party did you vote for?"

Poland: Religious affiliation/attendance by vote in last election

	Regular Catholic	Infrequent Catholic	Regular Protestant	Infrequent Protestant	Other	None	ALL
	%	%			N	N	%
POC	9	6					8
Christian parties	13	2					11
KLD, URP	8	12			(1)		9
UD	25	39				(6)	28
Solidarity	9	5				(1)	8
Peasant parties	13	5					11
KPN	10	10					9
SLD	5	13				(3)	7
Other parties	9	9				(2)	9
Base:	*343*	*71*	*0*	*0*	*1*	*13*	*428*

Source: ISSP 1991 (weighted)

Full party names are:

POC   Centre Alliance
KLD   Liberal Democratic Alliance
URP   Real Political Union
UD   Democratic Union
KPN   Independent Poland Confederation
SLD   Left-Democracy Alliance

The following categories are combined in the table: Catholic Election Action (44) and Christian Democracy (2) as 'Christian parties'; Peasant Party 'Programme Alliance' (30), Election Committee 'Peasant Alliance' (16) and Peasant Election 'Piast' (2) as 'Peasant parties'; Liberal-Democratic Alliance (33) and Real Politic Union (4) as 'KLD, URP'; Polish Beer Friends Party (17), Solidarity of Work (6), Democratic-Societal Movement (1), National Party (1), 'For Wielkopolska and Poland' (1), Coalition of Polish Green and Ecological parties (5), Democratic Party (4), 'In Solidarity with the President' (1), Party 'X' (2) and 'Other parties' (2) as 'Other parties'.

The following categories are excluded from the table: 'Don't know' (87), 'Not answered' (7), 'Did not vote' (532).

The vote question in Poland asked which party or candidate the respondent voted for in April 1990.

USA: religious affilation/attendance by party identification

	Regular Catholic	Infrequent Catholic	Regular Protestant	Infrequent Protestant	Other	None	ALL
	%	%	%	%	%	%	%
Republican	29	29	35	33	7	19	31
Independent	33	41	28	33	35	50	33
Democrat	39	30	37	33	50	29	35
Other parties		1	1		7	3	1
Base:	*200*	*157*	*447*	*357*	*54*	*91*	*1306*

Source: ISSP 1991 (unweighted)

The following categories are combined in the table: 'Strong Democrat' (190) and 'Not strong Democrat' (270) as 'Democrat'; 'Independent, near Democrat' (122), 'Independent' (162) and 'Independent, near Republican' (152) as 'Independent'; 'Not strong Republican' (248) and 'Strong Republican' (150) as 'Republican'.

The following categories are excluded from the table: 'Not answered' (5).

The party identification question in USA asks: "Generally speaking, do you usually think of yourself as a Republican, Democrat, Independent or what? (If Republican or Democrat) Would you call yourself a strong or not a very strong Republican or Democrat? (If Independent) Do you think of yourself as closer to the Republican or Democratic party?"

West Germany: affiliation/attendance by party identification

	Regular Catholic	Infrequent Catholic	Regular Protestant	Infrequent Protestant	Other	None	ALL
	%	%	%	%	N	%	%
CDU-CSU	65	31	45	26	(5)	16	34
FDP	6	12	14	13	(1)	14	12
SPD	24	50	31	52	(4)	55	45
Green	5	6	7	9	(3)	16	9
Other parties	1		3				
Base:	*162*	*250*	*71*	*390*	*13*	*110*	*996*

Source: ISSP 1991 (unweighted)

Full party names are:

CDU-CSU   Christian Democratic/Social Union
FDP   Free Democrats
SPD   Social Democrats
NDP   National Democratic Party

The following categories are combined in the table: NPD (1) and Republikaner (3) as 'Other parties'.

The following categories are excluded from the table: 'None/no party' (79), 'Refused' (92), 'Don't know/undecided' (146), 'Not answered' (26).

The vote question in West Germany asks "If there is a general election next Sunday, which party would you elect with your second vote?".

4 What citizens want from the state

*Peter Taylor-Gooby**

What do people in different countries expect from their governments? In particular, how far do they want government to extend? These questions are at the centre of politics in many countries and increasingly affect international debates, such as the controversy about the future of the European Community.

Two recent international events in particular have fractured the old order. First, the reforms initiated by Gorbachev in 1985 had by 1989 led to the collapse of Soviet hegemony in eastern Europe and the break-up of the Soviet Union itself. Then the United States, in pursuit of a 'new world order', led a coalition of nations, assembled under the United Nations flag, to the Gulf War victory of 1991, confirming the new, unchallenged US hegemony in world affairs. Alternatives to the 'Western idea' of free market economies within social or liberal democracies were fast disappearing.

At the national level too, governments were facing new dilemmas. A combination of slow growth, high unemployment and escalating national debt had, by the end of the 1970s, marked the end of the Western economic postwar boom. Governments could no longer be confident that the resources to enable them to spend their way out of recession would be available. At the same time, demographic changes (in particular the rising number of elderly people) and the costs of high unemployment were placing fresh pressures on state spending - a problem exacerbated as always by the uncomfortable habit of voters to insist on tax cuts and

---

* Professor of Social Policy, University of Kent

improvements in public services simultaneously. In any case, governments more or less everywhere nowadays are faced with the problem of satisfying incompatible expectations on the part of their electorates.

Developments within the European Community have brought some of these problems to the forefront. In particular, moves towards 'ever closer union' have been hotly disputed in many member states, sharpening the debate about the proper role and responsibilities of the state *vis-à-vis* its citizens.

All three issues - the changing world order, balancing demands for lower taxes against those for higher spending, and conflicts over the future direction of the EC - are bound to be reflected in changing social attitudes. Fukuyama, the most influential proponent of 'convergence theory' - the thesis that all the different world ideologies are about to come together - rests his arguments on the notion that history is driven more by dominant ideas than by economic or social forces. What has happened recently, he argues, is that the ideology of parliamentary democracy accompanied by economic individualism has become the dominant world order, as has a commitment to free enterprise economics and a distaste for state intervention in the market place. He sums up the twentieth century as 'an unabashed victory of economic and political liberalism...the triumph of the West, of the Western idea...' (Fukuyama, 1989, p. 3).

Opponents of this convergence theory argue that, while ideology is important, so are more mundane issues such as the role of economic growth rates, industrial structure and demography in maintaining or enlarging differences in politico-economic patterns from country to country (see Taylor-Gooby, 1991, pp. 60-65).

How have governments responded to the pressure for higher spending and lower taxes? In short, in almost all the advanced countries, taxation has become *less* progressive over the past decade, although revenues have increased. For instance, in the fourteen principal OECD countries, marginal tax rates for high earners fell by an average of 18 per cent between 1975 and 1990 (Heidenheimer *et al*, 1990, p. 211). One reason for this trend towards regressive taxation may be that the increasing ability of high earners to pay for private provision makes them less willing to help pay for core welfare services. In addition, the increasing mobility of capital and skilled labour makes it difficult for governments to operate a tax regime in respect of business and industry substantially different from that in other countries. High business taxes would simply drive investment elsewhere. So, unless the mass of the population pays more in taxes, it seems unlikely that governments can substantially improve welfare provision.

These trends highlight the importance of social attitudes, both at a national level - as a measure of the strength of feeling about the need for improved welfare - and at an international level. For instance, as the EC determines key issues of fiscal and economic policy and of social provision, public attitudes are bound to play a major role in influencing the potential or otherwise for closer European union.

The samples

This chapter examines data from the 1985 and 1990 ISSP 'role of government' questionnaire modules. It looks especially at questions of ideological convergence and differentiation, the conflict between the desire for better standards of social provision and for lower taxes, and attitudes towards economic and political rapprochement between EC countries.

The period between the two surveys coincides more or less with the emergence of the USA as the undisputed world superpower, and with the beginning of the decline into recession and decreased public spending in many countries. This was the period too in which the foundations for Maastricht were being laid (notably in the Val Duchesse agreement and the Single European Act, which was passed in member states in 1986/87).

The 1985 survey covers six countries (Australia, Austria, Britain, Italy, the United States and the former West Germany). The 1990 survey covers all of these except Austria, and also includes the former East Germany, Hungary, Republic of Ireland, Northern Ireland and Norway, although fieldwork in the Republic of Ireland and Italy was not carried out until early 1991.

We have decided not to restrict the analysis to those countries surveyed in *both* years since the additional information enables us to examine a wider range of countries and regimes. Moreover, results from the extended range of countries will provide a useful benchmark against which to measure changes when this module is repeated in 1996.

Convergence in the boundaries of government responsibility

If the proponents of 'convergence theory' are correct in predicting the demise of rival national political ideologies, we might expect that popular ideas about the role of government would also be drawing together. Thus, a comparison of the results from the 1985 and 1990 surveys should reveal evidence of a trend away from the relics of socialist and welfarist ideas towards undiluted free-market ideas. Such a trend may, for instance, be reflected in beliefs about what aspects of politico-economic life ought (or ought not) to be the government's responsibility, and in opinions about specific policies such as nationalisation, economic intervention and public spending. So the first step is to test the extent to which public attitudes have changed in the five-year period towards the general issue of where the legitimate boundaries of state responsibility ought to lie.

We looked first at the 1990 responses to a question on whether "it should or should not be the government's responsibility" to provide a number of services ranging from core welfare provision (health care, retirement pensions, housing, benefits for unemployed people), to more active economic interventions (price control, the right to work, help for industry), to active policies for redistribution between rich and poor, and for more equal access to higher education. The tables below show the percentages in each country who answered that the given service should 'definitely' be the state's responsibility. Although the answers reveal a common pattern of citizen demands from government, clear national differences do exist.

The most obvious common feature is the priority given to health care and adequate pensions in all the countries surveyed as compared with the provision of decent housing and help for unemployed people.

% saying definitely govt. responsibility to provide:	Britain	W. Germany	E. Germany	Hungary	Italy	Ireland	Norway	N. Ireland	USA
Health care	85	57	82	75	88	83	84	83	40
Decent pensions	79	54	85	77	82	81	86	81	40
Decent housing	47	24	49	35	45	56	38	56	21
Decent unemployment benefits	32	35	52	21	32	46	42	46	14

Source: ISSP 1990 data

As the table shows, established mass services - in particular health care and pensions - that do not involve direct intervention in the labour market, or in existing commodity markets, are clearly highly popular in all countries, though much less in the USA than in Europe. Within Europe, West Germans are the most fainthearted and Italians the most enthusiastic in their support for improved mass services.

The next table covers economic interventions and policies designed to achieve greater equality of opportunity (and of outcome). It is apparent immediately that these 'interventionist' policies are a great deal less popular than are the welfare ones. In addition, differences between countries are greater on these issues.

% saying definitely govt. responsibility to:	Britain	W. Germany	E. Germany	Hungary	Italy	Ireland	Norway	N. Ireland	USA
Provide jobs for all	24	30	63	52	38	38	52	35	16
Control prices	48	20	50	50	67	59	58	52	19
Aid industrial growth	43	12	35	41	29	54	23	45	25
Reduce income differences	42	22	48	47	38	52	39	47	17
Help low-income students	49	31	59	39	53	64	38	55	31

Source: ISSP 1990 data.

National differences are of two principal kinds. First, public opinion is much more 'statist' in some countries than in others. Thus, support for 'interventionist' policies is strongest in the former East Germany, Hungary, Ireland, Italy, Northern Ireland and Britain, while people in the United States and the former West Germany are more suspicious of the role of government.

The second kind of difference reflects distinctive national rather than ideological concerns, and the story is more complex. In countries such as Italy, Ireland and East Germany there is strong support for statism across the board, while in Norway and Britain, the support is more selective and is concentrated on traditional service-oriented welfare statism rather than on economic intervention or consciously redistributive policies. Americans are distinctive: they support government intervention in fostering equal opportunities in education, but are extremely wary of interventionist polices in all the other areas.

So, despite some common threads running through the data, there was in 1990 no apparent cross-national consensus or 'convergence'. Moreover, when we examine movements in attitudes towards these issues between 1985 and 1990 in the five countries for which we have data across time, we find no discernible trend towards international convergence.

Indeed, despite quite a bit of movement in both directions, the differences between countries are remarkably robust. True, overall support for state responsibility has tended to increase slightly in the United States over the period, but in West Germany it has declined in some areas and remained stable in others. In both Britain and Italy, opinion has moved one way on some measures and in the opposite direction on others. Notably, however, there is no single issue on which attitudes have moved in the same direction in all the countries. In short, the evidence does not sustain a theory of increasing international consensus.

We explored these responses to governmental responsibilities further by means of 'factor analysis' in order to discover whether or not there was a persistent basic *structure* to these attitudes in both years. And indeed there was, to a remarkable extent, in all five countries. (In no instance did an attitude load predominantly on one factor in 1985 and predominantly on another in 1990). Although there are three minor shifts in emphasis - towards government aid for industry in Britain and towards provision for unemployed people in Germany, which doubtless reflect objective changes in circumstances, the basic picture is consistent over time.

The factor analysis also brings out the distinctive structure of attitudes in the United States, where the commitment to economic liberalism is reflected in a unidimensional structure of attitudes. In all other countries, attitudes to the core services (health care and provision for pensioners) stand out as a separate attitudinal factor. Where countries vary most is in their attitudes to economic issues of price control, wage control, and help for unemployed people.

There is thus a sharp division in all countries between strong support for direct mass provision of health care and pensions, and more ambivalence about attitudes to those services which involve government intervention in either the operation of markets or the redistribution of wealth. Secondly, there is a clear distinction between countries, notably the United States, where there is resistance to the intervention of government in more or less any of these areas of social and economic life, and those, notably Italy and the former socialist countries in Europe, where a great deal is demanded of the state. The other nations occupy intermediate positions. And this pattern seems to have remained undisturbed, at least in the five countries for which we have trend data, during the turbulence between 1985 and 1990.

Convergence in economic and industrial policies

Two dominant areas of policy debate over recent years have been the privatisation of state enterprises and the extent and direction of government intervention in the economy. The convergence thesis implies that nations are moving towards a common model based on private ownership, free enterprise and limited state spending. From this perspective, the traditional mixed economy should be in retreat.

An insight into the level of support for government intervention in industry is provided by a series of questions covering attitudes to state ownership of the electricity and steel industries (in Norway, aluminium) and of banking. The answers do indeed show not only that public support for state ownership is limited in all the countries, but that such limited support as there was is either static or waning.

The almost complete lack of support for state ownership in the United States, the higher (though still modest) level of support in East Germany, Italy and Britain, and the somewhat greater enthusiasm in Hungary, reflects the pattern of support for 'statism' revealed in the earlier analysis of attitudes to state responsibilities.

% supporting state ownership

		Australia	Britain	West Germany	Italy	USA
Electricity	1985	37	26	19	36	6
	1990	38	30	16	28	6
Steel	1985	5	19	9	22	6
	1990	5	14	6	18	3
Banks	1985	5	10	5	24	3
	1990	7	7	7	21	4

		East Germany	Hungary	Ireland	Norway	Northern Ireland
Electricity	1990	30	40	18	28	28
Steel	1990	27	27	9	8	17
Banks	1990	20	28	10	7	9

Overall, the responses reflect the recent actual shift towards privatisation in most advanced economies. We cannot yet tell from these answers alone, however, whether this indicates a general mood of disillusionment with government economic intervention or just a resigned acquiescence in what seems to be an irreversible trend in public policy. Other answers throw light on this. For instance, the ISSP questionnaire included the following question designed to tap public attitudes to government intervention in eight different areas of the economy.

> *Here are some things the government might do for the economy. Please show which actions you are in favour of and which you are against.*

The first table below gives the pattern of results, showing only those 'strongly in favour' of each policy, in the five countries for which we have trend data; the second table shows only the 1990 figures for those countries that did not field a 1985 module.

Strongly in favour of government intervention

		Australia	Britain	Germany	Italy	USA
		%	%	%	%	%
Wage control	1985	14	10	11	31	9
	1990	8	7	9	22	7
Price control	1985	24	20	28	54	8
	1990	15	15	20	42	9
Spending cuts	1985	33	11	40	35	41
	1990	26	11	38	28	37
Create new jobs	1985	25	37	30	56	28
	1990	16	27	31	46	25
Deregulate business	1985	19	13	14	12	18
	1990	10	8	10	9	11
Support new technology	1985	38	37	31	27	22
	1990	32	35	28	21	26
Support declining industries	1985	15	19	25	35	17
	1990	9	18	26	30	15
Reduce working week	1985	7	16	22	26	6
	1990	4	10	23	22	8

	East Germany 1990	Hungary 1990	Norway 1990	Northern Ireland 1990
	%	%	%	%
Wage control	50	16	8	9
Price control	62	19	13	19
Spending cuts	38	53	27	11
Create new jobs	68	47	28	30
Deregulate business	14	40	13	7
Support new technology	54	56	27	31
Support declining industries	51	29	12	22
Reduce working week	47	21	6	12

Overall support is strongest for job creation policies, for the promotion of new technology, and for cuts in state spending - except amongst the British and Northern Irish (who may have thought that the cuts were already too deep) - and weakest for wage control, a reduction in the regulation of business and shortening the working week. While there is some enthusiasm for government investment, there is little overall support for substantial direct government intervention into the operation of market capitalism.

Notably however, there has, on all these items, been a remarkably consistent decline between 1985 and 1990 (shown in the first table above) in the level of support for economic intervention on all eight items. Some of the shifts may be explained by changes in objective circumstances: for instance, the fall in support for price control may simply reflect a fall in levels of inflation over the period, where in 1990 only the East Germans among all the nations (and for self-evident reasons) were strong proponents of statutory controls on prices (although they were keen on wage controls too). But the overall shift is undeniably a *general* pattern, and it gives some support to the convergence theory - at least as far as these important indicators are concerned.

In general, the country differences in attitudes to interventionist policies follow the pattern of attitudes to statism discussed earlier. Thus, the United States and Australia are the least interventionist, and the east Europeans (Hungary and, especially, East Germany) are the most interventionist. It is interesting that Norway, often seen as typifying the highly interventionist Scandinavian post war governments, scores lower than average in its support for all eight interventionist measures.

There are also, as before, a number of country-specific variations. West Germans are conspicuous in their support for aid to declining industries and a reduction in the working week; Australia and Britain in particular favour government support for new technology; Hungary (in contradiction to its general position) favours cuts in state spending as well as more de-regulation of business; Italy, alone among the Western economies, displays very high support for price controls. These variations doubtless reflect national factors, such as the reliance on a subsidised manufacturing base in Germany, the widespread concern in Australia and Britain about import penetration from more technically advanced economies, the experience of state socialism in Hungary and of inflation in Italy.

These national variations apart, there is clear evidence of an *international* movement of attitudes on these eight measures, away from the relatively interventionist position of the mid-1980s and earlier, towards a relatively free-market ideology in 1990. The change is most striking in attitudes to price and wage control. It is too early to talk of a definite trend (the next measure in two or three years' time, with a larger number of countries to look at, will confirm or disprove the existence of an international trend), but the consistent, unidirectional movement in attitudes that we have recorded so far is impressive indeed.[1]

So there appears to be a clear pattern of attitudes to the role of government in many countries: increasingly, public expectations of governments are that they should meet people's immediate and obvious needs, but that they should not intervene too much in the workings of the market economy. This pattern hardly fits a model of a fast developing *ideological* convergence, or - as Fukuyama calls it - 'the end of history'. Despite the very substantial shifts in the world political order between 1985 and 1990, all we have found so far is that economic intervention by government, never very popular in the first place, has now become even less so. Detailed examination of the data still show real and sustained differences in attitudes between countries that are much too complex to be captured in a one-dimensional model of change.

It is thus still appropriate to describe the United States as 'liberal' in the sense that Americans are the least likely to see a role for government across the board (see Davis, 1986; Smith, 1989). Australians follow this pattern in many respects too. In contrast, the former central European communist states and Italy tend to favour widespread intervention. Other countries, including Britain, come somewhere in between, preferring selective intervention, principally on welfare matters such as health care.

Squaring the spending circle

The demand for more spending

Between 1970 and 1985, public spending in industrial nations increased steadily from about 30 per cent to about 40 per cent of national product (OECD, 1993). The two biggest items of social spending in most countries are still pensions and health care. Because the main beneficiaries of health care and pensions are elderly people, demographic change means that the cost of maintaining current standards in these services is set to increase greatly. And this sort of state spending has strong public support. Nonetheless, most advanced countries took steps in the 1980s to limit their welfare responsibilities. For instance, pension reforms have been undertaken in Britain in 1986, in the United States in 1987, in Germany in 1989, and in Italy in 1992. While none of these reforms will actually reduce the total current burden on the public purse, they are all designed to limit the scale of future increases in demand.

But although pressures for higher government spending nowadays are becoming greater, it is becoming more and difficult for governments to expand tax revenues. As noted earlier, one reason for this is that the relatively poor - who generate the bulk of tax revenues - are already bearing more of the tax burden than they used to in many countries. However, the conflict between demands for higher spending and for lower taxes is hardly a new one, and perceived popular expectations have always played a crucial role in determining the outcome.

The ISSP dealt with the issue in two ways. First, a number of questions asked about the extent to which people wanted more state spending on a range of services. And a second set of questions asked about the extent to which people were keen on the adoption of a number of different taxation strategies - in particular on where the tax burden should fall. The questionnaire listed a number of important categories of state spending and asked whether people "would like to see more or less government spending" on each, using a five-point scale from 'much less' to 'much more'. To mitigate the obvious drawback of this question as it stands, a postscript was added: "Remember, if you say 'much more', it might require a tax increase to pay for it".

The table below gives the percentage of respondents who replied 'much more', despite the implied discouragement. Despite many national differences in provision, there is a clear overall cross-national pattern: health care and the environment tend to be very high priorities, as do pensions and education, while defence and culture are always low priorities, as is unemployment benefit. Notably, environmental spending receives relatively low priority in Britain, Northern Ireland and the United States despite the fact that these three countries (especially, of course, the USA) make a substantial contribution to world pollution. In stark contrast, in West Germany environment is comfortably the dominant target for extra spending.

% in each country calling for 'much more' public spending
on each of nine possible targets (1990)

	Australia	Britain	West Germany	Hungary	Italy	Northern Ireland	Norway	USA
Environment	17	15	61	36	26	14	25	16
Health Care	16	36	36	59	39	42	25	20
Police and Law	14	11	12	14	17	10	13	11
Education	18	27	20	42	23	24	11	26
Defence	5	2	2	3	2	5	1	3
Pensions	12	29	16	41	26	43	16	13
Unemployed People	2	8	9	10	15	20	4	7
Culture	2	2	5	16	10	2	2	3

Note: these questions were not fielded in the Republic of Ireland and East Germany.

Reassuringly, calls for extra spending follow the pattern set by opinions on where state responsibility should lie. So again we see substantially more support for increased spending generally in Hungary and Italy, followed by Northern Ireland and Britain, though in this case little support for extra spending in Norway, except on the environment. Americans and Australians are once again the least keen on increased state spending, although there is considerable commitment to more investment in education in the USA (probably associated with the widespread commitment to an ideology of opportunity there), and to law and order in Australia.

These responses bring out powerfully the problems that modern governments face in reconciling demands for extra spending with existing revenues. In general, the areas accorded low priority tend to account for a small proportion of state spending, while the high priority areas - especially health care, pensions and education - are much more costly. When we compare these responses with those given to the same question five years earlier, the most striking change, both overall and in individual countries, is the greater priority given to environmental spending.

Redistribution

Direct taxation has tended to become rather less progressive worldwide, with governments tending to place greater reliance on indirect taxation to maintain revenues. Unfortunately, although the ISSP question did explicitly link public spending to higher taxes, the survey did not ask any direct questions about people's willingness or otherwise to pay increased taxes, or whether they preferred direct to indirect taxation. It did, however, include questions about support for progressive taxation - that is, whether those with high incomes should pay a greater proportion of their income in tax, a smaller proportion or the same proportion. Both in 1985 and in 1990, the answers show strong support for progressive taxation. Once again, the lowest support for progressive taxes comes from the United States and Australia, but even in those countries there is majority support and virtually no-one who advocates the better-off paying a *smaller* proportion of income in tax than the less well-off. Nowhere else is the proportion opposed to progressive taxation greater than 17 per cent in either year.

% expressing support for progressive taxation

	Austra-lia	Britain	W. Ger-many	E. Ger-many	Hungary	Ireland	Italy	N. Ireland	Nor-way	USA
1985	65	76	90	-	-	-	86	-	-	58
1990	66	85	87	95	85	83	84	86	75	62

As the table above shows, there is little change in attitudes to this issue over time, except, notably, in Britain, where support for progressive taxation has grown markedly during a period when it was most under threat. The strongest support for highly progressive taxation is in East Germany, but there is not much to separate most of the other European countries in their attitudes to this issue. Only in Norway is the level of support for progressive taxes surprisingly moderate, especially given the strong social democratic tradition of that country. Once again, the real divide is between social democratic (and former communist) Europe on the one hand, and the liberal democracies of the United States and Australia on the other.

The widespread enthusiasm we have found for progressive taxation is, of course, against the trend of government policy in many countries, not least Britain. Moreover, in response to another ISSP question as to whether or not government should reduce income differences between higher and lower income groups, the pattern of opinion is similar - though at a lower level of support. Notably, we find more support for redistribution on this question than we did on another very similar question (referred to earlier) on whether it was the government's responsibility to reduce the gap between *rich and poor* (as opposed to the broader category of higher and lower income groups). Could this reveal, perhaps, a lack of positive commitment to tackle major inequalities in society, and merely a desire that the better-off should bear a greater burden of the cost of public services that they also enjoy?

% expressing support for reducing income differences between those with high and those with low incomes*

	Australia	Britain	W. Germany	E. Germany	Ireland	Italy	N. Ireland	Norway	USA
1985	45	52	56	-	-	67	-	-	30
1990	42	57	56	75	69	70	64	56	34

* This question was not fielded in Hungary in either year.

It is clear then, at least in principle, that most people would impose higher taxes on those with higher incomes in order to finance improvements in the most popular (or the most neglected) areas of provision. On this important issue, governments in a wide spectrum of nations seem to be out of step with public opinion. But the supreme unanswered question remains unanswered: despite an apparent *ideology* of equity, would people really be prepared to accept the consequences of the tax and spending policies they advocate?

The gap between rich and poor

We have been talking about high income groups, low income groups, rich and poor, as if they had a standard meaning within any one society, let alone a range of societies. It is helpful, therefore, to use data from another ISSP module for a better idea of how people in different societies see their own income distributions, particularly the perceived pay differences between a variety of occupational groups.

The 1987 ISSP module asked a series of questions about what income respondents thought 11 different occupations (such as doctors, skilled factory workers, unskilled workers and chairmen of large companies) were *actually* paid, and how much income they felt each occupation *should* be paid. These data enable us to explore differences between the patterns of perceived actual and appropriate rewards. We confined our analysis to six countries - Hungary and Poland (representing former communist economies), Austria and West Germany (representing Western European social democracies), and Britain and the USA (representing the more *laissez-faire* Anglo-Saxon economies).

First we show the average rank order of occupations that resulted when respondents in the six countries were asked about the *actual* wages or salaries of each occupation.

Average ranking of perceived actual earnings of 11 occupations (1987)

	Hungary	Poland	Austria	West Germany	Britain	USA
Cabinet minister	1	1	2	2	2	3
Chairman	2	3	1	1	1	1
Shopkeeper	3	2	4	4	4	4
Bricklayer	4	4	8	9	6	5
Doctor	5	8	3	3	3	2
Bus driver	6	7	7	7	8	7
Skilled factory worker	7	6	6	6	5	6
Farm worker	8	5	10	11	10	10
Bank clerk	9	10	5	5	7	8
Unskilled factory worker	10	9	11	10	11	11
Secretary	11	11	9	8	9	9

As can be seen from the table, there is considerable consensus across these six countries in respect of the perceived actual levels of monetary rewards for the 11 occupations. Cabinet ministers and chairmen of large companies are thought to earn higher salaries than the other occupations, while unskilled factory workers and secretaries are thought to be among the lowest earners. The average rankings of middle-earning jobs, such as shopkeepers and bus drivers, were also close to one another in all six countries. Indeed, for all these exemplars of the occupational pay structure, we were somewhat surprised at the level of shared perceptions that existed.

However, even with these broad perceptions in common, it is clear that there are distinctive national patterns in perceptions about existing income differences, as well as broad East/West contrasts in the rankings. Apart from the fact that the two eastern European nations believe cabinet ministers' earn more than company chairmen (no doubt reflecting the dominance of the communist party in the former reward structure), Western nations tend to put doctors in the top three in the average ranking of actual perceived incomes, while Hungary and Poland reflect reality in these countries by assigning them lower rankings (of five and eight respectively). The Americans are particularly likely to believe that doctors are relatively highly paid, a perception which probably also reflects reality.

Moreover, the large differences that exist in the average rankings of perceived actual income for three other listed occupations (bricklayers, bank clerks and farm workers), all reflect differences in the occupational income structure between the market-led west and the monetary rewards mandated by the former communist economies. The relatively high average rankings of bricklayers, for instance, in both Hungary and Poland probably reflects the long-term dominance of skilled construction work in those countries, and the large difference between east and west in the ranking of farm workers' incomes probably reflects the relatively privileged position of farmers in the more agriculturally-inefficient Eastern bloc.

Of course, the relative rankings of the perceived average income of the eleven occupations tell us little about what people think different occupations *should* be worth. The table below shows the same six countries, and the same eleven occupations, and gives the rankings of the average wage or salary respondents felt people in each occupation *ought* to receive.

Average ranking of earnings that people in each of 11 occupations ought to receive (1987)

	Hungary	Poland	Austria	West Germany	Britain	USA
Cabinet minister	1	1	2	2	2	3
Chairman	2	2	1	1	1	1
Shopkeeper	5	3	4	4	4	4
Bricklayer	4	5	8	7	6	6
Doctor	3	4	3	3	3	2
Bus driver	6	7	7	8	9	7
Skilled factory worker	7	8	6	5	5	5
Farm worker	8	6	10	10	7	8
Bank clerk	10	9	5	6	8	9
Unskilled factory worker	9	10	11	11	11	11
Secretary	11	11	9	9	10	10

Surprisingly, perhaps, we find even more agreement between countries about the relative ranking of what the eleven occupations ought to be worth. The average rankings are largely similar, with three exceptions. First, the two middle European social democracies (Austria and West Germany) rank the desirable earnings of bricklayers much lower than either the two communist or the two *laissez-faire* economies. Second, Hungary and Poland tend to downgrade (in comparison with all western nations except the USA) the desirable earnings of bank clerks, revealing that the manual/non-manual divide is not only factually, but also normatively, weaker in the eastern bloc than in market systems (though this may of course be changing). A possible explanation for the relatively low American ranking of this occupation is that in the United States,

unlike Europe, bank clerks are overwhelmingly likely to be female.
Third, the largest difference once again in the normative rankings of
incomes is the relative position of farm workers in the East and West,
with Hungarians and Poles according them a much higher ranking -
further evidence of the distinctly privileged position of the eastern
agricultural sector.

In confirmation of the findings referred to earlier, the most striking
finding from an analysis of the perceived gaps in people's earnings is that
in all six countries, regardless of political history and economic
philosophy, the bulk of respondents wish to cut the salaries of (most of)
the better-off, and to raise the wages off (most of) the worse-off. Other
than this general redistributive pattern, the occupational structure within
each country seems to have a more decisive influence on answers than
does any generalised pattern of perceptions. (But see Evans *et al,* 1992;
and Kelley and Evans, forthcoming, for some elegant and informative
summaries of the differences between Australia and Hungary.) Thus,
respondents in all countries would cut the salaries of cabinet ministers
and company chairmen, though - as we shall see - by wildly varying
amounts, and increase the wages of manual workers, again by
substantially different margins. But there are exceptions to that general
tendency. The Poles, for instance, feel that doctors' salaries are much too
low, and even the British feel that doctors could have just a bit more
reward than now.

We went on to examine the *size* of the gaps between respondents'
perceptions of what *is* and what *ought* to be, via an analysis of their
estimates of actual and desired earning levels). We found that
Hungarians and Poles believe that the highest paid occupations in their
countries earn about five times as much as the lowest paid ones, and that
this is considered too big a margin; according to respondents' estimates,
they ought to earn only around three to four times as much. In contrast,
respondents in the four western countries think that the average highest
earners get between twelve and fifteen times more than the lowest paid
workers, but that they *should* earn only about seven times as much.

So, the influence of the *status quo* prevails (or, more strictly, of the
perceived *status quo* - though overall the perceptions are fairly accurate).
All these countries are redistributive in their attitudes, but some are more
redistributive than others, depending on where they start from.

Income inequality and social solidarity

The consistent support we found for progressive taxation suggests that any
increase in spending is bound to bear more heavily on the pockets of the
better-off, who will get relatively less benefit from it. This in turn will
impose a strain on social solidarity. In order to address this issue, we first
consider how people on different levels of household income (the most
useful measure of economic position presently available across nations)

vary in their attitudes to government responsibilities and to extra state spending.

The relationship between household income and economic well-being is, of course, complex and depends upon factors such as job security, levels of household expenditure, and views about inflation. We examined differences between the attitudes of people in the lowest and highest income quartile[*] in each country to indicate the extent to which public spending policies were likely to generate pressure on social solidarity.

It will come as no surprise that the better-off are generally rather less inclined than the worse-off to support extensive state programmes. After all, they may well end up paying for them. The gap between income groups in their attitudes generally narrowed between 1985 and 1990, indicating a growing consensus on what governments should be doing. The former West Germany, so often cited as a model of corporatist agreement in industrial relations and in politics, does indeed exhibit the strongest consensus, but on several issues (notably price control, industrial policy and the reduction of income differences) there is a noticeable income group gap between East and West Germany, which suggests that reunification may yet disturb national harmony. As expected on this issue by now, it was the *laissez-faire* regimes of the United States and Australia that show the least consensus.

But in all countries, the greatest controversy surrounds the egalitarian policy of reducing income differences and the strongly interventionist policies of guaranteeing a right to work and imposing price control. It is in these challenges to the mixed economy that there is the most marked disagreement between richer and poorer groups, especially in Britain. Yet it must be admitted that, even among the lower income groups in many countries, support for radical change is limited. Equally, the higher income groups in many countries are disinclined to see a reduction in government spending, particularly on the environment, education, law enforcement and, in West Germany and Italy, the arts.

As expected, perhaps, the greatest areas of disagreement between rich and poor in society are over health expenditure, pensions (the most expensive state service), and unemployment benefits. And the most polarised countries (though somewhat less so than before) on these issues are Britain and Italy.

In general too, controversy between rich and poor over these issues is in decline, despite the increase in poverty over the period in many of the countries surveyed, and despite the pursuit of market-oriented fiscal and economic policies which tend to give disproportionate benefit to better-off groups.

---

[*]   Respondent's own income for West Germany in 1985.

The EC countries

The three countries surveyed in both years (Germany - the united country for the 1990 survey - Britain and Italy) contain just over half of the 1990 EC population between them, and account for just over 60 per cent of the total EC domestic product (EC, 1992). They command 30 out of 76 votes in the Council of Ministers, 243 out of 518 seats in the European Parliament and 72 out of 189 seats on the Economic and Social Commission. Their governments broadly represent the chief political ideologies that exist in the EC - relatively 'right-wing' Britain, Christian Democrat Germany and the left-leaning coalitions of Italy. Analysing the views of the populations of these countries may reasonably be taken to represent most of the main currents in opinion on the role of government in EC member states.

The key question in current EC politics is whether the move towards closer economic co-operation following the Single European Act will lead to even closer economic and political alignment. The complex debates on these issues that took place over the period between the two surveys led to the Maastricht treaty of 1992, which emphasizes free enterprise as the cornerstone of a united Europe, accompanied by strict limits on fiscal policy and the supervision of a common currency by central banks. The social policy chapter (from which Britain opted out) refers to services for workers as a particular subset of society, but its scope may be widened at a later date; and the Treaty's environmental policy is built around the regulatory principle that the polluter must pay.

Our analysis here focuses once more on the question of whether there is convergence in attitudes among the EC countries surveyed both in 1985 and 1990. The main issues concern the range of government responsibilities and the direction of economic policy. The questions on extra government spending were not asked in the former East Germany.

Earlier discussion of these issues revealed a common overall pattern containing national differences; and this is the case for these EC countries too. Thus, all three nations enthusiastically support the state's involvement in health care and pensions, much less so in housing and job creation or other provision for the unemployed. Nor are redistributive policies strongly endorsed. In all cases, the former West Germany stands out as less interventionist than either its own eastern counterpart, or than Britain and Italy. But when we combine the average scores for East and West Germany and then weight them by population, as we have done in the second column of the table, it shows how much closer to its EC counterparts in its public attitudes to interventionism the new Germany may well become, or has become.

Economic Intervention in the EC: 1990

	Britain	United Germany (derived)	Italy	West Germany	East Germany
Wage control	7	19	21	9	50
Price control	16	31	52	20	62
Spending cuts	11	38	28	38	38
Job creation	28	41	44	31	68
Deregulation	8	11	10	10	14
New technology	35	35	21	28	54
Support declining industry	19	33	29	26	51
Reduce the working week	11	29	22	23	47

Note: the United Germany score is the average of East and West Germany, weighted by population

The earlier analysis of attitudes to state spending shows a substantial similarity between the countries, except in the high priority given to the environment and the lower priority for health care in the former West Germany. Unfortunately, these questions were not asked in the survey in the former East Germany.

In relation to the policies of Maastricht, the signs are hard to interpret. Certainly, public attitudes seem to support the general drift of policy which is for government to take an overall responsibility while letting the market decide on the detail.   But there is no clear trend towards ideological convergence, even within the EC. Moreover, to the extent that there is consensus among the citizenry in the three EC countries analysed here, it still does not seem to correspond closely to the market-orientated policies of their governments, especially in Britain: thus the British public resembles its counterparts elsewhere in the views they expresses rather more than British public policy sometimes does. But the same might now be true for Germany where a clear polarisation of opinion between east and west is a real danger.

Ironically, the particular policy areas about which the public express most immediate concern - health care, pensions and environmental issues - are those in which the EC has so far shown least interest.

Conclusion

This discussion leads to three conclusions. First, the convergence thesis is not endorsed by the evidence, despite a clear cross-national movement between 1985 and 1990 in public sympathy away from economic interventionism by governments towards a more free-market approach. In other respects, people remain as keen as, or keener than, before on policies which give high priority to cherished welfare state services. Within this framework, there are, however, distinctive national patterns of ideology which do not seem subject to rapid change. In particular the USA and, to a lesser extent Australia, remain unrepentantly non-interventionist in comparison with Europe, east and west.

Secondly, the problem of reconciling spending demands and the tax base is unlikely to go away or get any easier, especially since enthusiasm for extra spending is strongest in the most costly policy areas, and because demographic change is moving in an unfavourable direction. There is substantial support (in principle, at any rate) for progressive taxes that would support positive redistributive policies and more social spending. There is also a surprising measure of consensus between higher and lower income groups, and between countries, in their attitudes to the responsibilities of government for sustaining various welfare services.

Thirdly, public attitudes to many of the issues covered in this chapter were (and are) out of sympathy with the prevailing international mood of politicians and governments in favour of market-led provision. Within the EC, for instance, although there is certainly public suspicion of economic interventionism by governments - which clearly fits the free enterprise philosophy of the Maastricht treaty - there is also an apparently ingrained belief in high public spending, or at any rate in policies which would make it inevitable.

In short, the conflict between trying to minimise taxes and maximise spending shows no sign of diminishing, and the future is likely to prove just as diverse as the past, despite prophesies about the 'end of history'.

Note

1. Factor analysis of these economic intervention variables again confirms the existence of a common basic structure that is remarkably consistent over the period. The responses to both 1985 and 1990 surveys generate three underlying factors across all countries: attitudes towards regulation of wages and prices; attitudes towards the free market policies of spending cuts and deregulation; and the more interventionist theme of support for new technology, declining industries, job creation and a reduction in the working week.

References

Davis, J.A. (1986), 'British and American attitudes: similarities and contrasts', in Jowell, R., Witherspoon, S. and Brook, L. (eds.), *British Social Attitudes: the 1986 Report,* Aldershot: Gower.

European Community (1992), *Eurostat,* 29th edition, Luxembourg: EC.

Evans, M.D.R., Kelley, J. and Kolosi, T. (1992), 'Images of class: public perceptions in Hungary and Australia', *American Sociological Review,* Vol. 57 (August: pp. 461-482).

Fukuyama, F. (1989), 'The End of History', *The National Interest,* No. 16, pp. 3-18.

Heidenheimer, A., Heclo, H. and Adams, C. (1990), *Comparative Public Policy,* New York: St. Martin's Press.

Kelley, J. and Evans, M.D.R. (forthcoming), 'Legitimate inequality: attitudes towards inequality in nine nations', *American Journal of Sociology.*

Organisation for Economic Cooperation and Development (OECD) (1988), *The Future of Social Protection,* Paris: OECD.

Organisation for Economic Cooperation and Development (OECD) (1993), *Economic Outlook,* No. 54, Paris: OECD.

Smith, T. W. (1989), 'Inequality and Welfare', in Jowell, R., Witherspoon, S. and Brook, L. (eds.), *British Social Attitudes: Special International Report,* Aldershot: Gower.

Taylor-Gooby, P. (1991), *Social Change, Social Welfare and Social Science,* Harlow: Harvester/Wheatsheaf.

5 Satisfying work - if you can get it

*John Curtice**

Much of the impetus for research into job satisfaction came from claims that a more satisfied workforce is a more productive one (for a review, see Gruneberg,1976; Hirszowicz,1981). However, although some studies have found a relationship between satisfaction and productivity, it has generally been weaker than expected (Katzell and Yankelovich, 1975). Whereas good fringe benefits or friendly supervision may have contributed to job satisfaction, they apparently did not make people work harder; indeed, the possibility that job satisfaction was a *consequence* of working in a productive environment could not be discounted (Lawler and Porter, 1969).

But this does not mean that job satisfaction is unimportant. On the contrary, there is considerable evidence that dissatisfied workers are more likely to change jobs and be absent from work (see, for example, Brown *et al,* 1983, Gruneberg, 1979), and these characteristics in a workforce are costly both to employers and to the national economy. It is also argued that job satisfaction is a crucial ingredient of a good quality of life, since the average full-time worker spends around a third of his or her waking hours at work. There is a long tradition in sociology going back to Hegel and Marx which portrays the development of the 'alienated worker' as a social evil. Indeed, some writers claim a link between job satisfaction and mental health, or health in general, with a particular emphasis on the role

---

* Senior Lecturer in Politics and Director of the Social Statistics Laboratory, University of Strathclyde.

of occupational stress (see for example, Kornhauser, 1965; Clegg *et al,* 1987; Kasl, 1973).

In this chapter we explore what it is that makes some workers more satisfied than others, using data collected from eleven different national surveys as part of the *International Social Survey Programme* (ISSP) in 1989. In particular we examine whether women are more or less satisfied at work than men, and whether their sources of satisfaction with their jobs are the same as, or different from, men's. Since many women work part-time, we also look at the similarities and differences in job satisfaction of full and part-time workers.

All datasets have their advantages and drawbacks, and this one has unique advantages in its coverage of such a large and diverse range of countries. But, as with all cross-national datasets, its very diversity creates the worry that we may not always be measuring quite the same thing in each country, despite careful translations, or that sampling biases or 'design effects' may not be quite the same universally. On the other hand, as will be seen, the apparent *similarities* between countries are often much more impressive than the differences. Suffice it to say that the differences we report between countries, especially fine distinctions or rank orders, should be treated with due caution.

Levels of job satisfaction

Job satisfaction has been defined as 'the total body of feelings that an individual has about his job...in effect weighing up the sum total of influences on the job...' (Gruneberg, 1976). In the spirit of this definition one of the ISSP questions simply asked respondents who were currently in work how satisfied they were in their (main) job. Respondents were free to give one of seven answers ranging from 'completely satisfied' to 'completely dissatisfied'. In the following table we show the proportion in each of eleven countries who said they were 'completely' or 'very' satisfied.

Levels of job satisfaction

	% 'completely'/ 'very' satisfied
Irish Republic	51
United States	50
Austria	47
West Germany*	44
Norway	42
Northern Ireland	41
Netherlands	40
Britain	39
Israel	36
Italy	34
Hungary	13

* The survey was undertaken in 1989, before the unification of Germany.

The country which clearly stands out in this table is Hungary, where only one in eight workers are very or completely satisfied with their job. The next most dissatisfied workforces are in Italy and Israel, where in each case around one in three workers are very satisfied or better. Among the remaining countries the variation is modest, ranging from around 40 to 50 per cent expressing high satisfaction, with Britain bringing up the rear (at 39 per cent), and the USA and the Irish Republic heading the list (at 50 per cent and 51 per cent respectively). The relatively high level of satisfaction among American workers replicates the findings of previous research (Blauner, 1960; Yankelovich *et al*, 1983).

   But in any event dissatisfaction with one's job is rare among nearly all workers. The figures above report only those who are *very* or *completely* satisfied with their job. In line with other surveys of job satisfaction (Brown *et al*, 1983), between 80 and 91 per cent of workers in all countries except Hungary claim to be at least *satisfied* with their job.

Hard work?

How might we account for differences in the level of job satisfaction? One possible answer is that different workers have different experiences at work. In the survey, we asked workers whether they found their work stressful or exhausting.

% saying 'always' or 'often'	Find work stressful	Come home exhausted
Irish Republic	15	30
United States	38	36
Austria	38	32
West Germany	36	31
Norway	33	37
Northern Ireland	29	41
Netherlands	23	17
Britain	30	44
Israel	27	48
Italy	29	38
Hungary	27	45

Interestingly, the southern Irish, the most satisfied with their work, are also distinctively less likely to describe their work as stressful. But in case one is tempted to conclude from this that job satisfaction is simply determined by the absence or otherwise of stress, it is worth noting that the other distinctly 'satisfied' nation (the United States) reports one of the *highest* levels of stress. Indeed, along with Austrians and West Germans, Americans are at the top of the stress league table. Meanwhile it is the

Israelis, Hungarians and the British who are the most likely to report coming home from work 'exhausted'. Again, however, there is no sure link between tiring work and job satisfaction; the Italians, for instance, who are among the most 'dissatisfied' workers, are no more than average in their propensity to find work exhausting (or, for that matter, to find it stressful).

The rewards of work

Turning from negative to positive features of work, rewards can be both extrinsic, such as the pay received, and intrinsic, such as the stimulation of interesting work. We asked respondents what rewards they felt they derived from work by asking them whether they agreed or disagreed with a number of statements including 'My income is high', 'My job is secure' and 'My job is useful to society'. How workers responded to these items in each country is shown in the table below.

Rewards of work

% agreeing	Secure job	High income	Useful to society
Austria	87	29	73
West Germany	83	30	68
Italy	71	28	60
Hungary	70	10	85
Irish Republic	69	23	71
Netherlands	69	16	62
United States	68	25	69
Norway	63	19	72
Northern Ireland	62	19	73
Israel	61	27	65
Britain	59	18	56

Again there is no clear-cut relationship between these variables and reported levels of job satisfaction. Respondents in all countries are generally much more likely to say they have a secure job or that their job is useful to society than that they have a high income. Although Hungarians are the least likely to report having a high income, they are nonetheless by far the most likely to feel that their job is useful to society. If income and job security were everything, then it is clear from the figures above that Austrians and West Germans would be the most satisfied with their jobs. Yet, though relatively satisfied (as we have noted), neither the Austrians nor the Germans express the same level of job satisfaction as either the Irish (Republic) or the Americans, neither of whom appear to be particularly satisfied with their income levels.

There may, however, be some clues here as to why British workers are relatively dissatisfied. As the table above shows, the British are not only among the least likely to feel that their jobs are secure or useful to society, but they are also among the least likely to say that they are well-rewarded financially. The Northern Irish share the British gloom about job security and income, but are rather more likely to regard their jobs as useful to society.

So far we have looked at all workers in each country and taken a broadbrush look at job satisfaction and work experience to see how they might be related. We clearly need to do this more systematically. But, first, what about men and women within each country? Do they feel the same way about their jobs?

The gender paradox

Traditionally, a woman's place has supposedly been in the home. Nowadays, in most western economies, more and more women go out to work (Bean, 1989). In consequence, their attitudes towards work have been of increasing interest to sociologists, psychologists and labour market economists (for a review, see Hakim, 1991). These explorations have uncovered a paradox. For the most part women are employed in less desirable jobs, with lower incomes, poorer promotion prospects, less job security and fewer fringe benefits. Yet many studies have found that women, particularly women working part-time, are nonetheless more likely than men to be satisfied at work, and this remains the case even when the objective differences in their situations are taken into account (Blanchflower and Oswald, 1992; Clarke, 1993; though for a dissenting note see Gruneberg, 1979). It seems as though women expect less from work, or at least something different.

The relatively high job satisfaction of part-time women workers is of particular interest given recent labour market trends. Over the last two decades, part-time workers have become an increasing proportion of all workers in most western countries. And even in those countries, such as Italy and the USA, where women are *least* likely to dominate part-time employment, they still account for two out of three of all part-time workers. In other countries, such as Austria and Germany, as many as nine out of ten part-timers are women (OECD, 1993). In fact it is the expansion of part-time work in many countries which has made a significant contribution to the growth of the labour force in general and to the increase in women's participation in the labour market in particular (de Neuborg, 1985).

The preponderance of women, especially married women, among part-time workers[1] is apparent in our survey[2]. They are also clearly less well paid.

Who works full- and part-time?

% who are	Full-time	Part-time
Women	35	77
Married women	19	58
Earnings in lowest quartile*	10	54

* The percentage of workers in each category whose reported income was among the lowest 25 per cent in their country.

The apparent 'gender paradox', particularly among part-time workers, is illustrated in the table below which shows, for each country, the levels of job satisfaction of full-time men, full-time women and part-time women.[3]

Levels of job satisfaction

% 'completely' or 'very' satisfied	Full-time men	Full-time women	Part-time women
Irish Republic	48	58	48
United States	46	53	52
West Germany	42	40	50
Austria	42	50	56
Norway	41	41	42
Britain	39	35	46
Netherlands	38	40	45
Northern Ireland	36	44	50
Israel	36	34	43
Italy	34	34	35

* Information on hours worked to identify full and part-time workers not available for Hungary.

Given that women are in many respects worst off at work in objective terms, we would expect them to be less satisfied than men are with their jobs. Yet in four countries (the Irish Republic, the United States, Austria and Northern Ireland), full-time women are noticeably more satisfied than full-time men, and only in Britain is there any evidence that the opposite is true. Meanwhile, part-time women workers (objectively the worst off) are substantially more satisfied than full-time male workers in no less than seven of the ten countries in the table, and nowhere are they less satisfied. Our surveys clearly confirm previous research that women, in the majority of countries, do indeed tend to be more satisfied than men with their work.

Yet, as the next table shows, many women are all too aware that, economically, they are not as well-off at work as men are. First comparing full-time men with full-time women, we find that in eight of our ten countries (Austria and Northern Ireland are the exceptions) the men are considerably more likely to say they have a high income. The same is true in *all* countries when we compare full-time men with part-time women.

Job has high income

% agreeing	Full-time men	Full-time women	Part-time women
West Germany	35	28	24
United States	34	20	14
Italy	32	24	24
Austria	30	32	26
Israel	30	24	16
Irish Republic	27	19	14
Norway	26	12	13
Britain	21	14	11
Netherlands	20	11	9
Northern Ireland	19	21	14

Nonetheless, even if their incomes are lower, part-time women workers may have other compensations from their jobs. Hakim (1991), for instance, argues that for many women what matters most is the convenience of a job that can be fitted in with domestic and childcare duties. Certainly, as the next table shows, part-time women in most countries are, as expected, more likely than full-timers (men or women) to report that their job has flexible working hours.

Flexible working hours

% agreeing that 'my job has flexible working hours'	Full-time men	Full-time women	Part-time women
Italy	43	37	57
Irish Republic	43	33	43
United States	42	41	67
Israel	42	37	56
Norway	39	32	44
Netherlands	38	35	31
Northern Ireland	34	30	38
Britain	32	30	55
West Germany	29	22	38
Austria	24	24	31

So even if this factor helped to account for the job satisfaction of part-time women, it hardly explains why across countries, full-time women tend to be more satisfied than full-time men with their jobs. As the table above shows, full-time women seem, if anything, to be *less* likely than their male counterparts to have jobs with flexible hours. They are, incidentally, in answer to another question in the survey, also more likely to "come home from work exhausted". However, this could of course be because they are returning home to as unequal a proportion of household work as their part-time or non-working counterparts face (Witherspoon and Prior, 1991). Meanwhile, part-time women (with the clear exception of those in the Irish Republic) tend to find their work either less tiring than men do (most notably in Britain and the United States), or at any rate no more tiring.

Perhaps we could make rather more progress in unravelling the paradox if we looked at what women want from work. Maybe a high income is less important to women workers than men? We may also find that the convenience of flexible hours is particularly important to part-time women. Perhaps women who, even in their paid employment are more likely to be take on the role of 'carers', simply place more emphasis on the social or moral worth of a job. (For similar arguments see Gruneberg, 1979; Rose, 1988; Gallie and White, 1993.)

In the next table we examine how important various aspects of a job are to the three groups of workers. To simplify matters here we do not divide respondents into their countries because the results are broadly consistent from one country to another.

% saying job attribute 'very important' or 'important'	Full-time men	Full-time women	Part-time women
Secure job	92	94	96
High income	82	80	75
Useful to society	67	72	77
Flexible hours	50	58	62

There is certainly a little support here for the claim that women look for something different from work. Both full and part-time women are more likely than full-time men to say they value flexible hours and a job which is useful to society. Part-time women also place a little less emphasis on a high income. However, these differences are hardly large ones. And even among part-time women, the economic benefits of a job such as job security and a high income are regarded as more important than the job's convenience, as measured by 'flexible hours'. So these findings still do not resolve the paradox.

In any event this is not necessarily the best way to identify what contributes most to job satisfaction for different kinds of workers. People cannot necessarily identify accurately the features in their job that are most important to them or that give rise to most satisfaction. They may, for instance, refer to those features of their present job that they enjoy, rather than to what they would actually prefer in a job. An alternative approach is to examine systematically the correlation between our respondents' reports of their experience of work and their level of job satisfaction. If, for example, having 'flexible hours' really is more important to women than to men, we should find that, other things being equal, women respondents who actually have flexible hours would be more likely than their male counterparts with flexible working hours to report a high level of job satisfaction. It is to this systematic identification of what contributes to the job satisfaction of different groups of workers that we now turn.

The correlates of job satisfaction

To unpick the relationship between our respondents' experience of work and their overall job satisfaction, we use a technique known as 'stepwise multiple regression'[4]. This technique first identifies which single feature is most closely correlated with reported job satisfaction and produces an equation summarising its apparent impact on job satisfaction. It then takes each remaining variable and tests which one best explains the variation in respondents' reported job satisfaction that has not already been successfully accounted for by the first feature. In this way an equation is built up adding one feature at a time, until all those items which are statistically significant are included. The equation states, for each feature, how much overall job satisfaction is increased or reduced by a one unit rise in the value of that feature, assuming no change in the value of the other features.

Initially this exercise was undertaken separately in each country to see whether what mattered to workers was similar or different from country to country,[5] and it emerged clearly that there were very few differences. For example, the two primary components of job satisfaction in virtually all countries were whether the respondent's job is interesting or boring, and management/employee relations. Further, in all but two countries (Norway and Israel), at least one of the economic benefits of the job (that is its income, security, or opportunities for advancement) came in the top five.

This similarity (as well as the pattern of similarities that we have already reported) suggests that we can reasonably safely pool the data from the different countries in this analysis.[6]

The following variables were entered into the equations[7].

Hard physical work	Interesting work
Dangerous conditions	Independent working
Unhealthy conditions	Bored at work
Physically unpleasant conditions	
	Flexible working hours
Work helps others	Secure job
Useful to society	High income
	Opportunities for advancement
Leisure time	
Come home exhausted	Management/employee relations
Stressful work	Relations with colleagues

In the following table we show the first five features which were entered into the equation for each of the three groups of workers we have been examining - full-time men, full-time women, and part-time women. The 'beta' values in the table are the (standardised) partial regression coefficients, telling us simply how strongly on average the particular feature influences job satisfaction levels. So, the higher the beta value for a feature (that is, the closer it is to 1), the greater is its impact on people's overall satisfaction at work. A negative beta value for a feature (such as for 'boredom' in all three columns) shows simply that it is inversely related to job satisfaction. The R^2 value at the base of each column of the table tells us how much of the variation in people's overall job satisfaction is explained by *all* the features included in the equation[8]. The higher the R^2 value, the more successfully we have accounted for the variation in our respondents' job satisfaction.

The results are striking. We can see immediately that for the most part the features of a job which most contribute to job satisfaction are the same for full-time men, full-time women and part-time women. In each case the first five features which are introduced into the equation (the only ones shown below) are exactly the same. Further, the amount by which each of these aspects of a job influences job satisfaction, as measured by the beta coefficient, is largely similar in each equation as well.

Regression analysis of job features
correlated with job satisfaction

Full-time men		Full-time women		Part-time women	
Feature	Beta	Feature	Beta	Feature	Beta
Interest	.25	Interest	.24	Management relations	.24
Management relations	.20	Management relations	.23	Interest	.19
Boredom	-.17	High income	.13	Boredom	-.21
High income	.12	Boredom	-.14	Stressful	-.12
Stressful	-.07	Stressful	-.10	High income	.10
(+ 8 items)		(+ 7 items)		(+ 7 items)	
R^2 = 42%		R^2 = 37%		R^2 = 40%	

That we should derive almost identical equations for full-time men and full-time women is probably not surprising[9]. A number of writers have suggested that those women who remain in or return to full-time employment after the birth of their first child have a strong commitment to work and look for the same sorts of rewards from work as men do (Hakim, 1991). Our results clearly lend weight to that view.

But that the sources of job satisfaction for part-time and full-time women should be very similar is certainly surprising. As noted, it has often been argued that part-time women are *most* concerned to find work that is compatible with domestic duties. And although part-time respondents did rate flexible hours higher than their full-time counterparts did - suggesting perhaps that it may be a factor in whether or not to enter the labour market at all - our analysis suggests that it does not contribute significantly to their satisfaction with work once they are in a job.

So if both part-time and full-time women largely derive satisfaction from the same things at work as men, why are women and especially part-time women more satisfied at work than men? One clue lies in the features which actually appear in our equations. Satisfied workers are not simply those who are well rewarded. Even among full-time men, their income is a less important source of satisfaction than either the intrinsic interest of their work or the quality of the relationship between management and staff. Therefore, if economic rewards of work are not of primary importance in determining job satisfaction of either men or women, then neither are the 'objective' economic disadvantages for women that we noted earlier.

What our regression equations have done, of course, is to tell us which features of workplace experience we should focus on. So, in the following table we report the percentage of workers who say that their job has each of these five crucial features.

Whose job has the crucial features?

	Full-time men	Full-time women	Part-time women
Interest	76	77	72
Management relations	67	71	75
Boredom	26	24	22
High income	28	21	15
Stressful	32	34	22

Interest: 'strongly agree'/'agree' job is interesting; management relations: 'very good'/'good' management/employee relations; boredom: 'always'/ 'often'/sometimes' bored at work; high income: 'strongly agree'/'agree' job pays high income; stressful: work 'always'/'often' stressful.

Once again, what we discover is that the reported workplace experience of full-time men, full-time women and part-time women does tend to be similar. But as we saw earlier, women, particularly part-time women, are less likely to say that their income is high. And now we can also clearly see apparent compensations, particularly for part-time women workers - in particular that their work is less stressful and that they work in jobs where management-worker relations are better.

In short, we have evidence here which suggests that while the economic circumstances of part-time work are indeed disadvantageous, there may be real psychological compensations. Of course, in reporting lower levels of stress, part-time workers may be referring not only to the amount of stress generated by their work, but also to the relative ease of combining work with other aspects of their lives. So we should evidently be more wary than some writers have been of assuming that part-time work is objectively always second best. Certainly, if only economic factors are taken into account in the analysis, the 'gender paradox' is indeed perplexing (see for example Clarke, 1993), but this may be an artefact of having excluded important non-economic factors from the analysis.

Even so, we have not yet fully solved the 'gender paradox'. The fact is that the level of job satisfaction of full-time and part-time women is still slightly higher than we would anticipate even after taking into account their reported workplace experience. To see this we have first of all to construct a regression equation for all three groups of workers together. Then we create variables which identify the full and part-time female workers in our surveys. If women's job satisfaction is significantly higher than that of full-time men, then these variables will be introduced into our equation with a positive beta coefficient.

So far as full-time women are concerned this simply does not happen. Their level of satisfaction is indeed no higher than we would expect given their reported workplace experience. But of course it was the part-time women, not the full-timers, who were generally most satisfied in our survey. And indeed the variable which identifies these women does enter into the equation. True, the beta coefficient is not large, just .03, but it does indicate that, even after allowing for their reported workplace experience, part-time women *are* still marginally more satisfied at work than we would expect.[10] So, rather than a 'gender paradox', we have a 'part-time paradox' (see also Hakim, 1991; Weaver, 1979)

Lower expectations?

How might we solve this 'part-time paradox'? One possible answer is that part-time workers have lower expectations of work than full-time workers and are more easily satisfied by any given objective set of circumstances. Previous research has repeatedly demonstrated the importance of workers' expectations. For example, people with a higher level of education have been shown to have higher expectations of being able to control their work tasks than those with less education (Ross and Reskin, 1992).

Expectations of work are not simply formed outside the workplace; they can also be shaped by the actual experience of work. For example, if people start off with high expectations and then find it impossible to secure high paid employment, they may then lower their expectations accordingly. But expectations are extremely difficult to measure. To compare the influence of the prior work expectations of full and part-time workers we would need to interview them repeatedly over a considerable period of time. And we interviewed our respondents at only one point in time.

Nonetheless, we do have some evidence about the 'work commitment' of our respondents which might be relevant. By 'work commitment' we mean the extent to which an individual is committed to doing a job even when financially he or she does not need to work. Sometimes referred to as the 'work ethic', such a high commitment to work is often seen as a stimulus to national economic success because it produces a reliable yet economically undemanding workforce (Yankelovich *et al*, 1983).

Naturally, work commitment is in no sense a simple substitute for expectations. The relationship between the two is by no means necessarily straightforward or strong (see, for example, Rose 1988; Gallie and White, 1993). Nevertheless, it has been argued that there is a relationship between the work commitment of part-time workers, their expectations of work and their job satisfaction. In particular, it is argued that part-time women workers are often not the principal breadwinners in their families; they can therefore choose whether or not to remain in the labour market and, if so, for how many hours they work (Kalleberg and Loscocco, 1983). In consequence, part-time women workers are said to have a lower commitment to work than full-time workers (Warr, 1982). Part-time workers are thus to some extent a self-selected group who work for a supplementary wage and expect little else from their jobs (Hakim, 1991).

But does our survey confirm the basis of this argument that part-time workers are less committed to work? Respondents were asked whether they agreed or disagreed with the following two statements:

A job is just a way of earning money - no more

I would enjoy having a paid job even if I did not need the money

Those with a strong work commitment would be expected to disagree with the first statement and agree with the second. The following table shows the percentage amongst our three groups of workers who did precisely that.

Work commitment of full- and part-time workers[*]

	Full-time men	Full-time women	Part-time women
Just a way of earning money (*% dis*agree)	57	66	63
I would enjoy a paid job even if I did not need the money (% agree)	62	69	72

[*] See Appendix III for exact question wording.

As can be seen, the results do *not* confirm the premise that part-time women workers are less committed to work than are full-time workers. It is not even clear that they are less committed than full-time women workers, who themselves demonstrate a slightly higher level of 'work commitment' than their male colleagues. This difference between male and female full-time workers is perhaps an indication that, as some writers have argued, women who work full-time are more likely to do so out of choice (Hakim, 1991). In any event, these data do not lend any clear support to the argument that part-time women workers necessarily expect less from work. So we are still left with the 'part-time paradox'.

Returning to national differences

Our regression equations were of some help in accounting for the levels of satisfaction of men and women workers. But earlier in this chapter we also found it difficult to account for some of the national differences in levels of job satisfaction. Can we do any better in explaining those differences now?

   To answer this question we can repeat the procedure we used to see whether the job satisfaction of women workers is higher than expected once we take into account their reported workplace experience. But instead of introducing into our analysis variables which identify the full and part-time women workers in our surveys, we now introduce variables that tell us in which country each worker lives. If the level of satisfaction in a country is significantly higher than we would expect, the variable for that country will be introduced with a positive coefficient. If the level of satisfaction is less than we would expect, the variable will be introduced with a negative coefficient. The following table shows only those countries which proved to have significant positive or negative coefficients when we analysed men and women full-time workers together.

The unusual countries

	Beta Coefficient
United States	+ .23
Northern Ireland	+ .17
Irish Republic	+ .14
Israel	-.12
West Germany	-.09

The table shows the unstandardised partial regression coefficients for those countries whose level of job satisfaction is significantly statistically different at the five per cent level.

We are evidently still unable to account for the high level of satisfaction among workers in the United States or the Irish Republic, nor the low level in Israel. For instance, on the basis of their reported workplace experience, American workers ought to be no more satisfied than British workers are. Either our survey has failed to tap some feature of workplace experience of particular importance to American workers, or else American culture beyond the workplace has a significant impact on Americans' reported satisfaction at work.

   Nonetheless, we can perhaps now account for the low level of job satisfaction among British and Italian workers that we identified earlier. For instance, of the five key features of workplace experience we have identified as most crucial to job satisfaction, we find that British workers score low on two: they are particularly likely to bored at work and particularly unlikely to describe their income as high.

Although the level of job satisfaction among Northern Irish workers is not particularly high, it is still higher than one would expect given their reported workplace experience. This may be because the Northern Irish report particularly poor management-employee relations. Meanwhile, our earlier suspicion that West German workers ought to be more satisfied, given the frequency with which they report having a high income, is also shown to be well-founded.

Conclusions

The increased participation of women in the labour market has been one of the most important social trends of the last two decades. Its implications for the orientations that workers have to work has fostered considerable debate (Rose, 1988). On the one hand it has been argued that women are less committed to paid work and have different job expectations from those of men. Thus, it is argued, the increased participation of women in the labour market is gradually changing the values held by workers as a whole, presenting employers and managers with new challenges as to how to get the best out of their workforces. On the other hand, it has been argued that as more women enter the labour market, so their work orientations will change and become more like those of men (Crompton and Sanderson, 1986; Gallie and White, 1993).

Our analysis clearly lends support to the second conclusion. The features of their work which give them most satisfaction are largely the same for men and women. If anything, women are more committed to work than men. Whatever the position may have been twenty years ago, there is no reason to believe, on the evidence of this survey, that the continued growth of female and part-time employment will cause any fundamental change in the attitudes that workers have to their jobs.

Equally, our findings suggest that the continued growth of part-time work will have at most a marginal impact on the overall level of job satisfaction in the workforce. This is not to say that full-time work and part-time work are viewed as similar experiences. Part-time workers are aware of the economic disadvantages of their jobs. But these disadvantages have, perhaps, been accorded too much importance in previous studies of women and work, compared with the non-economic advantages of part-time work (and, for that matter, with some of the disadvantages of full-time work). In our survey, for instance, full-time workers are much more likely to report that their jobs are 'stressful', and - so far as job satisfaction is concerned - this helps to counterbalance their relative economic advantages.

Moreover there is some evidence from Britain at least that stress is becoming more widespread at work (Gallie and White, 1993). True, some of our respondents' stress may have been a reflection of the difficulties of balancing the demands of full-time work and domestic responsibilities. But these problems are hardly likely to become any less commonplace if the increased participation of women in the workforce continues. And on the evidence of this survey such difficulties should not be ignored.

Notes

1. Finding a valid measure of part-time work that can be operationalised consistently between countries is never easy. Teachers may say they work less than 30 hours a week (based on the number of hours in the classroom) but in practice they may be working full-time to fulfil those duties. In some countries (such as Italy) it is not uncommon for individuals to hold more than one part-time job while in others (such as the United States) holding a part-time job while engaged in full-time education is not uncommon. The statistical bureau of each country - and the survey organisations which contribute to ISSP - do not adopt a consistent definition of the number of hours of work which constitute full-time work. However, all but one of the countries contributing to the 1989 ISSP collected information on the number of hours the respondent worked in his or her main occupation, and this was used to create a systematic definition of part-time and full-time workers. Information on hours worked was not available for Hungary, which has therefore had to be omitted from this analysis. For all other countries, part-time workers are those working between 10 and 30 hours a week in their main occupation. Full-time workers are those working more than 30 hours a week. Not surprisingly, perhaps, the adoption of this constant definition reduces the variation in the proportion of all workers who are part-time between countries to a rather smaller range than is implied by OECD data. With the exception of Norway (28 per cent), the proportion of part-time workers in the ISSP survey ranges only from 11 per cent (Austria) to 17 per cent (Britain).
2. The country patterns in the survey were largely, but not entirely, as one would anticipate from OECD data. Thus the countries with the highest proportion of part-timers who were female were Britain (93 per cent), Netherlands (90 per cent), West Germany (87 per cent), Austria (82 per cent) and Northern Ireland (82 per cent). The lowest proportions were in the Irish Republic (58 per cent), the USA (65 per cent) and Italy (69 per cent). The figure for the Netherlands is higher, and that for the Irish Republic lower, than might have been anticipated. It is also worth noting that, in countries for which data were available, part-timers were more likely to be employed in service industries and (with the exception of Israel) in the public sector. With the exception of the USA they are, however, less likely to be self-employed. Self-employed people have a higher level of satisfaction than employees (Blanchflower and Oswald, 1992), but their relative scarcity amongst part-time workers means that this does not help account for the relatively high level of job satisfaction of part-timers.
3. There were too few part-time male workers in most of the surveys to analyse their levels of satisfaction separately and they are consequently excluded from the analysis. The unweighted sample sizes for each of these categories are as follows:

	Full-time men	Full-time women	Part-time women
West Germany	353	181	82
Britain	373	179	135
United States	405	315	90
Austria	482	270	94
Netherlands	427	121	136
Italy	326	160	68
Irish Republic	281	127	42
Northern Ireland	187	82	53
Norway	566	278	206
Israel	298	205	122

4. Note that this technique assumes that the dependent variable, in this case job satisfaction, is an interval level variable. An alternative procedure would be to use ordered logit or probit analysis (see for example, Blanchflower & Oswald, 1992; Clarke, 1993), which would simply assume that the job satisfaction data is ordinal. Regression is used here for ease of interpretation. Note that we have been able, using multiple regression, to replicate Blanchflower and Oswald's finding using ordered probit that the self-employed are more satisfied than employees, which suggests that the analysis of this data is robust against choice of statistical technique.

5. We looked at full- and part-time workers separately in each country although the results reported in this paragraph are based on all workers in each country.

6. These surveys in combination do not, of course, represent any identifiable universe. Further, the sample sizes of the individual country surveys are not proportionate to population and no attempt has been made to weight the surveys to render them proportionate. Our assumption is that because the relationship between workplace experience and job satisfaction is largely similar in each country, our findings will be robust in the face of such considerations.

7. The grouping of these variables reflects the results of a factor analysis undertaken country by country to identify the structure of intercorrelations between the various measures of workplace experience. For the most part the results in each country were similar to each other. Thus for example, in each country respondents who thought that management/employee reactions were good also felt that they had good relations with colleagues. Together, they appear to constitute a 'workplace relations' dimension.

8. Note that none of the individual features we have not listed adds as much as one per cent to the R^2 in any of the equations and collectively they add no more than three per cent.

9. Indeed as many as the first seven variables to be introduced into these two equations are identical to each other. The additional variables are 'relations with colleagues' (beta for men, .10; for women, .08) and 'good opportunities for advancement' (.08 in both cases).

10. The size of this beta coefficient is in fact only slightly smaller than the beta coefficient that we get if we simply regress job satisfaction on our part-time women identifier without introducing any of our measures of workplace experience. This indicates that our regression analysis has not particularly helped to explain why part-time women tend to be *more* satisfied than full-timers, but that the reported workplace experience of part-time women does not give us any reason to expect them to be *less* satisfied. In other words the perceived advantages of 'part-time' work, such as lower stress, do more or less counterbalance the disadvantages, such as lower pay, but they are not sufficient to explain why part-time workers tend to be more satisfied than full-time workers.

References

Bean, R. (ed.) (1989), *International Labour Statistics: a handbook, guide and recent trends*, London: Routledge.

Blanchflower, D. and Oswald, A. (1992), 'Entrepreneurship, Happiness and Supernormal Returns: Evidence from Britain and the US', *National Bureau of Economic Research Working Paper No. 4228*, Cambridge, Massachusetts.

Blauner, R. (1960), 'Work satisfaction and industrial trends in modern society', in Galenson, W. and Lipset, S.M., *Labour and Trade Unionism*, New York: Wiley.

Brown, R., Curran, M. and Cousins, J. (1983), 'Changing attitudes to employment?', *Department of Employment Research Paper No. 40*, London.

Clarke, A. (1993), 'Job Satisfaction and Gender: Why are Women So Happy at Work?', *BHPS Discussion Paper, No. 4*, Colchester: University of Essex.

Clegg, C., Wall, T. and Kemp, N. (1987), 'Women on the Assembly Line: a comparison of main interactive explanations of job satisfaction, absence and mental health', *Journal of Occupational Psychology*, XL, pp. 273-87.

Crompton, R. and Sanderson, K. (1986), 'Credentials and Careers: Some Implications of the Increase in Professional Qualifications Amongst Women', *Sociology*, XX, pp. 25-42.

de Neuborg, C. (1985), 'Part-time work: an international quantitative comparison', *International Labour Review*, CXXIV, pp. 559-76.

Gallie, D. and White, M. (1993), *Employee Commitment and the Skills Revolution*, London: Policy Studies Institute.

Gruneberg, M. (ed.) (1976), *Job Satisfaction - A Reader*, London: Macmillan.

Gruneberg, M. (1979), *Understanding Job Satisfaction*, London: Macmillan.

Hakim, C. (1991), 'Grateful slaves and self-made women: fact and fantasy in women's work orientations', *European Sociological Review*, VII, pp. 101-21.

Kalleberg, A. and Loscocco, K. (1983), 'Aging, Values, and Rewards: Explaining Age Differences in Job Satisfaction', *American Sociological Review*, XLVIII, pp. 78-90.

Kasl, S. (1973), 'Mental Health and work environment: An examination of the evidence', *Journal of Occupational Medicine*, XV, pp. 509-18.

Kornhauser, A. (1965), *Mental Health of the Industrial Worker: A Detroit Study*, New York: Wiley.

Lawler, E. and Porter, L. (1969), 'The effect of performance on job satisfaction', *Industrial Relations,* VIII, pp. 20-8.

OECD (1993), *Employment Outlook July 1993*, Paris: OECD.

Rose, M. (1988), 'Attachment to Work and Social Values', in Gallie, D. (ed.), *Employment in Britain*, Oxford: Blackwell.

Ross, C. and Reskin, B. (1992), 'Education, Control at Work and Job Satisfaction', *Social Science Research*, XXI, pp. 134-48.

Warr, P. (1982), 'A national study of non-financial employment commitment', *Journal of Occupational Psychology*, LV, pp. 297-312.

Weaver, C. (1979), 'The irony of the job satisfaction of females', *Personnel Administration*, May, pp. 70-4.

Witherspoon, S. and Prior, G. (1991), 'Working Mothers: Free to Choose?', in Jowell, R., Brook, L. and Taylor, B., with Prior, G. (eds.), *British Social Attitudes: the 8th Report*, Aldershot: Dartmouth.

Yankelovich, D. *et al* (1983), *Work and Human Values: An International Report on Jobs in the 1980s and 1990s*, New York: Aspen Institute.

6 Class conflict and inequality

*Geoffrey Evans**

This chapter is primarily a tale of two countries. The United States has often been presented as the exemplar of a classless society. As such, its praises have been sung by many observers and, even if social scientists have not always concurred with this view, the American public has often been thought to do so.[1] In contrast, despite the Prime Minister's well-publicised aspirations to a 'classless society', Britain is usually seen as very much a class-conscious and class-divided nation, with a long history of inequalities in many areas of life, such as educational achievement, health, income, psychological well-being and, of course, class attainment itself.[2] Surely, then, we are likely to find sharp and persistent differences within the British public in how people perceive class divisions, and - given class-party relationships in Britain - we are also likely to find cleavages on these sorts of issues along party political lines.

However, these familiar images of American classlessness and British class-dividedness are, of course, only images. They are bound to blur as we consider the evidence a little more carefully. Indeed, although admittedly there are methodological problems in collecting and interpreting the available data, such sources as there are suggest, for instance, that income inequality is rather more pronounced in the USA than it is in Britain (Taylor and Jodice, 1982; Smeeding *et al,* 1990). Moreover, several authors have suggested that class divisions in the two

* Geoffrey Evans is the Research Fellow in the Centre for European Studies, Nuffield College, Oxford, and lectures at the London School of Economics.

societies have more in common than has been assumed, and that the political attitudes of Americans are indeed conditioned by their position in the class structure (Vanneman, 1980; Robinson and Bell, 1978; Bell and Robinson, 1980).[3] In *British Social Attitudes: Special International Report*, Smith has also shown that Americans are no less likely than the British to perceive class conflict in their society (Smith, 1989, p. 71) . If so, it would be surprising if social class in the USA did not influence social attitudes there, as it undoubtedly does in Britain.

It has also been argued that in recent years the influence of class on social and political attitudes in Britain has declined as other factors have become more important. In particular, increases in social mobility and in levels of education are supposedly weakening the class-party relationship in Britain, and being replaced partially by the influence of factors such as state and private sector employment and home ownership (see, for example, Franklin, 1985; Robertson, 1984; Dunleavy and Husbands, 1985).

So the received wisdom about class divisions in Britain and the classless nature of the USA has been challenged. But up to now there have been few opportunities to examine the issue using cross-national evidence. Clearly, British data alone cannot provide clearcut answers to questions about whether Britain is especially (or even uniquely) divided on social class lines. Nor is it entirely satisfactory to look at just Britain and the USA. They may differ, but are they exceptional? Answers to this question require comparable information about other advanced industrial nations, which allow both Britain and the USA to be compared with suitable benchmarks (see Davis and Jowell, 1989). We can then find out if Britain and the USA are indeed exceptional in, for example, their self-reported class identity or their attitudes towards inequality, rather than simply show that they are more (or less) similar to each other.

Measuring beliefs and attitudes towards class

The data in this chapter are derived from surveys undertaken in 1987 in seven ISSP member countries: Australia, Austria, Britain, Hungary, the Netherlands, the United States and West Germany.[4] Switzerland, although not an ISSP member, also fielded the questionnaire, and we have drawn on their data too. Not all of the questions we shall examine were asked in all countries, but the great majority were. We can therefore contrast Britain and the USA not only with a range of West European democracies, but also with Australia - a country with a long colonial past, but (in common with the USA) a 'self-made' nation that 'grew up' democratic and capitalist (Smith, 1989, p. 60). Hungary, in sharp contrast, was still part of the communist bloc when the survey was conducted.

As well as looking at a range of countries, we need also to consider a variety of indicators relating to class inequality[5], rather than focusing on only one (and so run the risk of producing misleading results).[6] Among those examined are self-assessed social class, attitudes towards social inequality and policies to redistribute wealth, beliefs about inequalities of opportunity, and support for class-based parties. Together these measures should provide a wealth of information about the public's understanding of class-related inequality.

Smith (1989) has already shown that - in Britain and elsewhere - most people not only think there is too much inequality, but also endorse a variety of strategies to reduce it. Nonetheless, while recognising the importance of social background and contacts in 'getting ahead in life', most people also believe that meritocratic factors, such as hard work, ambition and education, are the most important. Many people also believe that opportunities for advancement exist for people 'like themselves' and, except in Hungary and Italy, that levels of class conflict are low.[7] Nevertheless, although these findings are of interest, they address only one aspect of the importance of class position in a country in creating *divisions* over such issues. The crucial test of the degree of class-dividedness of a country is the extent to which people's objective class positions are linked to their attitudes. So this chapter will try to answer two questions. First, how different are the attitudes of the working classes and the middle classes in each country? And, secondly, how substantial is the link between class position and class identity, taking into account differences between *all* the classes?

Our categorisation of social class in each country is derived from respondents' own job descriptions coded into one of nine categories. People's employment status (self-employed *versus* employee) is asked separately. These two questions are combined to arrive at a measure of 'objective' social class ('class position') that approximates the one devised by John Goldthorpe and his colleagues, and used before in the *British Social Attitudes* series and in Goldthorpe's own cross-national research (Erikson and Goldthorpe, 1992). The measure used here has the following categories:

Salariat:	professional and managerial
Routine non-manual:	routine non-manual, sales and service workers [8]
Petty bourgeoisie:	self-employed and small-scale employers
Skilled manual:	skilled manual workers (including their supervisors)
Working class:	semi- and unskilled manual workers

In all countries except Hungary there were too few agricultural workers to examine separately; they have therefore been grouped with the working class.

Class and social identity

If class position is an important social characteristic, it should be reflected in people's own class identity. As Hodge and Treiman (1968) pointed out, the strength of association between 'objective' and self-assessed class position reveals the degree of crystallisation of class-consciousness within each economic group. Thus cross-national differences in the strength of such links should reveal the degree of salience that class position has in each country.

In the first table we present the percentages reporting themselves as 'working class' (or 'lower class' or 'poor') cross-analysed by 'objective' class position.[9] At the bottom of the table is a statistic ('eta') that indicates the overall strength of association between these two variables: the higher the eta, that is the closer it is to 1, the greater is the strength of association. (Tables that follow are organised similarly for the other variables we shall be examining.[10])

Before considering the distribution of responses we should note that self-reported social class is not measured in exactly the same way in each country. (It is a 'background variable' which is not standardised in the ISSP, because each country already has a standard way of measuring it.) For instance, although most countries have categories for the 'lower class' and 'upper class', in Britain 'poor' is preferred for the former and the latter is omitted. Britain has an 'upper working class' category and the Netherlands one for the 'lower middle class', while other countries use neither of these terms. Clearly, these sorts of variations in response categories will influence the distribution of answers. Nevertheless, the differences between the formats adopted in each country are not great - in all cases there is a four or five point scale which includes 'middle class' and 'working class'. Moreover, the differences in format reflect the judgment of the researchers in each country on how to measure class identity most accurately within each cultural context. Consequently, it is acceptable to compare the overall *strengths of association* between class identity and objective class position across countries, despite the variations in the way the data were collected.

Association between objective and subjective class position

% in each 'objective' class category calling themselves 'working class'	Britain	USA	Aus-tralia	Austria	West Germany	Nether-lands	Switzer-land
Salariat	16	26	17	1	1	1	3
Routine non-manual	52	48	43	21	12	17	37
Petty bourgeoisie	34	53	49	34	10	10	17
Skilled manual	64	64	65	54	49	39	59
Working class	76	66	79	73	68	58	65
Eta	.47	.30	.41	.51	.55	.51	.37

As can be seen, the link between objective class position and class identity tends to be strong. Respondents whose job classifies them objectively as 'working class' tend also to identify themselves as such, and *vice versa* for respondents categorised objectively as 'middle class'. In four nations - Britain, Germany, the Netherlands and Austria - the eta coefficient is around .50. In two others - Switzerland and Australia - it is around 10 points below that. Although these two groups of countries differ significantly in the strength of the association between objective class position and class identity, in all of them the percentage 'gap' between working class and salariat falls within a relatively narrow range. The only noticeable outlier is the USA (with an eta coefficient of .30). In other words, class divisions appear to be rather more blurred to Americans than to the other nationalities represented here.

As far as Britain is concerned, then, the impact of class position on identity is not especially strong in comparison with the other countries. But the USA is exceptional. And this is consistent with orthodoxy, suggesting that (on this measure at least) the USA is a less class-conscious society than any of the others surveyed.[11]

Class and beliefs about the extent of inequality

Although the strength of association between 'objective' and self-rated social class is an important indicator of class divisions in a society, it is of course not the only relevant one. Even if people's sense of class identity is weak, they may nonetheless have firm views about the extent of, and need for, class-related social inequality. As we noted, class-related attitudes matter more: people's objective class positions (derived from occupational details) may well influence their beliefs regardless of how they label themselves or, indeed, whether or not they label themselves at all.

Do classes share views on inequality? We address this issue first by examining responses to the statement that:

Differences in income in [respondents' country] *are too large*

Response categories were on a five-point scale, ranging from 'strongly agree' to 'strongly disagree'. The table below shows that in most countries there are predictable differences between classes. As with class identity, however, Britain is not exceptional: although it is not lacking in class divisions, those of other countries - Austria and the Netherlands - are even more pronounced (as measured by the eta below). Of the western countries, the USA again is comfortably the least divided.[12] What is especially remarkable about this table is the pattern of responses given by the Hungarian sample. In Hungary, as in the USA, there is near consensus across classes on the matter of perceived inequality.

Class position and perceived social inequality

% in each class agreeing that there is too much inequality	Britain	USA	Aus- tralia	Austria	W. Ger- many	Hun- gary	Nether- lands	Switzer- land
Total	74	56	57	87	72	73	64	65
Salariat	64	53	48	69	60	74	38	55
Routine non-manual	73	54	61	88	72	74	64	71
Petty bourgeoisie	69	53	52	86	59	72	60	66
Skilled manual	85	61	70	93	77	74	76	73
Working class	81	59	72	88	83	71	83	70
Agricultural labourers	-	-	-	-	-	78	-	-
Eta	.21	.08	.20	.25	.19	.06	.30	.18

Class and beliefs about opportunity

Given the widespread inequality of achievement between social classes, we might expect that people in different social strata would be likely to explain success and failure in different ways. Working-class people, for instance, might perhaps be more inclined to see success in terms of the advantages associated with money and connections, and less inclined to see it as resulting from personal qualities. The middle class, in contrast, has been thought to have a meritocratic conception of achievement which emphasises hard work and ability (Goldthorpe *et al,* 1969). In an ideal world, equality of opportunity - if not of outcome - might prevail, inequalities arising only from the fact that some people make less than others do of the chances offered to them. To what extent do people see their own countries as achieving this ideal? To what extent do people in *all* classes believe that individuals are responsible for their own success and failure, regardless of the advantages and disadvantages associated with their social origins. This ideal has been described as 'the dominant ideology' (Huber and Form, 1973), or as 'the success ideology' (Ichheiser, 1949). In western societies it has been seen as the basis for the acceptance of social inequalities by the working classes and other disadvantaged groups. In the USA in particular, home of the Horatio Alger myth and the 'American Dream' of equality of opportunity, acceptance of this ideology has been said to explain the political quiescence of the working class (see Kluegel and Smith, 1986; Huber and Form, 1973).

The questionnaire has 13 items covering ways of 'getting ahead in life', and respondents are invited to say how important they think each of these is. The following three are particularly relevant to inherited class advantages: 'coming from a wealthy family'; 'having well-educated parents'; 'knowing the right people'. Three others are useful counterpoints, focusing instead on personal characteristics and behaviour: 'ambition'; 'natural ability'; 'hard work'. Responses to all these questions, ranging from 'not important at all' to 'essential' have been scored from one to five, and the answers summed to make a scale. In the scale, scores have then been derived (by dividing the mean score of the three explanations referring to individual characteristics and behaviour by the mean score of the class-related explanations) in order to mitigate the tendency among some respondents to rate all explanations as either particularly important or particularly unimportant. A score of 1.0 indicates that both types of explanations were accorded equal importance. The *lower* the score, that is the closer it is to zero, the more inclined are people to believe that personal attributes as opposed to social class are the most important for getting ahead in that country.

Class position and beliefs about achievement

Mean score on the achievement scale:	Britain	USA	Aus- tralia	Austria	W. Ger- many	Hun- gary	Nether- lands	Switzer- land
Total	.71	.69	.65	.87	.86	.79	.76	.81
Salariat	.69	.68	.62	.82	.86	.77	.73	.77
Routine non-manual	.68	.66	.62	.85	.85	.80	.74	.83
Petty bourgeoisie	.71	.61	.66	.83	.80	.72	.71	.80
Skilled manual	.71	.70	.66	.91	.86	.80	.77	.87
Working class	.76	.76	.72	.91	.87	.81	.82	.82
Agricultural labourers	-	-	-	-	-	.82	-	-
Eta	.12	.18	.14	.12	.08	.17	.10	.21

The scores on the scale average around 0.78. Thus, in general, respondents do give more weight to personal attributes than to class-related explanations of getting ahead in life. Moreover, there is a fair amount of agreement across social classes about the weight attributed to personal *versus* class-related causes of achievement: the 'etas' are generally lower than they were in the previous tables (despite the use of a multiple item measure which would be expected to increase the magnitude of association between the scale and other variables). True, working-class people tend to be a little more inclined to see origins as important, while the middle class attribute a little more importance to personal qualities, but the differences are not great. Neither are there striking cross-national differences. The Americans for once are not noticeably different from the Europeans on this measure. These answers suggest a shared acceptance by different classes in all these diverse countries of a dominant ideology of individualism. The USA does not, after all, appear to be unusual in having a widespread acceptance of an ideology of achievement, which (as some authors have suggested) has served to unify it.

The issue of class-based inequality of opportunity is also addressed by other questions. In particular, one question asked respondents about the opportunities they, and people like them, had to improve their living standards. Since this question is more personal, it may detect differences between classes that were not picked up by the more abstract questions about getting ahead. Indeed, it is clear from the next table that in most countries working-class people do perceive themselves to have less opportunity than those in the middle class to improve their lot. Once again, however, Americans are much less likely than any other nationality to see this as a debilitating disadvantage in their country: even among working-class Americans, two in three perceive opportunities for advancement to be relatively plentiful. Indeed, working class Americans perceive greater opportunities for improvement in their standard of living than do middle-class people in Britain! As can be seen from the eta scores, British respondents are the most divided over this issue. In Hungary alone the working class sees *more* opportunity than does the middle class: this may either reflect reality there in 1987 under the former communist regime, where there was a manipulation of actual opportunities by the state, or - more likely - belief among Hungarian workers in the egalitarian claims of the communist system, just as American workers believe in the American dream.

National differences can, of course, reflect many factors, among them variations in levels of social mobility and living standards. Nevertheless, the lack of any marked difference in the views of middle- and working-class Americans adds weight to explanations of American exceptionalism.

Class position and opportunities to improve standard of living

% in each class agreeing that they have a good chance to improve their standard of living	Britain	USA	Aus- tralia	Austria	W. Ger- many	Hun- gary	Nether- lands	Switzer- land
Total	36	71	58	45	36	32	22	56
Salariat	53	73	66	50	48	23	44	63
Routine non-manual	34	71	63	48	39	29	21	53
Petty bourgeoisie	49	86	58	29	41	38	23	59
Skilled manual	25	65	50	54	37	30	18	55
Working class	25	65	51	41	19	42	18	48
Agricultural labourers	-	-	-	-	-	39	-	-
Eta	.24	.12	.11	.19	.18	.16	.16	.11

Class and beliefs about the need for inequality

So far we have seen some class differences, usually in predictable directions, in perceptions of inequality in society. But, whether or not it is approved of in principle, inequality in practice may nonetheless be thought necessary to the successful operation of a market economy and to the achievement of high living standards by the majority. Such a functional justification of inequality may serve to link the working class with the middle class; they may share an acceptance of the need for unequal rewards. We addressed this issue by asking respondents whether they believed that:

> *Large differences in income are necessary for* [respondents' country's] *prosperity.*

First, we should note that a relatively small proportion of people in *any* of the countries is prepared to endorse this proposition. That aside, the pattern of responses shows that again the USA is distinctive. Indeed, more working-class Americans than middle-class Americans are prepared to endorse this functional justification of inequality of outcome. The same is true for Hungary: working-class and agricultural workers there are especially likely to endorse this instrumental justification for inequality. In most other countries there is much less disagreement (and in Britain virtual consensus) across social classes on this issue. Only in the Netherlands are there noticeable differences, but in this case in the expected direction.

We considered whether the tendency for working-class Americans to agree with these statements to a greater extent than their middle-class counterparts do might be attributed to 'acquiescence bias' arising from their lower levels of education (see Schuman and Presser, 1981). But since no such effect seems to be evident in other countries, this does not seem likely.

Class position and belief in the need for large differences in income

% in each class agreeing that large differences in income are necessary for prosperity	Britain	USA	Aus- tralia	Austria	W. Ger- many	Hun- gary	Nether- lands	Switzer- land
Total	26	31	28	25	24	24	15	16
Salariat	27	20	31	26	28	21	28	14
Routine non-manual	26	29	26	25	24	19	15	17
Petty bourgeoisie	26	27	32	12	33	30	19	14
Skilled manual	28	41	27	28	26	22	12	15
Working class	25	37	20	26	23	30	9	19
Agricultural labourers	-	-	-	-	-	31	-	-
Eta	.05	.19	.05	.08	.07	.11	.16	.09

Why then do the classes not divide in the expected way on this issue? Why are working-class people in some countries more likely (and in several others no less likely) than middle-class people to endorse an instrumental view of inequality? One explanation may be that such attitudes are derived from fundamental beliefs about human nature - notably that people will not work hard except for large and fitting rewards. Therefore, unless people with unusual abilities or special skills are paid differentially, they will not be motivated to work hard, to the detriment of the economy as a whole and, thereby, to working class people in particular. On this basis, inequality becomes necessary, or at least desirable, on pragmatic grounds. Given that the experience of most working-class people is very much one of work for wages rather than for promotion prospects, perquisites or other indirect rewards (see Evans, 1992b), then working-class people may well be inclined to adopt this much more pragmatic view, even if it does not coincide with their apparent class interests.

In confirmation, we see from the table below a widespread acceptance, across all social classes, of the need for large wage differentials to stimulate hard work. Again, the USA is distinctive in that working-class people are more prone to agree than are those in other classes. In sharp contrast, less than a quarter of working-class people in the Netherlands are prepared to endorse this proposition, suggesting once again that the

Dutch are less likely than the other nationalities are to defy the expected link between one's social class and one's views of egalitarianism.

Class position and belief in the need for large differences in pay to get people to work hard

% in each class agreeing that large differences in pay are necessary	Britain	USA	Aus-tralia	Austria	W. Ger-many	Hun-gary	Nether-lands	Switzer-land
Total	64	72	76	76	77	74	37	73
Salariat	65	68	77	83	75	75	56	68
Routine non-manual	65	71	72	76	77	78	36	71
Petty bourgeoisie	62	68	79	63	81	88	55	79
Skilled manual	62	68	75	78	79	75	26	78
Working class	66	79	74	78	77	71	23	72
Agricultural labourers	-	-	-	-	-	67	-	-
Eta	.06	.13	.06	.12	.06	.06	.25	.07

Class and support for redistribution

Do people's class identities and their perceptions of inequality in society affect their propensity to support policies that reduce class-related inequality? In each country several questions were asked about the role of government in the redistribution of resources, thus allowing us to compare levels of support for redistribution among the well-off and the less well-off. The issues we examined include support for income redistribution by government (which we interpret as support for the *principle* of redistribution); and the following strategies to promote it:

a guaranteed standard of living for the unemployed;[13]

more spending on benefits for the poor;

a guarantee of jobs for everyone;

a basic income for everyone.

Responses to these questions have been summed into a five-item scale of attitudes towards redistribution.[14]

From the table below we can see that in Britain there are far stronger links than in the other countries between one's social class and support for redistribution. As conventional wisdom suggests, on issues to do with the redistribution of income and resources, Britain is an especially class-divided society. Interestingly, Americans at last do *not* stand out on this scale from people in other countries in the way they have on a number of other issues. American manual workers *are* more inclined than are non-manual workers to favour redistribution, and the differences (as measured by eta) are at the same level as those found among the Austrians and the Dutch. This is particularly surprising, given not only the USA findings so far in respect of class identity, of perceptions of and justifications for inequality, but also the supposedly less ideologically extreme nature of American politics.

By far the weakest link between social position and attitudes towards redistribution is to be found in Hungary. Of course, this reflects in part the high level of consensus in Hungary on the desirability of government-directed redistribution, resulting in a rather more restricted range of responses than in the other countries. However, in neighbouring Austria, for instance, where there are also high levels of overall support for redistribution, there are nonetheless much clearer class divisions.

Class position and support for redistribution

Mean score[*] on the redistribution scale	Britain	USA	Aus-tralia	Austria	W. Ger-many	Hun-gary	Nether-lands	Switzer-land
Total	2.3	3.0	2.9	2.4	2.3	2.0	2.5	2.7
Salariat	2.7	3.2	3.1	2.6	2.5	2.1	2.8	2.9
Routine non-manual	2.4	3.1	2.9	2.5	2.3	2.0	2.5	2.6
Petty bourgeoisie	2.6	3.3	3.1	2.3	2.4	2.0	2.6	2.8
Skilled manual	2.1	2.9	2.8	2.4	2.2	1.9	2.4	2.4
Working class	1.9	2.7	2.7	2.1	2.0	1.9	2.2	2.4
Agricultural labourers	-	-	-	-	-	1.9	-	-
Eta	.34	.25	.21	.26	.22	.11	.25	.22

[*] The higher the mean score, the *less* the enthusiasm for redistributive policies

The story so far

Returning to the theme of Britain and the USA, in summary we have found that:

- The association between objective and subjective social class is fairly similar from country to country. In Britain there are fairly strong links between objective and subjective class, but this pattern is not significantly different from that in several other countries. In contrast, in the USA these links are weaker than average.

- Class divisions over perceived inequality are also less conspicuous in the USA than elsewhere. In Britain these divisions are on the strong side, but not exceptionally so.

- Beliefs about how people get ahead are similar across classes, and across countries, indicating a considerable degree of consensus about the paths to achievement.

- Class divisions over perceived opportunities for oneself and one's family to improve their standard of living are relatively strong in Britain and, once again, weak in the USA.

- Britain is the most class-divided nation in its support for policies of redistribution, and the USA is also fairly class-divided on this issue.

- Apart from the Netherlands and the USA, there are no very marked patterns by social class on the perceived need for incomes to be equal as a prerequisite for creating (or preserving) prosperity. But the pattern in the Netherlands is quite different from that in the USA. In the Netherlands the predicted differences occur, with middle-class people more supportive than working-class people of inequality in incomes; in the USA, however, working-class people are even more supportive than are the middle-classes of the need for inequality.

Among the other countries in the study, the Netherlands stands out as being relatively class-divided (particularly over inequality and government policies to promote redistribution), while Hungary stands out for its low level of class division - lower than its European counterparts and more consistently lower than even the USA. The USA is, however, distinctive in the west for its lack of clear-cut class divisions, except over the issue of redistribution. Paradoxically, the strongest single piece of evidence in support of the traditional view of Britain as an especially class-divided society is also over this issue of redistribution - a finding in opposition to recent claims that class is no longer an important basis of political cleavage in Britain. True, in respect of the link between subjective and objective social class, and a number of other attitudes and perceptions, Britain is certainly not exceptional. So why is the strength of the relationship between class and support for redistribution particularly strong in Britain? And why in particular is this also a big issue in the conspicuously non-class divided USA? We now turn to these questions.

Understanding national differences in class conflict

There are two main ways of interpreting differences between countries in the class-related political attitudes and behaviour of their citizens. The first and most common has been to see such attitudes and behaviour as reflections of national differences in levels of class-consciousness. According to this school, class differences reflect the degree to which different social classes have formed as distinct groups with distinct social identities, which in turn lead to different interests (see Giddens, 1973, for a discussion).[15] The second school is based on the notion that there are different political choices available to people in different classes. Thus, if the main political parties do not present clearly class-based programmes to the electorate, then the choices for members of different classes are not clearcut, and consequently people in different classes are less likely to perceive particular policies to be in their interests (or otherwise). So, if political parties are not themselves formed on class lines, class does not become salient in political or ideological divisions.[16] A working-class voter, for instance, cannot in these circumstances cast his or her vote automatically for a party of the 'left', so the links between class and voting behaviour remain weak (see Vanneman and Cannon, 1987).

The question of which of these influences is most important can be examined, at least in an exploratory way, by looking at the relationships between objective social class (class position), subjective class (or class identity), attitudes towards redistribution, and political partisanship. Important differences in the origins and nature of social identities and political attitudes have already been discovered. In Britain, for example, evidence from the *British General Election Study* series (see Heath *et al,* 1991, Chapter 5) indicates that class identity is a stable attribute, changing only gradually in proportion to the changes in sizes of social classes, and so maintaining a relatively constant relationship with objective social class. Class identity in Britain, where there *are* class-based parties, is therefore not likely to be as strongly influenced by day-to-day political issues as by the glacial, secular change associated with social structures. In other words, class identification reflects social factors rather than political ones (see Evans, 1992a).

Attitudes towards redistribution, like those towards other social policy issues are, of course, likely to be influenced by a person's social class, but they are also firmly within the realm of party politics. After all, changes over time in attitudes towards such issues bear no relation to changes in the size of social class groupings. They may more easily be explained as responses to political events (see for example the analysis of the reaction to Thatcherite policies among the British public in Heath *et al,* 1991, pp. 171-189).

This conclusion is supported by evidence from the ISSP survey. As we have seen, the link between objective social class and class identity is substantial and fairly similar across most of the ISSP nations. In contrast, the *attitudinal* divisions between classes on a variety of measures are relatively small, suggesting that such ideological divisions as do exist may reflect influences other than class identity - including, of course, differences between countries in the political importance attached to the redistribution of wealth.

Let us now link these considerations to cross-national differences. If national differences in class divisions are due to differences in levels of class consciousness, then there should be a link between the strength of association between class position and class identity on the one hand, and between the strength of association between class position and attitudes towards redistribution on the other. However, if differences in the extent of class divisions are attributable to differences in *political* factors, rather than to class consciousness, then they should be linked with the strength of party divisions over redistribution. So, if class consciousness is the key to understanding class politics, we should find evidence of subjective class identity accompanying the development of class polarisation over redistribution; if, however, the link between class and attitudes towards redistribution is merely a reflection of the way these issues have been politicised, then levels of class identity will not be as important as the degree of partisan division over the issues.

First we examine the degree to which attitudes to redistribution are politicised in each of the countries - as indicated by the strength of association between political partisanship and attitudes towards redistribution:

Partisanship and support for redistribution

Mean score* on the redistribution scale	Britain	USA	Aus-tralia	Austria	West Germany	Nether-lands	Switzer-land
Total	2.3	3.0	2.9	2.4	2.3	2.5	2.7
'Left-wing'	1.8	2.7	2.6	2.3	2.0	2.1	2.3
'Centre'	2.2	3.1	2.8	2.4	2.3	2.6	2.7
'Right-wing'	2.8	3.4	3.1	2.4	2.5	3.1	2.9
Eta	.53	.34	.33	.10	.26	.48	.20

* The higher the mean score, the *less* the enthusiasm for redistributive policies

As we have already seen, there is considerable support for redistribution in most countries. Nevertheless, in several the issue is still an important focus of ideological dispute between the parties of the left and right (as indicated by the relatively high eta scores). This is so despite recent claims about the emergence of a 'new political agenda' (Inglehart, 1990). Within that general picture, however, we can see that in Britain there are stronger links between support for redistribution and left-right partisanship than in any other country (with an eta coefficient of .53). The Netherlands is the nearest, and there are also divisions (although fairly moderate ones) in the USA and Australia. In contrast, Austria has almost no division in terms of partisanship.[17]

Linking this finding to other findings in this chapter, it is clear that Britain stands out as divided both by class and by political partisanship over the issue of redistribution, but not especially so either by class identity or by perceptions of the extent of, or need for, inequality as a prerequisite for prosperity.   Americans are also class-divided and politically-divided over redistribution, although not to the same extent as are the British; but in other respects, such as in class identity and perceptions of inequality, they are much less strongly divided according to objective social class.

The high level of class division over redistribution in Britain becomes easier to explain when we confirm that it is accompanied by pronounced party political divisions over redistribution.   Class division may thus reflect political factors rather than those derived from a strong sense of class identity.   This suggests that the basis of the divisions over redistribution lie not in aspects of Britain's social structure which make it unusual or even unique, but in something distinctive about its political culture.

By the same token, we can perhaps begin to understand the greater than expected class divisions over redistribution in the USA. The explanation of this may well lie in the political significance of attitudes towards 'big government'. So, while working- and middle-class Americans may have fairly similar beliefs in respect of class identity, shared beliefs in the availability of opportunity for personal advancement, and similar attitudes to inequality, they part ways in their attitudes to government intervention. Debates over welfare and other methods of redistribution were important features of the Reagan years and beyond, and it is not difficult to understand why people in different classes can come to have a growing awareness of where their interests lie in respect of such policies. There is plenty of evidence from other research to suggest that conflicting attitudes to inequality and redistribution can coexist with consensus over other policy matters that would appear *prima facie* to be closely related.[18]

Finally we should note that the association between subjective social class and attitudes towards redistribution is relatively weak in comparison with that between political partisanship and distribution - confirming yet again that attitudes to redistribution tend to be politicised, not an automatic function of class-consciousness.

Conclusion

It appears that received wisdom does, after all, have some basis in reality. The United States is indeed a relatively classless society in comparison with the western European nations included in our survey, and even in comparison with Australia.   Nevertheless there are surprises.   For instance, the two most politically distinctive societies - capitalist America and communist (as was) Hungary - are also the two least class-divided societies.   Whether or not post-communist Hungarian society is now beginning to develop the sorts of class divisions to be found in western

Europe is a matter of some interest and early findings suggest this might well be the case (Evans and Whitefield, 1993).

But received wisdom does less well in the case of Britain. Britain is not, after all, as class-bound as it is often painted (though it is *among* the most class-bound in most respects), except in respect of attitudes towards policies for reducing inequality. As we have seen, however, there may be special reasons for this, notably the politicisation of class-related issues like these. Now that the heated political debates of the late 1980s (when Thatcherism was at its peak and the Labour Party was more left-wing than now) have cooled somewhat, these class divisions over redistribution of income and resources may become less pronounced. If so, Britain may yet become more like other western European societies, and John Major may come closer to fulfilling his stated wish to turn Britain into a classless society.

Notes

1. The classic reference to American exceptionalism is de Tocqueville (1848). For more recent discussions see Shafer (1991), especially Lipset's contribution (Lipset, 1991). For rejections of the classless society argument see Vanneman and Cannon (1987), and Jackman and Jackman (1983). Kluegel and Smith (1986) present extensive evidence on American public opinion about inequality and its concern with issues of race rather than class.
2. Works on these issues are numerous: see Reid (1989), Halsey, Heath and Ridge (1980), Wilkinson (1986) and Goldthorpe (1987), to select just a few.
3. Note, however, that the usefulness of Robinson and Bell's work is limited by their use of extremely small and unrepresentative local area samples.
4. The survey was also conducted in Italy, but the question about respondents' social class was not asked in a comparable fashion.
5. A good example of the need for multiple indicators is presented by Vanneman (1980), who argues that the link between class and class identity in the USA is similar to that in Britain, but that the link between class and vote is far stronger in Britain than in the USA (see Vanneman and Cannon, 1987 for a more extended discussion). The implications of such inconsistencies will be discussed later when considering our own findings.
6. Interpretation of the reasons for differences between countries is not straightforward - since levels of inequality and policies to deal with the issue vary between them (Coughlin, 1980; Taylor-Gooby, 1989) - and are thus likely to lead to differences in levels of support for redistribution. Nevertheless, for the questions addressed in this chapter this is not a problem, as we are interested only in differences between countries in respect of *internal* patterns of relationships between attitudes and social background, rather than in levels of support among the population as a whole.
7. But not conflict between 'workers and management' or between 'rich and poor', which suggests that classes are often thought of as status groups, rather than conflicting groups in the Marxist sense, and probably as less extreme categories than are 'rich and poor'.
8. For all countries except Hungary, this class is somewhat more heterogeneous than its equivalent in the Goldthorpe schema. Ideally, some of the sales and service workers should be allocated to other classes, such as the working class or salariat. However, data were not collected in such a way that this could be done with sufficient precision.

9. In all countries, the vast majority of respondents chose working or middle class self-labels, with very few seeing themselves as upper class or poor (the question was not asked in Hungary).

10. For brevity and clarity in the tables that follow, we have looked at class divisions in isolation from other possible social bases of conflict. However, all of these data have also been examined using multivariate regression models which take into account the relationships between class, religion, age, sex etc., and then estimate the effect attributable to each particular social characteristic. The beta coefficients from these models tend to support the conclusions drawn from just the simple analyses presented here. The models confirm the importance of class, but also show that other structural characteristics contribute independently, but far less substantially, to the prediction of attitudes to inequality in all countries. (Detailed multivariate analyses of British data can be found in Evans, 1992a.)

11. In the USA the weakness of the class-identity link may in part be due to the tendency of black respondents to see themselves as working class, regardless of their 'objective' class: there is very little difference between classes in partisanship or identity amongst blacks, and a quite different pattern of social structuring than there is amongst whites. Given the small size of the black middle class, however, this factor is likely to be of only minor importance (see Sigelman and Welch, 1991, for more detailed consideration of these issues).

12. The Netherlands has exceptionally generous social security provision, which may account for the rejection of the statement about inequality by almost half of middle-class respondents - note that class divisions among the Dutch are unusually strong over this particular issue.

13. Not asked in Hungary; in 1987 unemployment did not exist there in the form found in the West.

14. Before scaling the items their dimensionality was assessed using principal components analysis. In all countries there was only one dimension, which means that individuals will tend to be similarly ranked on all the statements in the battery. The average Cronbach's Alpha coefficient for the scales was around an acceptable .70.

15. This thesis has tended to be assumed rather than tested. For example, discussions of American exceptionalism have assumed that a lack of socialism and class voting in the USA is due to a lack of class-consciousness among the working class. One approach to this problem (see Vanneman, 1980) is to measure class identity and political *attitudes* rather than political choices. Class identity and attitudes may well be indicators of differences between social groups that voting choices alone would not reveal.

16. This argument owes much to party identification theory (Campbell *et al*, 1960), in which it is argued that party affiliation influences political attitudes to a greater degree than *vice-versa*. The most prominent alternative view is that people are to some degree rational in their political choices, and that attitudes to redistribution do influence choice of party (Himmelweit *et al*, 1985; Franklin, 1985).

17. In Austria, attitudes towards redistribution are only weakly unidimensional, which suggests that the issue of redistribution is less well-defined as a political issue. It should be noted that similar patterns of cross-national difference are found even when using multivariate models that control for the association between partisanship and social class and a large number of other social characteristics.

18. Converse (1964) presents the seminal account of the nature and origins of inconsistency in mass political beliefs. Kluegel and Smith (1986) have undertaken a detailed examination of these characteristics of the American public.

References

Bell, W. and Robinson, R.V. (1980), 'Cognitive maps of class and racial inequalities in England and the United States', *American Journal of Sociology*, 86, pp. 320-49.

Campbell, A., Converse, P.E., Miller, W.E. and Stokes, D.E. (1960), *The American Voter*, New York: Wiley.

Converse, P.E. (1964), 'The nature of belief systems in mass publics', in Apter, D.E. (ed.), *Ideology and discontent*, New York: Free Press.

Coughlin, R. (1980), *Public opinion and welfare policy*, Berkeley: University of California Press.

Davis, J.A. and Jowell, R. (1989), 'Measuring national differences', in Jowell, R., Witherspoon, S. and Brook, L. (eds.), *British Social Attitudes: Special International Report*, Aldershot: Gower.

Dunleavy, P. and Husbands C. (1985), *British democracy at the crossroads*, London: Allen and Unwin.

Erikson, R. and Goldthorpe, J.H. (1992), *The constant flux*, Oxford: Clarendon Press.

Evans, G.A. (1992a), 'Is Britain a class-divided society? A re-analysis and extension of Marshall *et al*'s study of class consciousness', *Sociology*, 26, pp. 233-58.

Evans, G.A. (1992b), 'Testing the validity of the Goldthorpe class schema', *European Sociological Review*, 8, pp. 211-32.

Evans, G.A. and Whitefield, S. (1993), 'Identifying the bases of party competition in Eastern Europe', *British Journal of Political Science*, 23, pp. 521-48.

Franklin, M. (1985), *The decline of class voting in Britain*, Oxford: Oxford University Press.

Giddens, A. (1973), *The class structure of the advanced societies*, New York: Barnes and Noble.

Goldthorpe, J.H. [in collaboration with Llewellyn, C. and Payne, C.] (1987), *Social mobility and class structure in modern Britain*, 2nd Edition, Oxford: Clarendon Press.

Goldthorpe, J.H., Lockwood, D., Bechhofer, F. and Platt, J. (1969), *The affluent worker in the class structure!*, Cambridge: Cambridge University Press.

Halsey, A.H., Heath, A.F. and Ridge, J.M. (1980), *Origins and destinations*, Oxford: Clarendon.

Heath, A.F., Jowell, R., Curtice, J., Evans, G.A., Field, J. and Witherspoon, S. (1991), *Understanding political change: The British voter 1964-1987*, Oxford: Pergamon.

Himmelweit, H.T., Humphreys, P. and Jaeger, M. (1985), *How voters decide*, (revised edition), Milton Keynes: Open University Press.

Hodge, R.W. and Treiman, D.W. (1968), 'Class identification in the United States', *American Journal of Sociology*, 73, pp. 535-47.

Huber, J. and Form, W. (1973), *Income and ideology*, New York: The Free Press.

Ichheiser, G. (1949), 'Misunderstandings in human relations: a study in false social perception', *American Journal of Sociology*, 55, pp. 1-70.

Inglehart, R. (1990), *Culture shift in advanced industrial societies*, Princeton: Princeton University Press.

Jackman, M.R. and Jackman R.W. (1983), *Class awareness in the United States*, Berkeley: University of Los Angeles Press.

Kluegel, J. and Smith, E. (1986), *Beliefs about inequality*, New York: Aldine De Gruyter.

Lipset, S.M. (1991), 'American exceptionalism reaffirmed', in Shafer, B. (ed.), *Is America different?* Oxford: Clarendon Press.

Reid, I. (1989), *Social class differences in Britain*, (3rd edition), Glasgow: Fontana.

Robertson, D. (1984), *Class and the British electorate*, Oxford, Basil Blackwell.

Robinson, R. and Bell, W. (1978), 'Equality, success and social justice in England and the United States', *American Sociological Review*, 43, pp. 125-43.

Schuman, H. and Presser, S. (1981), *Questions and answers in attitude surveys: Experiments on question form, wording and context*, New York: Academic Press.

Shafer, B. (ed.) (1991), *Is America different?* Oxford: Clarendon Press.

Sigelman, L. and Welch, S. (1991), *Black Americans' views of racial inequality*, Cambridge: Cambridge University Press.

Smeeding, T., O'Higgins, M. and Rainwater, L. (eds.) (1990), *Poverty, inequality and income distribution in comparative perspective*, New York: Harvester Wheatsheaf.

Smith, T. (1989), 'Inequality and welfare', in Jowell, R., Witherspoon, S. and Brook, L. (eds.), *British Social Attitudes: special international report*. Aldershot: Gower.

Taylor, C. and Jodice D. (1982), *World handbook of political and social Indicators*, 3, pp. 1948-77, Köln: Zentralarchiv für Empirische Sozialforschung.

Taylor-Gooby, P. (1989), 'The role of the State', in Jowell, R., Witherspoon, S. and Brook, L. (eds.), *British Social Attitudes: special international report*, Aldershot: Gower.

de Tocqueville, A. (1848), *Democracy in the USA*, New York: Alfred A. Knopf.

Vanneman, R. (1980), 'U.S. and British perceptions of class', *American Journal of Sociology*, 85, pp. 769-790.

Vanneman, R. and Cannon, L. (1987), *The American perception of class*, Philadelphia: Temple University Press.

Wilkinson, R. (ed.) (1986), *Class and health*, London: Tavistock.

Appendix I
Technical details of the surveys

This appendix describes in brief the various surveys on which the data presented in this report are based. The data stem from annual national surveys conducted by countries participating in the International Social Survey Programme (ISSP). Since 1985, the members[1] of the ISSP have each undertaken to run a short survey on an agreed topic usually as a bolt-on to large national surveys. Further information about the annual national surveys conducted by the other countries participating in the ISSP between 1985 and 1993 may be obtained from the respective organisations that mount them, or from the West German *Zentralarchiv* at the University of Cologne; the details provided in this Appendix are derived from the ISSP Codebooks published by the *Zentralarchiv*.[2]

ISSP surveys

Britain: British Social Attitudes survey series

This annual survey series is now in its tenth year. It is designed and carried out by SCPR, core-funded by the Sainsbury Family Charitable Trusts and financially supported by additional contributors from government departments, other research bodies and foundations, quasi-government organisations and industry. Data are collected by personal interview and on a follow-up self-completion questionnaire (on which the ISSP questions are asked).

Each survey is designed to yield a representative sample of adults aged 18 and over living in private households in Britain. For the surveys undertaken between 1985 and 1990, the sampling frame used was the electoral register (ER); the sampling method during these years involved a multi-stage design, with four separate stages of selection:

- *parliamentary constituencies* (114 in 1985; 151 in 1986 and 1987; 152 in 1989 and 176 in 1990), stratified by Standard Region, population density and percentage owner-occupation, and selected systematically with probability proportionate to size of electorate;
- *polling districts* (p.d.);
- *addresses* (22 per p.d. in 1985; 30 in 1986; 29 in 1987; 30 in 1989; 26 in 1990) chosen with probability proportionate to their number of listed electors;
- *individuals* - one at each address (or household) chosen by a random procedure.

Since ER is increasingly considered to be a deficient sampling frame, the sampling frame for the 1993 module will be the Postcode Address File (PAF), a list of addresses - postal delivery points - compiled by the Post Office. It has greater coverage of addresses than ER, with no detectable bias in coverage. The decision to switch from ER to PAF was made after a 'splicing' experiment conducted in 1991 where half of the BSA sample was drawn from ER and half from the PAF. The purpose of the experiment was to investigate whether the switch would have any effects on response rates, on the demographic and socio-economic structure of the respondent 'population' and hence on the distribution of responses to particular questions. Any possible effects of the switch would be particularly serious for a time-series such as *British Social Attitudes,* where it is important to maintain year-on-year consistency. In the event, no sampling frame effects were discernible.

The sampling method in 1991 for the ER half of the sample was as described above, with 26 addresses chosen in each of 88 constituencies. The sampling method for the PAF half of the sample also involved a multi-stage design:

- *wards within 88 parliamentary constituencies*, selected with probability proportionate to the number of addresses listed in each PAF segment. Within each selected ward the PAF addresses were listed in alphanumeric order of postcode, the list split into three equal-sized segments, and one segment selected at random;
- *28 addresses* in each segment selected by starting from a random point on the list and choosing each address at a fixed interval;[3]
- *individuals* - one at each address chosen by a random procedure.

Fieldwork is carried out during the spring of each year, the bulk of interviewing typically taking place in April and May. In 1988 and 1992 the procedures differed because in general election years, SCPR carries out a post-election study of political attitudes in place of the regular BSA survey. Therefore, the 1988 ISSP module was fielded as part of the 1989

BSA survey. The 1992 module was a postal self-completion questionnaire sent to respondents to the 1991 survey who had said they were willing to help us again, had returned a self-completion questionnaire in 1991 and had *not* been selected to take part in the ISSP environment module pilot in April 1992. Response to the eight surveys was as follows:

	1985 module		1986 module		1987 module		1988[*] module	
	No	%	No	%	No	%	No	%
Addresses issued	2508		4530		4279		4560	
In scope (eligible)	2450	100	4454	100	4240	100	4370	100
Interview achieved	1804	74	3100	70	2847	67	3029	69
Self-completion q'aire returned	1530	62						
(i) Both versions	n/a		2737	61	2493	59	2604	60
(ii) ISSP version	n/a		1416	64	1212	57	1307	60
Proportion of respondents to the main q'aire who returned the ISSP q'aire		85		91		86		86

	1989 module		1990 module		1991 module		1992 module	
	No	%	No	%	No	%	No	%
Addresses issued	4560		4576		4752		2067	
In scope (eligible)	4370	100	4402	100	4378	100	1920	100
Interview achieved	3029	69	2797	64	2918	67		
Self-completion q'aire returned							1053	55
(i) Both versions	2604	60	2430	55	2481	57	n/a	
(ii) ISSP version	1297	59	1197	54	1257	57	n/a	
Proportion of respondents to the main q'aire who returned the ISSP q'aire		86		86		85		n/a

Note: Since 1986 two (randomly allocated) versions of the questionnaire have been fielded, the ISSP questions being carried out on one version only (except in 1989).

---

[*] The 1988 ISSP module was fielded in 1989 as part of that year's survey. The questions were asked on the A version of the self-completion questionnaire.

A more detailed statement of response, by questionnaire version and by Standard Region, is included in Appendix B of the annual Technical Reports of the *British Social Attitudes* survey.

Where necessary, two postal reminders were sent to respondents in an effort to obtain the self-completion supplement. Since the overall proportion returning the supplement each year is high, no weighting is applied to correct for differential non-response.

Each year the data are weighted. The procedures differ for the respective sampling frames. The ER sample weighting takes account of differences between the number of electors listed on the register for that address (which determined the original selection probability) and the number of eligible adults found at the address. However, the PAF does not list the number of persons at each address, and so the selection probabilities cannot take size of household into account. The data were weighted to take account of the fact that individuals living in large households have a lower chance than individuals in small households of being included in the sample. Neither does the PAF contain any information about how many 'dwelling units' there are at each address; so in cases where there are several dwelling units at the same postal address corrective weights need to be applied. To compensate for this, the weighting has to take account of the number of dwelling units at an address, as well as the number of adults in the selected unit. This means that the weights applied to the PAF sample are, in general, larger than those applied to the ER sample (see the annual Technical Reports). It also means that the total number of cases to which weights are applied is larger in the PAF than in the ER sample.

Users of the *Zentralarchiv* Codebooks should note that the tabulated data presented there are unweighted; for most purposes, analysts should use weighted data.

Full technical details of the eight surveys will be found in Witherspoon (1986), Brook and Witherspoon (1987), Brook and Witherspoon (1988), Brook, Taylor and Prior (1990), Brook, Taylor and Prior (1991), Brook Taylor and Prior (1992) and Brook, Dowds and Ahrendt (1994, forthcoming).

All reports can be obtained from SCPR or from the ESRC Data Archive at the University of Essex where the datasets are publicly available.

Northern Ireland: Northern Ireland Social Attitudes survey series

In 1989, the Nuffield Foundation and the Northern Ireland Office agreed to fund three extensions of the *British Social Attitudes Survey* to Northern Ireland. The survey has now received funding for three more years from all of Northern Ireland's government departments. The *Northern Ireland Social Attitudes* (NISA) survey has included ISSP modules from 1989 to 1991.

The survey is designed to yield a representative sample of all adults aged 18 or over living in Northern Ireland. The sample frame for the surveys is the rating valuation list. Before addresses are selected, the list is stratified into geographical areas. Within each stratum, a simple random sample of addresses is selected with probability proportionate to the number of addresses. A further selection stage is required to convert the listing of addresses to a listing of individuals. At each address, interviewers have to list all people aged 18 and over living at that address. From this listing of eligible adults, one respondent is selected by a random selection procedure.

Fieldwork is carried out by the Policy Planning and Research Unit (PPRU) in Belfast. In 1989 the survey was in the field during March and April, in 1990 between February and April, and in 1991 during February and March.

The response rates for the ISSP modules were as follows:

	1989 module		1990 module		1991 module	
	No	%	No	%	No	%
Addresses issued	1398		1400		1400	
In scope	1304	100	1277	100	1271	100
Interviews achieved	866	66	896	70	906	71
Self-completion q'aire returned	780	60	772	60	838	66
Proportion of respondents to the main q'aire who returned the ISSP q'aire		90		86		92

The data were weighted to adjust for the fact that individuals living in large households had a lower chance than individuals in small households of being included in the sample. Full technical details of the surveys can be found in Stringer and Robinson (1991, 1992 and 1993) and in the BSA Technical Reports for the 1989, 1990 and 1991 surveys. Further information may be obtained from:

Dr Kevin Sweeney
PPRU
Londonderry House
Chichester Street
Belfast BT1 4SX
UK

United States of America: General Social Survey

The *General Social Survey* (GSS) has been carried out annually since 1972 by the *National Opinion Research Center* (NORC), University of Chicago. The project is conducted for the National Data Program for the Social Sciences and is financially supported by the National Science Foundation. Data are collected mainly by face-to-face interview; the ISSP questionnaire modules are in a self-completion supplement, which most respondents fill in immediately after the interview and which is collected by the interviewer.

Each annual survey is designed to be representative of English-speaking persons within the USA, aged 18 years or over and living in non-institutional arrangements. The sample is a multi-stage probability sample, with three stages of selection:

- *primary sampling units*, comprising Standard Metropolitan Statistical Areas; or non-metropolitan counties, stratified before selection by region, age and race;
- *block groups and enumeration districts*, stratified before selection by race and income;
- *blocks*, selected with probability proportionate to size. (In the absence of block statistics, measures of size are obtained by field counting.)

Corrective weights were applied to the 1985 and 1987 data (see below) but not in any of the other years. The 1987 GSS dataset also contains an oversample of black respondents, but this is excluded from the ISSP dataset.

Fieldwork is carried out between February and April each year.

Response to the surveys carried out between 1985 and 1991 was as follows:

	1985 module		1986 module		1987[*] module		1988 module	
	No	%	No	%	No	%	No	%
Original sample	2201		2192		2250		2250	
Net sample (eligible)	1948	100	1944	100	1945	100	1916	100
Interviews achieved	1534	79	1470	76	1466	75	1481	77
Self-administered q'aire filled in	677	71	1428	73	1285	66	1414	74
% of respondents who filled in self-administered q'aire		90		97		88		95

	1989 module		1990 module		1991 module	
	No	%	No	%	No	%
Original sample	2250		2165		2312	
Net sample (eligible)	1981	100	1857	100	1950	100
Interviews achieved	1537	78	1372	74	1517	78
Self-administered q'aire filled in	1453	73	1217	66	1359	70
% of respondents who filled in self-administered q'aire		95		89		90

[*] The figures for 1987 are weighted.

The 1985 data have been weighted to correct for an unintentional overlap between the respondent selection procedures and form assignment procedures. The weighting compensated for this assignment bias and achieved a random distribution of affected variables (such as age, sex, labour force status and income) across assignments (see Smith and Petersen, 1986). The 1987 data have been weighted because of the black oversample. The weight factor makes the survey a representative cross-section by excluding the black oversample cases.

The GSS data are published annually in a cumulative Codebook produced by NORC and distributed by the Roper Center for Public Opinion Research, University of Connecticut. Further information may be obtained from:

> Dr. Tom W. Smith
> NORC
> University of Chicago
> 1115 East 60th Street
> Chicago, Illinois 60637
> USA

Australia: International Social Survey/Australia

The *International Social Survey/Australia* (ISS/A), and its predecessor, the *National Social Science Survey* (NSSS) were founded in 1984/85. ISS/A carries ISSP modules as part of their annual survey which is based on large representative national samples.

The ISS/A is primarily an academic research programme conducted by researchers affiliated to the Institute of Advanced Studies at the Australian National University (ANU). The first survey was funded primarily by the Australian Research Grants Commission; subsequent surveys have been supported primarily by the Research School of Social Sciences at the ANU, and secondarily by the Australian International Development Assistance Bureau, the Australian Institute of Criminology, the Australian Institute of Family Studies and other funders.

The ISS/A uses a simple random sample drawn from the (compulsory) electoral rolls. Sampled individuals are sent a questionnaire, addressed to them personally, followed about ten days later by a thank you/reminder letter. Non-respondents are pursued by up to four more mailings over the next six to nine months, including two mailings with fresh copies of the questionnaire, one by certified mail.

Comparisons with the 1986 Australian Census show that the ISS/A sample closely approximates the population in age, sex, place of residence, education, labour force participation, occupation and other characteristics.

The response rates for the five ISSP modules fielded by NSSS-ISS/A are as follows[4] :

- *Role of Government.* Respondents to the 1984/1985 NSSS were sent a postal self-completion questionnaire. The survey was in the field from November

1986 to July 1987. From the issued sample of 2509, 1528 completed questionnaires were returned, yielding a response rate of 61 per cent.

- *Social Networks and Support Systems.* The ISSP questionnaire was fielded as a supplement to the NSSS 1987 Election Panel and mailed to all original respondents whose addresses were known and who had not indicated that they were opposed to being contacted again. Data were collected in mid-1987. The completion rate was 60 per cent, yielding 1250 respondents.[5]

- *Social Inequality.* The third ISSP questionnaire was fielded as part of the fourth round of the NSSS. The sample was drawn at random from the national electoral rolls. The survey was carried out in two waves, starting in November 1987. The first wave yielded 1574 cases. Telephone contacts follow ups yielded an additional 89 cases, bringing the total of completed cases to 1663. The completion rate was 60 per cent.

- *Family and Changing Sex Roles.* The fourth ISSP questionnaire had a completion rate of 67 per cent, yielding 4514 cases.

- *Role of Government II (part replication).* The ISSP questionnaire was fielded as part of the NSSS 1990 Election Panel Survey. Respondents were sent a postal self-completion questionnaire. The survey was in the field from late 1989 to early 1990. The sample was drawn at random from the national electoral rolls. The completion rate was 84 per cent, yielding 2398 respondents.

None of the datasets was weighted.

Additional details about the ISS/A sampling and mailing procedures will be found in Kelley *et al* (1987). The ISS/A-NSSS datasets are archived at the Social Science Data Archive at ANU. Further information may be obtained from:

Dr. Jonathan Kelley
Department of Sociology
Research School of Social Sciences
The Australian National University
Canberra ACT 0200
Australia

Germany: ALLBUS

ALLBUS *(Allgemeine Bevölkerungsumfrage der Sozialwissenschaften)*, conducted biennially since 1980, is the German general social survey and, like BSA and the GSS, is a replicating time-series. It is the joint responsibility of the *Zentrum für Umfragen, Methoden und Analysen* (ZUMA) in Mannheim and the *Zentralarchiv für Empirische Sozialforschung* (ZA) in Cologne. In 1990, ALLBUS was extended to cover the former GDR (see below).

Each survey is designed to be a representative sample of adults (aged 18 and over) living in private households in Germany. A three-stage stratified design is used: selection of sampling points; selection of households within those points by a random route method; and at each household selection of an eligible German national (from 1991 on,

German speaking foreigners are also eligible for inclusion). The ISSP data are collected on a self-completion questionnaire, usually filled in following the main ALLBUS interview. Fieldwork was carried out as follows:

1985	*Role of Government*	:	May - August 1985 (mail survey)
1986	*Social Networks*	:	March - May 1986 (ALLBUS)
1987	*Social Inequality*	:	September - October 1987 (SOWI-BUS)
1988	*Family and Changing Sex Roles*	:	April - July 1988 (ALLBUS)
1989	*Work Orientations*	:	November - December 1989 (SOWI-BUS)
1990	*Role of Government* II	:	March - May 1990 (WESTERN ALLBUS) December 1990 (EASTERN ALLBUS)
1991	*Religion*	:	May - July 1991 (ALLBUS Baseline)
1992	*Social Inequality* II	:	May - June 1992 (ALLBUS)
1993	*Environment*	:	May - July 1993 (SOWI-BUS)

The table below shows the response rates achieved in each year. The 1985 module was fielded on its own, and the 1987, 1989 and 1993 modules were carried out as supplements to another general social survey, *Sozialwissenschaften-Bus* (SOWI-BUS).

	1985 module		1986 module		1987 module	
	No	%	No	%	No	%
Issued	2704		5512		2896	
Adjusted sample (eligible)	2513	100	5275	100	2580	100
Achieved interviews	n/a		3095	59	1655	64
Completed ISSP q'aire	1048	42	2809	53	1397	54
% of respondents who returned the ISSP q'aire	n/a			91		84

	1988 module		1989[*] module		1990 module	
	No	%	No	%	No	%
Issued	4620		2688		5204	
Adjusted sample (eligible)	4509	100	2398	100	5054	100
Achieved interviews	3070	68	1622	68	3051	60
Completed ISSP q'aires	2994	66	1464	61	2812	56
% of respondents who returned the ISSP q'aire		98		90		92

---

[*] The figures for adjusted sample represent the reduced ISSP sample size. Because of an unsystematic mistake, questionnaires were sent to interviewers in 24 sample points which should have been excluded from the ISSP sample.[6]

The two surveys that were administered after 1990 (when ALLBUS was extended to cover the former GDR) achieved the following response rates:

	1991				1992			
	West Germany		East Germany		West Germany		East Germany	
	No	%	No	%	No	%	No	%
Issued	2900		2720		4650		2100	
Adjusted sample	2875	100	2712	100	4625	100	2100	100
Achieved interviews	1517	53	1544	57	2400	52	1148	55
Completed ISSP q'aires	1346	47	1486	55	2297	50	1094	52
% of respondents who returned the ISSP q'aire		89		96		96		95

The 1986 dataset was the only one to be weighted (to correct for non-response). Further details are given in Hippler (1986); Erbslöh and Wiedenbeck (1987); Braun, Trometer and Wiedenbeck (1989); Wasmer, Koch and Wiedenbeck (1990); Bandilla *et al* (1992) and Braun *et al* (1993). Further information may be obtained from:

Dr. Peter Ph. Mohler
ZUMA
B2,1 PO BOX 12 21 55
68072 Mannheim
Federal Republic of Germany

Austria

The first ISSP modules to be fielded in Austria (*Role of Government I*, 1985; and *Family Networks and Support Systems*, 1986) were administered on a self-completion supplement to the *Sozialer Survey Österreich (SSÖ)*, conducted in 1986 by the Institut für Soziologie (IS) at the University of Graz. The SSÖ is being carried out again in 1993 and will carry the 1993 ISSP questionnaire module. In the intervening years, ISSP modules have been administered face-to-face on other surveys carried out by the IS.

The SSÖ sample, and that of the other surveys containing the ISSP modules, is designed to be representative of adults in the Republic of Austria and is three-stage.

- *sampling points* are selected within each Bundesland (region) according to the population size of each point;
- *households* within each sampling point are selected using addresses drawn randomly from the electoral register;
- *individuals* (aged between 16 and 69) are randomly selected for interview in each household, using a fixed random number.[7]

For further details see Haller and Holm (1987) and IS (1988).

The 1985 *Role of Government* and 1986 *Social Networks* modules were administered during May and June 1986 to a random half of those responding to the main SSÖ questionnaire; the 1987 *Social Inequality* and the 1988 *Family and Changing Sex Roles* modules were administered by personal interview in June and July 1988; the 1989 *Work Orientations* ISSP module, also conducted by personal interview, was fielded in April and May of that year. Response rates achieved on each interviewing round are shown below:

	1985 module		1986 module		1987[*] module		1988[*] module		1989[*] module	
	No	%	No	%	No	%	No	%	No	%
Issued addresses	2820		2820		1400		1400		2840	
Adjusted sample (eligible)	2763	100	2763	100	1361	100	1361	100	2772	100
Achieved interviews	2016	72	2016	72	972	71	972	71	1997	72
Completed ISSP questionnaires	987	36	1027	37						

[*] carried out by personal interview

The 1990 and 1991 modules were not fielded in Austria.

The five datasets have been weighted to restore correct population proportions based on an achieved sample of 1000 adults (IFES-weighting). Further information may be obtained from:

Professor Dr. Max Haller *or* Dr. Franz Höllinger
Institut für Soziologie der Universität Graz
Universitätsplatz 4/III
A-8010 Graz
Austria

Hungary

Each year *Tärsadalomkutátsi Informatikai Egyesülés* (TÁRKI) carries out a national survey representative of the population of Hungary aged 18 and over. Samples are selected in two stages, the first consisting of a cluster of 'settlements' and the second of individuals. Random selection of individuals is based on files at the Population Register Bureau which provide names, home addresses and year of birth. Thus, the representativeness of the issued sample is controlled in respect of region, age and gender. The fieldwork method is personal interview.

Respondents are drawn either from a 'fresh' sample or from a 'follow-up' sample of people interviewed earlier. For fresh samples, the Population Register Bureau usually provides 50 to 100 per cent substitute addresses in addition to those issued for the 'main' sample. Thus, for a survey of 3000 cases interviewers would be given 3000 main addresses and 1500 to 3000 substitute addresses. When an interview cannot be achieved, a substitute address is randomly selected. This procedure ensures that the final sample consists of 3000 cases.

For both fresh and follow-up samples, the datasets are weighted as necessary to make them representative of the population in terms of region, age-group, gender and education.

For the 1986 *Social Networks* module, a subsample of 1000 adults representative of the population as a whole was drawn from the 6000 nationwide random sample of TÁRKI I respondents. A further subsample of 2000 younger people (aged 18-39) was drawn to boost the number of young people answering the ISSP questionnaire, but has not been included in the response data shown below. Fieldwork took place in autumn 1986.

For the 1987 *Social Inequality* module, a random nationwide subsample of 3000 adults was drawn from the 6000 nationwide random sample of TÁRKI I respondents. Fieldwork took place in spring 1987. The 1988 *Family and Changing Sex Roles* module was administered to a subsample of respondents to the 1987 survey. Fieldwork was carried out in June and July 1988. For the 1989 *Work Orientations* module, a random nationwide sample of 1000 addresses was drawn from the Population Register Bureau files, and 500 substitute addresses issued. Fieldwork was carried out in spring 1989.

The 1000 nationwide random subsample for the 1990 *Role of Government* module was drawn from the 3000 nationwide random sample of the TÁRKI A survey respondents, interviewed in spring 1988. Five hundred substitute addresses were also provided. Interviews were carried out in spring 1990. For the 1991 *Religion* module, a random subsample of 1000 adults and 500 substitute addresses was drawn from the 3000 nationwide random sample of TÁRKI B survey respondents, interviewed in spring 1989.

For each of the ISSP modules carried out by TÁRKI, the following number of questionnaires were received:

	1986 module	1987 module	1988 module	1989 module	1990 module	1991 module
Issued addresses	1000	3000	1965	1000	1000	1000
Completed ISSP questionnaires	912	2604	1737	1000	977	1000
Response rate	91%	87%	88%	n/a[*]	n/a[*]	n/a[*]

[*] Response rates are not shown since substitute addresses were drawn.

Further information may be obtained from:

> Professor Dr. Tamás Kolosi *or* Dr. Peter Robert
> TÁRKI
> Victor Hugo u. 18-22
> 1132 Budapest
> Hungary

Italy: Indagine Sociale Italiana

The *Indagine Sociale Italiana* (ISI) is an annual series of surveys, carried out by the *Ricerca Sociale e di Marketing Institute* (EURISKO) in Milan. Since 1985, the surveys have included the ISSP questionnaire modules, administered either as a self-completion supplement to the main ISI interview or as an interviewer-assisted supplement.

The sample for each ISI survey is designed to be representative of the population of Italy aged between 18 and 74. A national two-stage probability sample is used selecting:

- *at first stage*, small geographical areas or administrative units to yield a probability sample of primary sampling units (PSUs); areas and units had been pre-stratified according to sex, age and population density;
- *at the second stage*, a pre-specified number of households (or dwellings units) within each PSU.

Finally, within each selected household, one adult (aged 18-74) is selected by quota sampling methods.

Response rates are not available from the ZA Codebooks.

Fieldwork on the modules was carried out as follows:

1985	*Role of Government*	:	September & October 1985
1986	*Family Networks and Support Systems*	:	March & April 1987
1987	*Social Inequality*	:	March & April 1987
1988	*Family and Changing Sex Roles*	:	Not available
1989	*Work Orientations*	:	Not available
1990	*Role of Government* II	:	April 1990
1991	*Religion*	:	Not available

Corrective weights were applied to the data for all six surveys to adjust for population size, sex, age and occupation (based on 1981 Census estimates).

Further information may be obtained from:

Prof. Gabriele Calvi *or* Dr. Paolo Anselmi
Ricerca Sociale e di Marketing Institute (EURISKO)
Via Monte Rosa 15
20149 Milano
Italy

Netherlands

The Netherlands has no single annual or biennial national survey on which to field the ISSP module. Instead, the *Sociaal en Cultureel Planbureau* (SCP) in Rijswijk regularly conducts surveys on social and cultural welfare issues in the Netherlands, as mandated by its terms of reference (see SCP, 1986). To date, the 1987, 1988, 1989 and 1991 ISSP modules have been fielded, administered as self-completion supplements to the nationwide survey *Cultural Changes in the Netherlands.* Samples are drawn from a list of all Dutch addresses as used by the postal service. All towns with 20,000 addresses or more are selected, with a sample of smaller towns chosen at random (their chance selection being proportionate to their size).

At each sampling point, interviewers are provided with a 'starting address', from which they proceed to other addresses according to strict 'random route' guidelines. If they fail to achieve an interview at any address (after at least three calls), they are given a new 'starting address' and seek an interview in the same way. To achieve 2000 interviews, 2424 'starting addresses' are provided.

At each household, the interviewer attempts to interview the 'head of household'; where there are two 'heads' (for example, husband and wife) one is selected for interview according to predetermined rules.

Fieldwork details are as follows:

			Achieved interviews
1987	*Social Inequality*	: September–December 1987	1638
1988	*Family and Changing Sex Roles*	: November–January 1989	1737
1989	*Work Orientations*	: September–January 1990	1690
1991	*Religion*	: Throughout the year	1635

Because substitute 'starting addresses' are used, it is not possible to calculate non-response to the main (face-to-face) questionnaire according to the usual rules. However, response to the ISSP self-completion questionnaire is usually about 80 per cent (that is, it is filled in by about four out of five respondents to the main questionnaire).

No weights were applied to the data.

Further information may be obtained from:

> Dr. Carlo van Praag *or* Dr. Jos Becker
> Sociaal en Cultureel Planbureau
> JC van Markenlaan 3
> Postbus 37
> 2280 AA Rijswijk
> Netherlands

Republic of Ireland

In common with some other ISSP member countries, the Republic of Ireland has no regular national survey on which to field the annual ISSP module. Since 1988, however, ISSP modules have been fielded as part of nationwide *special purpose* surveys.

For each survey, two-stage probability samples were drawn, the first stage being District Electoral Divisions and the second, electors aged 18 and over. The number of achieved interviews in each year is as follows:

			Achieved interviews
1986	*Family Network and Support Systems*	: September-December 1990	975
1987	*Social Inequality*	: September-December 1990	975
1988	*Family and Changing Sex Roles*	: November 1988-January 1989	1005
1989	*Work Orientations*	: Dates unavailable	972
1990	*Role of Government* II	: September-December 1991	1005
1991	*Religion*	: September-December 1991	1005

The methods used to select individuals for interview, and response rates achieved, are not available from the ZA Codebooks. Further information may be obtained from:

> Dr. Liam Ryan *or* Andrew Greeley
> Social Science Research Centre
> University College Dublin
> Dublin 4
> Republic of Ireland

Norway

The *Norwegian Social Science Data Services* (NSD) became a member of the ISSP in 1989 and to date has fielded five modules. Norway has no regular annual national survey on which to field the ISSP modules, but instead carries them out as postal self-completion surveys. They are financed by the Research Council of Norway.

The 1989 *Work Orientations* module was administered on a self-completion supplement to a random sample of persons aged 16-74 interviewed as part of the Labour Force Survey. Respondents were selected through a two-stage sampling procedure. Municipalities – the primary sampling units (PSUs) – are stratified according to location, industrial structure and population size, with cities of more than 30,000 inhabitants forming separate strata. One PSU is selected from each stratum. For each of the municipalities selected at the first stage a register of households is then randomly selected from each of the municipalities' registers, in such a way that each household has an equal probability of selection. Fieldwork was conducted by the Central Bureau of Statistics of Norway in April and May 1989.

Since 1990, fieldwork has been conducted by the NSD, between February and July each year, by means of 'stand-alone' postal self-completion questionnaires. A simple random sample of persons aged 16-79 is drawn from the Central Register of Persons. The datasets are not weighted, except in 1992, when response among elderly women was especially low.

The response rates achieved were as follows:

	1989 module		1990 module		1991 module		1992 module		1993 module	
	No	%	No	%	No	%	No	%	No	%
Addresses issued	2488		2500		2500		2500		2300	
In scope	2470	100	2425	100	2420	100	2420	100	2231	100
ISSP q'aires received	1848	75	1571	63	1506	62	1538	64	1414	63

The datasets include a weight based on the estimating procedures in the main survey. Further information may be obtained from:

> Knud Knudsen
> NSD, Norwegian Social Science Data Services
> Hans Holmboesgt 22
> 5007 Bergen
> Norway

Israel

The Department of Sociology and Anthropology of the University of Tel Aviv joined the ISSP in 1988 and has fielded questionnaire modules since 1989. Information is only available only for the 1990 *Role of Government II* module, which was administered to 991 respondents selected by area probability sampling. Respondents were interviewed face-to-face, and fieldwork took place in December 1991. Further information may be obtained from:

> Professor Noah Lewin-Epstein
> Department of Sociology and Anthropology
> Tel Aviv University
> PO Box 39040 Ramat Aviv
> 69978 Tel Aviv
> Israel

Switzerland

Switzerland is not one of the ISSP member nations, but in 1987 the Soziologisches Institut der Universität Zurich fielded a questionnaire replicating the 1987 Social Inequality module. The Institute used a two-stage stratified random sample designed to be representative of adults (aged 16 and over) resident in Switzerland (including foreign workers). The first selection stage involved selecting 129 'representative Swiss communities'; at the second stage, addresses were selected according to random principles (See Hischier and Zwicky, 1988).

The questionnaire was postal and included some questions repeated from a Swiss survey of 1975. German, French and Italian versions were used, and an incentive payment of SFR50 was made to those returning a completed questionnaire. Returns were received between October and December 1987. Response was as follows:

	1987	
	No	%
Questionnaires mailed	2,046	
(Assumed to be) eligible	1,925	*100*
Completed questionnaires	987	*51*

The dataset was not weighted.

New ISSP members

Several ISSP members have joined recently but details of survey methodology are not yet available. Further information may be obtained directly from the contact names and addresses listed below:

Bulgaria:

Yuri Aroyo, Lilya Dimova
Institute for Trade Union and Social Research
1 Macedonia Square
1040 Sofia
Bulgaria

Canada:

Alan Frizzell
School of Journalism/Mass Communications
Survey Center
Carleton University
346 St. Patrick's Building
Ottawa
Canada K1S 5B6

Czech Republic:

Petr Mateju
Institute of Sociology
Czechoslovak Academy of Sciences
Jilska 1
110 00 Praha 1
Prague
Czech Republic

Japan:

Shigeru Yokoyama
Broadcasting Culture Research
NHK (Japanese Broadcasting Corporation)
2-1-1 Atago
Minato-Ku
Tokyo
105 Japan

New Zealand:

Philip Gendall
Department of Marketing
Faculty of Business Studies
Massey University
Palmerston North
New Zealand

The Philippines:

Mahar Mangahas, Mercedes Abad
Social Weather Stations, Inc.
Philippine Social Science Center
Commonwealth Avenue
Diliman, Quezon City 1101
The Philippines

Poland:

Bogdan Cichomski
Institute for Social Studies
University of Warsaw
Stawki 5/7
00-183 Warsaw
Poland

Russia: Tatyana Zaslavskaya, Ludmilla Khakhulina
                               The Soviet Center for Public Opinion
                                and Market Research
                               17, ul. 25 Oktyabrya
                               Moscow 103642
                               USSR

Slovenia: Niko Tos
                               Public Opinion and Mass Communications Research Centre
                               University of Ljubljana
                               Kardeljeva ploscad 5
                               61109 Ljubljana
                               Slovenia

Sweden: Steffan Svallfors
                               Department of Sociology
                               University of Umeå
                               901 87 Umeå
                               Sweden

ISSP members archive the data with the Zentralarchiv in Cologne. Further information may be obtained from:

Rolf Uher
Zentralarchiv für Empirische Sozialforschung
Bachemer Strasse 40
5000 Köln 41
Germany

Notes

1. ISSP membership has risen from its four 'founding fathers' in 1985 to 21 countries in 1993.
2. 1985: Ref. ZA-No. 1490; 1986: Ref. ZA-No. 1620; 1987: Ref. ZA-No. 1680; 1988: Ref. ZA-No. 1700; 1989: Ref. ZA-No. 1840; 1990: Ref. ZA-No. 1950; 1991: Ref. ZA-No. 2150; 1992: Ref. ZA-No. 2240.
3. More addresses were selected on the PAF half of the sample than on the ER half, because the PAF contains a higher proportion of 'deadwood' addresses (such as unoccupied addresses or those that are business premises only).
4. NSSS did not carry the 1988, 1989, 1991 and 1992 ISSP modules.
5. Some additional data on social support systems were collected as part of this study. They are available on request from Dr Clive Bean, Department of Sociology, Research School of Social Sciences, ANU.
6. Users of the data have the choice of whether to use the original sample or the reduced sample. Instructions can be found in the Zentralarchiv's 1989 ISSP Codebook (ZA-No. 1840).
7. In 1989, eligible respondents were aged 14 years or older.

References

Bandilla, W., Gabler, S. and Wiedenbeck, M. (1992), *Methodenbericht zum DFG-Projekt ALLBUS Baseline-Studie 1991*, ZUMA-Arbeitsbericht, No. 92/04, Mannheim: ZUMA.

Braun, M., Trometer, R. and Wiedenbeck, M. (1989), *Methodenbericht zur Allgemeinen Bevölkerungsumfrage der Sozialwissenschaften, ALLBUS 1988*, ZUMA-Arbeitsbericht, No. 89/02, Mannheim: ZUMA.

Braun, M., Eilinghoff, C., Gabler, S. and Wiedenbeck, M. (1993), *Methodenbericht zur Allgemeinen Bevölkerungsumfrage der Sozialwissenschaften, ALLBUS 1992*, ZUMA Arbeitsbericht No. 93/01, Mannheim: ZUMA.

Brook, L. and Witherspoon, S. (1987), *British Social Attitudes, 1986 Survey:* Technical Report, London: SCPR.

Brook, L. and Witherspoon, S. (1988), *British Social Attitudes, 1987 Survey:* Technical Report, London: SCPR.

Brook, L., Taylor, B. and Prior, G. (1990), *British Social Attitudes, 1989 Survey:* Technical Report, London: SCPR.

Brook, L., Taylor, B. and Prior, G.(1991), *British Social Attitudes, 1990 Survey:* Technical Report, London: SCPR.

Brook, L., Taylor, B. and Prior, G. (1992), *British Social Attitudes, 1991 Survey:* Technical Report, London: SCPR.

Brook, L., Dowds, L. and Ahrendt, D. (forthcoming), *British Social Attitudes, 1992 ISSP Survey:* Technical Report, London: SCPR.

Erbslöh, B. and Wiederbeck, M. (1987), *Methodenbericht zur Allgemeinen Bevölkerungsumfrage der Sozialwissenschaften, ALLBUS 1986*, ZUMA-Arbeitsbericht, No. 1987/04, Mannheim: ZUMA.

Haller, M. and Holm, K. (eds.) (1987), *Werhaltungen und Lebensformen in Österreich. Ergebnisse des Sozialen Survey 1986*, Munich/Vienna: R. Oldenburg Verlag and Verlag für Geschichte und Politik.

Hippler, H. J. (1986), *Methodenforschung im Rahmen des International Social Survey Project (ISSP) 1985*, ZUMA-Nachrichten, No. 19, pp. 64-75, Mannheim: ZUMA.

Hischier, G. and Zwicky H. (1988), *Die Erhebung der Daten und ihre Bestimmungsgründe*, Soziologisches Institut der Universität Zurich, Zurich: SI

IS (Institut für Soziologie der Universität Graz) (1988), *Codebuch mit Methodenbericht, Linearauszahlung und Fragebogen (ISSP-87 Ungleichheit; ISSP-88 Familie)*, Graz: IS.

Kelley, J., Cushing, R. G. and Headley, B. (1987), *The Australian National Social Science Survey, 1984-1985*, Social Science Data Archive, Australian National University.

SCP (Social and Cultural Planning Office) (1986), *Social and Cultural Report 1986*, Rijswijk: SCP.

Smith, T.W. and Petersen, B.L. (1986), 'Problems in Form Randomization on the General Social Surveys', in *GSS Technical Report No. 53*, Chicago: NORC.

Stringer, P. and Robinson, G. (1991), *Social Attitudes in Northern Ireland: 1990-1991 edition.* Belfast: The Blackstaff Press.

Stringer, P. and Robinson, G. (1992), *Social Attitudes in Northern Ireland: 1991-1992 edition.* Belfast: The Blackstaff Press.

Stringer, P. and Robinson, G. (1993), *Social Attitudes in Northern Ireland: 1992-1993 edition.* Belfast: The Blackstaff Press.

Wasmer, M., Koch, A. and Wiedenbeck, M. (1990), *Methodenbericht zur Allgemeinen Bevölkerungsumfrage der Sozialwissenschaften*, ALLBUS, Mannheim: ZUMA.

ZA (Zentralarchiv für Empirische Sozialforschung) (1986), *International Social Survey Programme: Role of Government I - 1985*, Codebook ZA-No. 1490, Mannheim: ZA.

ZA (Zentralarchiv für Empirische Sozialforschung) (1987), *International Social Survey Programme: Social Networks and Support Systems - 1986*, Codebook ZA-No. 1620, Mannheim: ZA.

ZA (Zentralarchiv für Empirische Sozialforschung) (1988), *International Social Survey Programme: Social Inequality - 1987*, Codebook ZA-No. 1680, Mannheim: ZA.

ZA (Zentralarchiv für Empirische Sozialforschung) (1990), *International Social Survey Programme: Family and Changing Sex Roles - 1988,* Codebook ZA-No. 1700, Mannheim: ZA.

ZA (Zentralarchiv für Empirische Sozialforschung) (1991), *International Social Survey Programme: Work Orientations - 1989,* Codebook ZA-No. 1840, Mannheim: ZA.

ZA (Zentralarchiv für Empirische Sozialforschung) (1991), *International Social Survey Programme: Role of Government II - 1990,* Codebook ZA-No. 1950, Mannheim: ZA.

ZA (Zentralarchiv für Empirische Sozialforschung) (1992), *International Social Survey Programme: Religion - 1991,* Codebook ZA-No. 2150, Mannheim: ZA.

Appendix II
Notes on the tabulations

1.   Tables at the end of chapters are percentaged vertically; tables within the text are percentaged as indicated.

2.   In all of the tables, whether in the text or at the end of chapters, a percentage of less than 0.5 is indicated by '*'.

3.   In the great majority of tables, percentages have been rounded up or down to the nearest whole %. Percentages of 0.5 have been rounded up (e.g. 38.5% = 39%).

4.   In some tables the proportions of respondents answering 'don't know' or not giving and answer are omitted. This, together with the effects of rounding and weighting, means that percentages will not always add to 100 per cent.

Appendix III
The questionnaires

The findings which are reported in Chapters 1-6 are based on six *International Social Survey Programme* (ISSP) questionnaire modules run in 1985, 1987, 1988, 1989, 1990 and 1991. The English language versions of the questionnaires are reproduced below. Question numbers of the English language version correspond to the question numbers used in SCPR's *British Social Attitudes* survey.

INTERNATIONAL SOCIAL SURVEY PROGRAMME

1985 MODULE

ROLE OF GOVERNMENT

(ENGLISH LANGUAGE VERSION)

- 1 -

2.01 Suppose a newspaper got hold of confidential government papers about defence plans and wanted to publish them.

PLEASE TICK ONE BOX (✓)

Should the newspaper be allowed to publish the papers? [1]

OR

Should the government have the power to prevent publication? [2]   20.07

Can't choose [8]

b) Now suppose the confidential government papers were about economic plans.

PLEASE TICK ONE BOX (✓)

Should the newspaper be allowed to publish the papers? [1]

OR

Should the government have the power to prevent publication? [2]   20.08

Can't choose [8]

2.02 In general, would you say that people should obey the law without exception, or are there exceptional occasions on which people should follow their consciences even if it means breaking the law?

PLEASE TICK ONE BOX (✓)

Obey the law without exception [1]

Follow conscience on occasions [2]   20.09

Can't choose [8]

/continued over ...

- 2 -

2.03 There are many ways people or organisations can protest against a government action they strongly oppose. Please show which you think should be allowed and which should not be allowed by ticking a box on each line.

Should it be allowed?

PLEASE TICK ONE BOX ON EACH LINE

	Defin-itely	Proba-bly	Probably not	Definitely not	Can't choose	OFFICE USE ONLY
A. Organising public meetings to protest against the government	[1]	[2]	[3]	[4]	[8]	20.10
B. Publishing pamphlets to protest against the government	[1]	[2]	[3]	[4]	[8]	20.11
C. Organising protest marches and demonstrations	[1]	[2]	[3]	[4]	[8]	20.12
D. Occupying a government office and stopping work there for several days	[1]	[2]	[3]	[4]	[8]	20.13
E. Seriously damaging government buildings	[1]	[2]	[3]	[4]	[8]	20.14
F. Organising a nationwide strike of all workers against the government	[1]	[2]	[3]	[4]	[8]	20.15

2.04 There are some people whose views are considered extreme by the majority.

a) First, consider people who want to overthrow the government by revolution. Do you think such people should be allowed to ...

PLEASE TICK ONE BOX ON EACH LINE

	Defin-itely	Proba-bly	Probably not	Definitely not	Can't choose	OFFICE USE ONLY
i) ... hold public meetings to express their views ?	[1]	[2]	[3]	[4]	[8]	20.16
ii) ... teach 15 year olds in schools ?	[1]	[2]	[3]	[4]	[8]	20.17
iii) ... publish books express-ing their views?	[1]	[2]	[3]	[4]	[8]	20.18

b) Second, consider people who believe that whites are racially superior to all other races. Do you think such people should be allowed to ...

PLEASE TICK ONE BOX ON EACH LINE

	Defin-itely	Proba-bly	Probably not	Definitely not	Can't choose	OFFICE USE ONLY
i) ... hold public meetings to express their views?	[1]	[2]	[3]	[4]	[8]	20.19
ii) ... teach 15 year olds in schools ?	[1]	[2]	[3]	[4]	[8]	20.20
iii) ... publish books express-ing their views?	[1]	[2]	[3]	[4]	[8]	20.21

- 4 -

2.07 The government has a lot of different pieces of information about people which computers can bring together very quickly. Is this ...

PLEASE TICK ONE BOX

... a very serious threat to individual privacy, [1]

a fairly serious threat, [2]

not a serious threat, [3]

or - not a threat at all to individual privacy? [4]

Can't choose [8]

20,31

2.08 Some people think those with high incomes should pay a larger proportion (percentage) of their earnings in taxes than those who earn low incomes. Other people think that those with high incomes and those with low incomes should pay the same proportion (percentage) of their earnings in taxes.

Do you think those with high incomes should ...

PLEASE TICK ONE BOX

... pay a much larger proportion, [1]

pay a larger proportion, [2]

pay the same proportion as those who earn low incomes, [3]

pay a smaller proportion, [4]

or - pay a much smaller proportion? [5]

Can't choose [8]

20,32

2.09 What is your opinion of the following statement: it is the responsibility of the government to reduce the differences in income between people with high incomes and those with low incomes.

PLEASE TICK ONE BOX

Agree strongly [1]

Agree [2]

Neither agree nor disagree [3]

Disagree [4]

Disagree strongly [5]

20,33

- 3 -

2.05 Suppose the police get an anonymous tip that a man with a long criminal record is planning to break into a warehouse.

PLEASE TICK ONE BOX ON EACH LINE

Do you think the police should be allowed, without a Court Order....

	Defin-itely [1]	Proba-bly [2]	Probably not [3]	Definitely not [4]	Can't choose [8]	
i) ... to keep the man under surveillance?						20,22
ii) ... to tap his telephone?						20,23
iii) ... to open his mail?						20,24
iv) ... to detain the man overnight for questioning?						20,25

b) Now, suppose the tip is about a man _without_ a criminal record.

PLEASE TICK ONE BOX ON EACH LINE

Do you think the police should be allowed, without a Court Order ...

	Defin-itely [1]	Proba-bly [2]	Probably not [3]	Definitely not [4]	Can't choose [8]	
i) ... to keep the man under surveillance?						20,26
ii) ... to tap his telephone?						20,27
iii) ... to open his mail?						20,28
iv) ... to detain the man overnight for questioning?						20,29

2.06 All systems of justice make mistakes, but which do you think is worse?

PLEASE TICK ONE BOX

to convict an innocent person? [1]

OR

to let a guilty person go free? [2]

Can't choose [8]

20,30

/continued over ......

2.10 Please show whether you agree or disagree with each of the following statements.

PLEASE TICK ONE BOX ON EACH LINE

	Agree strongly	Agree	Neither agree nor disagree	Disagree	Disagree strongly	OFFICE USE ONLY
A. A person whose parents are rich has a better chance of earning a lot of money than a person whose parents are poor	1	2	3	4	5	20.34
B. A person whose father is a professional person has a better chance of earning a lot of money than a person whose parents are poor	1	2	3	4	5	20.35
C. In Britain what you achieve in life depends largely on your family background	1	2	3	4	5	20.36

2.11 Would you say that opportunities for university education are, in general, better or worse, for women than for men?

PLEASE TICK ONE BOX (✓)

		OFFICE USE ONLY
Much better for women	1	
Better for women	2	
No difference	3	20.37
Worse for women	4	
Much worse for women	5	
Can't choose	8	

2.12 How about job opportunities for women: do you think they are, in general, better or worse than job opportunities for men with similar education and experience?

PLEASE TICK ONE BOX (✓)

		OFFICE USE ONLY
Much better for women	1	
Better for women	2	
No difference	3	20.38
Worse for women	4	
Much worse for women	5	
Can't choose	8	

2.13 And how about income and wages: compared with men who have similar education and jobs - are women, in general, paid better or worse than men?

PLEASE TICK ONE BOX (✓)

		OFFICE USE ONLY
Women are paid much better	1	
Women are paid better	2	
No difference	3	20.39
Women are paid worse	4	
Women are paid much worse	5	
Can't choose	8	

2.14 Here are three things the government might do. Some people are in favour of them while other people are against them. Please tick one box for each statement to show how you feel.

PLEASE TICK ONE BOX ON EACH LINE

	Strongly in favour	In favour	Neither in favour nor against	Against	Strongly against	OFFICE USE ONLY
A. The government should increase opportunities for women in business and industry	1	2	3	4	5	20.40
B. The government should increase opportunities for women to go to university	1	2	3	4	5	20.41
C. Women should be given preferential treatment when applying for jobs or promotions	1	2	3	4	5	20.42

2.15 And now a few questions about education:

Here are some things that might be taught in school. How important is it that schools teach each of these to 15 year olds?

PLEASE TICK ONE BOX ON EACH LINE

	Essential, must be taught	Very important	Fairly important	Not very important	Not needed, should not be taught	Can't choose	OFFICE USE ONLY
A. Reading, writing and mathematics	1	2	3	4	5	8	20.43
B. Sex education	1	2	3	4	5	8	20.44
C. Respect for authority	1	2	3	4	5	8	20.45
D. History, literature and the arts	1	2	3	4	5	8	20.46
E. Ability to make one's own judgements	1	2	3	4	5	8	20.47
F. Job training	1	2	3	4	5	8	20.48
G. Science and technology	1	2	3	4	5	8	20.49
H. Concern for minorities and the poor	1	2	3	4	5	8	20.50
J. Discipline and orderliness	1	2	3	4	5	8	20.51

- 7 -

2.16 How do you feel about opportunities for young people to go to university?

PLEASE TICK ONE BOX

Should opportunities be ...

	(✓)	OFFICE USE ONLY
... increased a lot,	1	
increased a little,	2	20.52
kept the same as now,	3	
reduced a little,	4	
or - reduced a lot?	5	
Can't choose	8	

2.17 Some people think the government should provide financial assistance to university students. Others think the government should not provide such aid. In each of the circumstances listed below should the government provide grants that would not have to be paid back, provide loans which the student would have to pay back, or should the government not provide any financial assistance?

PLEASE TICK ONE BOX ON EACH LINE

	Government should give grants	Government should make loans	No Government assistance	Can't choose	OFFICE USE ONLY
A. For students whose parents have a low income	1	2	3	8	20.53
B. For students who have outstanding exam results in secondary school	1	2	3	8	20.54
C. For students who have average exam results and middle income parents	1	2	3	8	20.55

/continued over ...

- 8 -

2.18 Sometimes public authorities intervene with parents in raising their children. Please show in each of the following cases how far you think public authorities should go in dealing with a 10 year old child and his or her parents:

PLEASE TICK ONE BOX ON EACH LINE

	Take no action	Give warnings or counselling	Take the child from its parents	Can't choose	OFFICE USE ONLY
A. The child uses drugs and the parents don't do anything about it	1	2	3	8	20.56
B. The child frequently skips school and the parents don't do anything about it	1	2	3	8	20.57
C. The parents regularly let the child stay out late at night without knowing where the child is	1	2	3	8	20.58
D. The parents fail to provide the child with proper food and clothing	1	2	3	8	20.59
E. The parents regularly beat the child	1	2	3	8	20.60
F. The parents refuse essential medical treatment for the child because of their religious beliefs	1	2	3	8	20.61
G. The parents refuse to send their child to school because they wish to educate the child at home	1	2	3	8	20.62
H. The parents allow the child to watch violent or pornographic films	1	2	3	8	20.63

2.19 Do you think that ......

PLEASE TICK ONE BOX ON EACH LINE

	Agree strongly	Agree	Neither agree nor disagree	Disagree	Disagree strongly	OFFICE USE ONLY
A. ... the wearing of seat belts in cars should be required by law?	1	2	3	4	5	20.64
B. ... smoking in public places should be prohibited by law?	1	2	3	4	5	20.65
C. ... all employees should be required to retire at an age set by law?	1	2	3	4	5	20.66

- 9 -

2.20 Please show whether you agree or disagree with each of the following statements.

PLEASE TICK ONE BOX ON EACH LINE

	Agree	Disagree	Can't choose	OFFICE USE ONLY
A. The public has little control over what politicians do in office	1	2	8	20.67
B. The average person can get nowhere by talking to public officials	1	2	8	20.68
C. The average citizen has considerable influence on politics	1	2	8	20.69
D. The average person has much to say about running local government	1	2	8	20.70
E. People like me have much to say about government	1	2	8	20.71
F. The average person has a great deal of influence on government decisions	1	2	8	20.72
G. The government is generally responsive to public opinion	1	2	8	20.73
H. I am usually interested in local elections	1	2	8	20.74
J. By taking an active part in political and social affairs the people can control world affairs.	1	2	8	20.75
K. Taking everything into account, the world is getting better	1	2	8	20.76

20.77-80

CARD 21

2.21 Here are some things the government might do for the economy. Please show which actions you are in favour of and which you are against.

PLEASE TICK ONE BOX ON EACH LINE

	Strongly in favour	In favour	Neither in favour nor against	Against	Strongly against	OFFICE USE ONLY
A. Control of wages by legislation	1	2	3	4	5	21.
B. Control of prices by legislation	1	2	3	4	5	21.08
C Cuts in government spending	1	2	3	4	5	21.09
D. Government financing of projects to create new jobs	1	2	3	4	5	21.10
E. Less government regulation of business	1	2	3	4	5	21.11
F. Support for industry to develop new products and technology	1	2	3	4	5	21.12
G. Supporting declining industries to protect jobs	1	2	3	4	5	21.13
H. Reducing the working week to create more jobs	1	2	3	4	5	21.14

- 10 -

2.22 Listed below are various areas of government spending. Please show whether you would like to see more or less government spending in each area.

Remember that if you say "much more", it might require a tax increase to pay for it.

PLEASE TICK ONE BOX ON EACH LINE

	Spend much more	Spend more	Spend the same as now	Spend less	Spend much less	Can't choose	OFFICE USE ONLY
A. The environment	1	2	3	4	5	8	21.15
B. Health	1	2	3	4	5	8	21.16
C. The police and law enforcement	1	2	3	4	5	8	21.17
D. Education	1	2	3	4	5	8	21.18
E. The military and defence	1	2	3	4	5	8	21.19
F. Old age pensions	1	2	3	4	5	8	21.20
G. Unemployment benefits	1	2	3	4	5	8	21.21
H. Culture and the arts	1	2	3	4	5	8	21.22

2.23 Do you consider the amount of income tax that your household has to pay is...

PLEASE TICK ONE BOX

		OFFICE USE ONLY
...much too high,	1	21.23
too high,	2	
about right,	3	
too low,	4	
or - much too low?	5	
Can't choose	8	
Does not apply	6	

/continued over ......

- 11 -

2.24 Do you consider the amount of tax that business and industry have to pay is too high or too low?

PLEASE TICK ONE BOX

(✓)

- Much too high   1
- Too high   2
- About right   3
- Too low   4
- Much too low   5
- Can't choose   8

OFFICE USE ONLY — 21,24

2.25 If the government had to choose between keeping down inflation or keeping down unemployment to which do you think it should give highest priority?

PLEASE TICK ONE BOX

(✓)

- Keeping down inflation   1
- Keeping down unemployment   2
- Can't choose   8

21,25

2.26 Do you think that trade unions in this country have too much power or too little power?

PLEASE TICK ONE BOX

(✓)

- Far too much power   1
- Too much power   2
- About the right amount of power   3
- Too little power   4
- Far too little power   5
- Can't choose   8

21,26

/continued over ...

- 12 -

2.27 How about business and industry? Do they have too much power or too little power?

PLEASE TICK ONE BOX

(✓)

- Far too much power   1
- Too much power   2
- About the right amount of power   3
- Too little power   4
- Far too little power   5
- Can't choose   8

OFFICE USE ONLY — 21,27

2.28 And what about the government, does it have too much power or too little power?

PLEASE TICK ONE BOX

(✓)

- Far too much power   1
- Too much power   2
- About the right amount of power   3
- Too little power   4
- Far too little power   5
- Can't choose   8

21,28

2.29 What do you think the government's role in each of these industries and services should be?

The government should

PLEASE TICK ONE BOX ON EACH LINE

	Own it	Control prices and profits but not own it	Neither own it nor control its prices & profits	Can't choose	
A. Electricity	1	2	3	8	21,29
B. Local public transport	1	2	3	8	21,30
C. The steel industry	1	2	3	8	21,31
D. Banking and insurance	1	2	3	8	21,32
E. The car industry	1	2	3	8	21,33

- 13 -

2.30 On the whole, do you think it should or should not be the
government's responsibility to ...

PLEASE TICK ONE BOX
ON EACH LINE

	Definitely should be	Probably should be	Probably should not be	Definitely should not be	Can't choose	OFFICE USE ONLY
A. ... provide a job for everyone who wants one	1	2	3	4	8	21.34
B. ... keep prices under control	1	2	3	4	8	21.35
C. ... provide health care for the sick	1	2	3	4	8	21.36
D. ... provide a decent standard of living for the old	1	2	3	4	8	21.37
E. ... provide industry with the help it needs to grow	1	2	3	4	8	21.38
F. ... provide a decent standard of living for the unemployed	1	2	3	4	8	21.39
G. ... reduce income differences between the rich and poor	1	2	3	4	8	21.40

2.31 If the government had a choice between reducing taxes and spending
more on social services, which should it do?

PLEASE TICK ONE BOX

	(✓)	OFFICE USE ONLY
Reduce taxes and spend less on social services	1	
OR Increase taxes and spend more on social services	2	21.41
Can't choose	8	

INTERNATIONAL SOCIAL SURVEY PROGRAMME

1987 MODULE

SOCIAL INEQUALITY

(ENGLISH LANGUAGE VERSION)

- 1 -

2.01 To begin, we have some questions about opportunities for getting ahead ...

Please tick one box for each of these to show how important you think it is for getting ahead in life ...

a) First, how important is coming from a wealthy family?

PLEASE TICK ONE BOX

(✓)
- Essential
- Very important
- Fairly important
- Not very important
- Not important at all
- Can't choose

17.09

b) Having well-educated parents?

PLEASE TICK ONE BOX

(✓)
- Essential
- Very important
- Fairly important
- Not very important
- Not important at all
- Can't choose

17.10

c) Having a good education yourself?

PLEASE TICK ONE BOX

(✓)
- Essential
- Very important
- Fairly important
- Not very important
- Not important at all
- Can't choose

17.11

d) Ambition?

PLEASE TICK ONE BOX

(✓)
- Essential
- Very important
- Fairly important
- Not very important
- Not important at all
- Can't choose

17.12

Please continue ...

- 2 -

e) Natural ability - how important is that for getting ahead in life?

PLEASE TICK ONE BOX

(✓)
- Essential
- Very important
- Fairly important
- Not very important
- Not important at all
- Can't choose

17.13

f) Hard work - how important is that?

PLEASE TICK ONE BOX

(✓)
- Essential
- Very important
- Fairly important
- Not very important
- Not important at all
- Can't choose

17.14

g) Knowing the right people?

PLEASE TICK ONE BOX

(✓)
- Essential
- Very important
- Fairly important
- Not very important
- Not important at all
- Can't choose

17.15

h) Having political connections?

PLEASE TICK ONE BOX

(✓)
- Essential
- Very important
- Fairly important
- Not very important
- Not important at all
- Can't choose

17.16

OFFICE USE ONLY

- 7 -

2.06 Next, **what do you think** people in these jobs **ought** to be paid
– how much do you think they **should** earn each year before
taxes, regardless of what they actually get?

*Please write in how much
they should earn each
year, before tax*

a) First, **about how much do you** think
a bricklayer **should** earn? .... £ ---------------- 18, 34-39

b) A doctor in general practice? .... £ ---------------- 18, 40-45

c) A bank clerk, how much should s/heearn? £ ---------------- 18, 46-51

d) The owner of a small shop? .... £ ---------------- 18, 52-57

e) The chairman of a large national
company? .... £ ---------------- 18, 58-64

f) A skilled worker in a factory? ...... £ ---------------- 18, 65-70

g) A farm worker? .... £ ---------------- 18, 71-76

h) A secretary? .... £ ---------------- 19, 09-14

i) A city bus driver? .... £ ---------------- 19, 15-20

j) An unskilled worker in a factory? ... £ ---------------- 19, 21-26

k) A cabinet minister in the national
government? .... £ ---------------- 19, 27-33

Please continue ...

- 8 -

2.07 Please show how much you agree or disagree with each statement.....

PLEASE TICK ONE BOX ON EACH LINE

	Agree strongly	Agree	Neither agree nor disagree	Disagree	Disagree strongly	Can't choose	
a) Differences in income in Britain are too large.	1	2	3	4	5	8	19,34
b) It is the responsibility of the government to reduce the differences in income between people with high incomes and those with low incomes.	1	2	3	4	5	8	19,35
c) The government should provide more chances for children from poor families to go to university.	1	2	3	4	5	8	19,36
d) The government should provide a job for everyone who wants one.	1	2	3	4	5	8	19,37
e) The government should spend less on benefits for the poor.	1	2	3	4	5	8	19,38
f) The government should provide a decent standard of living for the unemployed.	1	2	3	4	5	8	19,39
g) The government should provide everyone with a guaranteed basic income.	1	2	3	4	5	8	19,40

OFFICE USE ONLY

- 9 -

2.08 Generally, how would you describe taxes in Britain today ...

(We mean all taxes together, including national insurance, income tax, VAT and all the rest.)

a) First, for those with high incomes, are taxes ...

PLEASE TICK ONE BOX

(✓)

Much too high	1
Too high	2
About right	3
Too low	4
Much too low	5
Can't choose	8

Office use only: 19,41

b) Next, for those with middle incomes, are taxes ...

PLEASE TICK ONE BOX

Much too high	1
Too high	2
About right	3
Too low	4
Much too low	5
Can't choose	8

Office use only: 19,42

c) Lastly, for those with low incomes, are taxes ...

PLEASE TICK ONE BOX

Much too high	1
Too high	2
About right	3
Too low	4
Much too low	5
Can't choose	8

Office use only: 19,43

2.09 Do you think that people with high incomes should pay a larger share of their income in taxes than those with low incomes, the same share, or a smaller share?

PLEASE TICK ONE BOX

(✓)

Much larger share	1
Larger	2
The same share	3
Smaller	4
Much smaller share	5
Can't choose	8

Office use only: 19,44

Please continue ...

- 10 -

2.10 In all countries there are differences or even conflicts between different social groups. In your opinion, in Britain how much conflict is there between ...

PLEASE TICK ONE BOX ON EACH LINE

	Very strong conflicts	Strong conflicts	Not very strong conflicts	There are no conflicts	Can't choose	
a) Poor people and rich people?	1	2	3	4	5	19,45
b) The working class and the middle class?	1	2	3	4	5	19,46
c) The unemployed and people with jobs?	1	2	3	4	5	19,47
d) Management and workers?	1	2	3	4	5	19,48
e) Farmers and city people?	1	2	3	4	5	19,49
f) Young people and older people?	1	2	3	4	5	19,50

2.11 In our society there are groups which tend to be towards the top and groups which tend to be towards the bottom. Below is a scale that runs from top to bottom. Where would you put yourself on this scale?

PLEASE TICK ONE BOX

Top

	01
	02
	03
	04
	05
	06
	07
	08
	09
	10

Bottom

Office use only: 19,51-52

2.12 Please think of your present job (or your last one if you don't have one now). If you compare this job with the job your father had when you were 16, would you say that the level or status of your job is (or was) ...

(✓)

Much higher than your father's	1
Higher	2
About equal	3
Lower	4
Much lower than your father's	5
(I never had a job)	6
(Never knew father/father never had a job)	7

Office use only: 19,53

- 11 -

2.13a Here is a list of different types of jobs. Which type did your father have when you were 16?

(If your father did not have a job then, please give the job he used to have.)

PLEASE TICK ONE BOX

Professional and technical (for example: doctor, teacher, engineer, artist, accountant) ☐ 01
Higher administrator (for example: banker, executive in big business, high government official, union official) ☐ 02
Clerical (for example: secretary, clerk, office manager, bookkeeper) ☐ 03
Sales (for example: sales manager, shop owner, shop assistant, insurance agent) ☐ 04
Service (for example: restaurant owner, police officer, waiter, barber, caretaker) ☐ 05
Skilled worker (for example: foreman, motor mechanic, printer, tool and die maker, electrician) ☐ 06
Semi-Skilled worker (for example: bricklayer, bus driver, cannery worker, carpenter, sheet metal worker, baker) ☐ 07
Unskilled worker (for example: labourer, porter, unskilled factory worker) ☐ 08
Farm (for example: farmer, farm labourer, tractor driver) ☐ 09
(Never knew father/father never had job) ☐ 10

(Office use only: 19.54-55)

b) Was your father self-employed, or did he work for someone else?

PLEASE TICK ONE BOX

Self-employed, had own business or farm ☐ 1
Worked for someone else ☐ 2
(Never knew father/father never had job) ☐ 3

(Office use only: 19.56)

Please continue ...

(Office use only: 19.57)

- 12 -

2.14a And how about your first job - the first job you had after you finished full-time education?

(Even if that was many years ago, we would still like to know about it.)

PLEASE TICK ONE BOX

Professional and technical (for example: doctor, teacher, engineer, artist, accountant) ☐ 01
Higher administrator (for example: banker, executive in big business, high government official, union official) ☐ 02
Clerical (for example: secretary, clerk, office manager, bookkeeper) ☐ 03
Sales (for example: sales manager, shop owner, shop assistant, insurance agent) ☐ 04
Service (for example: restaurant owner, police officer, barber, waitress, caretaker) ☐ 05
Skilled worker (for example: foreman, motor mechanic, printer, seamstress, electrician) ☐ 06
Semi-skilled worker (for example: bricklayer, bus driver, cannery worker, sheet metal worker, baker) ☐ 07
Unskilled worker (for example: labourer, porter, unskilled factory worker) ☐ 08
Farm (for example: farmer, farm labourer, tractor driver) ☐ 09
(Never had a job) ☐ 10

(Office use only: 19.58-59)

b) Were you self-employed, or did you work for someone else?

PLEASE TICK ONE BOX

Self-employed, had own business or farm ☐ 1
Worked for someone else ☐ 2
(Never had a job) ☐ 3

(Office use only: 19.60)

(Office use only: 19.61-62)

- 13 -

2.15a And how about your job now?

(If you are not working now, please tell us about your last job.)

PLEASE TICK ONE BOX

	OFFICE USE ONLY

Professional and technical (for example: doctor, teacher, engineer, artist, accountant) ☐ 0 1

Higher administrator (for example: banker, executive in big business, high government official, union official) ☐ 0 2

Clerical (for example: secretary, clerk, office manager, bookkeeper) ☐ 0 3

Sales (for example: sales manager, shop owner, shop assistant, insurance agent) ☐ 0 4

Service (for example: restaurant owner, police officer, waitress, barber, caretaker) ☐ 0 5

Skilled worker (for example: foreman, motor mechanic, printer, seamstress, electrician) ☐ 0 6

Semi-skilled worker (for example: bricklayer, bus driver, cannery worker, carpenter, sheet metal worker, baker) ☐ 0 7

Unskilled workers (for example: labourer, porter, unskilled factory worker) ☐ 0 8

Farm (for example: farmer, farm labourer, tractor driver) ☐ 0 9

(Never had a job) ☐ 1 0

19.63-64

b) Are you self-employed, or do you work for someone else?

PLEASE TICK ONE BOX

Self-employed, have own business or farm ☐ 1

Work for someone else ☐ 2

(Never had a job) ☐ 3

19.65

INTERNATIONAL SOCIAL SURVEY PROGRAMME

1988 MODULE

WOMEN AND THE FAMILY

(ENGLISH LANGUAGE VERSION)

FIELDED IN BRITAIN
IN 1989

- 1 -

2.01 To begin, we have some questions about women.
Do you agree or disagree ...?

PLEASE TICK ONE BOX ON EACH LINE

	Strongly agree	Agree	Neither agree nor disagree	Disagree	Strongly disagree	Can't choose	OFFICE USE ONLY
a. A working mother can establish just as warm and secure a relationship with her children as a mother who does not work.							1808
b. A pre-school child is likely to suffer if his or her mother works.							1809
c. All in all, family life suffers when the woman has a full-time job.							1810
d. A woman and her family will all be happier if she goes out to work.							1811
e. A job is all right, but what most women really want is a home and children.							1812
f. Being a housewife is just as fulfilling as working for pay.							1813
g. Having a job is the best way for a woman to be an independent person.							1814
h. Both the husband and wife should contribute to the household income.							1815
i. A husband's job is to earn money; a wife's job is to look after the home and family.							1816

Do you agree or disagree ....

	Strongly agree	Agree	Neither agree nor disagree	Disagree	Strongly disagree	Can't choose	OFFICE USE ONLY
j. I would enjoy having a job even if I didn't need the money.							1817

Please continue ...

- 2 -

2.02 Do you think that women should work outside the home full-time, part-time or not at all under these circumstances?

PLEASE TICK ONE BOX ON EACH LINE

	Work full-time	Work part-time	Stay at home	Can't choose	OFFICE USE ONLY
a. After marrying and before there are children?					1818
b. When there is a child under school age?					1819
c. After the youngest child starts school?					1820
d. After the children leave home?					1821

2.03 Think of a child under 3 years old whose parents both have full-time jobs.

How suitable do you think each of these childcare arrangements would be for the child?

	Very suitable	Somewhat suitable	Not very suitable	Not at all suitable	Can't choose	OFFICE USE ONLY
a. A state or local authority nursery?						1822
b. A private creche or nursery?						1823
c. A childminder or baby-sitter?						1824
d. A neighbour or friend?						1825
e. A relative?						1826

2.04a If you were advising a **young woman**, which of the following ways of life would you recommend?

PLEASE TICK ONE BOX ONLY

		OFFICE USE ONLY
To live alone, without a steady partner?		
To live with a steady partner, without marrying?		
To live with a steady partner for a while, and then marry? (✓)		
To marry without living together first?		
Can't choose		1827

Please continue ...

- 3 -

2.04b If you were advising **a young man**, which of the following ways of life would you recommend?
PLEASE TICK ONE BOX ONLY

	(✓)
To live alone, without a steady partner?	
To live with a steady partner, without marrying?	
To live with a steady partner for a while, and then marry?	
To marry without living together first?	
Can't choose	

(Office use only: 1828)

2.05 Do you agree or disagree ...?
PLEASE TICK ONE BOX ON EACH LINE

	Strongly agree	Agree	Neither agree nor disagree	Disagree	Disagree strongly	Can't choose	
a. Married people are generally happier than unmarried people.							1829
b. Personal freedom is more important than the companionship of marriage.							1830
c. The main advantage of marriage is that it gives financial security.							1831
d. The main purpose of marriage these days is to have children.							1832
e. It is better to have a bad marriage than no marriage at all.							1833
f. People who want children ought to get married.							1834
g. A single mother can bring up her child as well as a married couple.							1835
h. A single father can bring up his child as well as a married couple.							1836
i. Couples don't take marriage seriously enough when divorce is easily available.							1837
j. Homosexual couples should have the right to marry one another.							1838

Please continue ...

- 4 -

2.06 All in all, what do you think is the **ideal** number of children for a family to have?
PLEASE WRITE THE NUMBER IN THE BOX

(Office use only: 1839-40)

2.07 In general, what do you feel about each of these family sizes?
PLEASE TICK ONE BOX ON EACH LINE

It is ...

A family with:	Very desirable	Desirable	Neither desirable nor un-desirable	Un-desirable	Very un-desirable	Can't choose	
a. No children?							1841
b. One child?							1842
c. Two children?							1843
d. Three children?							1844
e. Four children or more?							1845

2.08 Do you agree or disagree ...?
PLEASE TICK ONE BOX ON EACH LINE

	Strongly agree	Agree	Neither agree nor disagree	Disagree	Strongly disagree	Can't choose	
a. Children are more trouble than they are worth.							1846
b. Watching children grow up is life's greatest joy.							1847
c. Having children interferes too much with the freedom of parents.							1848
d. A marriage without children is not fully complete.							1849
e. It is better not to have children because they are such a heavy burden.							1850
f. People who have never had children lead empty lives.							1851

Please continue ...

- 5 -

2.09 In general, would you say that the law now makes it easy or difficult for people who want to get divorced?

PLEASE TICK ONE BOX ONLY

Very easy	1
Fairly easy	2
Neither easy nor difficult	3
Fairly difficult	4
Very difficult	5
Impossible	6
Can't choose	8

2.10 And in general, how easy or difficult do you think the law **should** make it for **couples without young children** to get a divorce?

PLEASE TICK ONE BOX ONLY

- Very easy
- Fairly easy
- Neither easy nor difficult
- Fairly difficult
- Very difficult
- Impossible
- Can't choose

1853

2.11 And what about **couples with young children**? How easy or difficult should the law make it for them to get a divorce?

PLEASE TICK ONE BOX ONLY

- Very easy
- Fairly easy
- Neither easy nor difficult
- Fairly difficult
- Very difficult
- Impossible
- Can't choose

1854

Please continue ...

- 6 -

2.12 When a marriage is troubled and unhappy do you think it is generally better for the **children** if the couple stays together or gets divorced?

PLEASE TICK ONE BOX ONLY

- Much better to divorce
- Better to divorce
- Worse to divorce
- Much worse to divorce
- Can't choose

2.13 And when a marriage is troubled and unhappy, is it generally better for the **wife** if the couple stays together or gets divorced?

PLEASE TICK ONE BOX ONLY

- Much better to divorce
- Better to divorce
- Worse to divorce
- Much worse to divorce
- Can't choose

1856

2.14 And when a marriage is troubled and unhappy, is it generally better for the **husband** if the couple stays together or gets divorced?

PLEASE TICK ONE BOX ONLY

- Much better to divorce
- Better to divorce
- Worse to divorce
- Much worse to divorce
- Can't choose

1857

2.15 Did your mother ever work for pay for as long as **one year** **after** you were born and **before** you were 14?

PLEASE TICK ONE BOX ONLY

- Yes, she worked
- No
- Did not live with mother

1858

1859

Please continue ...

– 41A –

		Worked full-time	Worked part-time	Stayed at home	Does not apply	Col/Code	Skip to
A903a)	INTERVIEWER TO COMPLETE: RESPONDENT IS:					1471	
	IF WOMAN:			Man		1 →	Q.904
				Woman		2 →	b)
	b) RESPONDENT IS: (SEE CODE 1, Q.900)			Married		1472 1	c)
				Not married		2	Q.904
	IF MARRIED WOMAN:					1473	
	c) RESPONDENT: Has children (SEE B/B GRID Q.901) OR Has had children (CODE 1 AT Q,902)					1 →	d)
				Has not		2 →	Q.904
	IF MARRIED WOMAN WITH CHILDREN (CODE 1 AT Q.903c) CARD FF d) Please use this card to say whether you worked full-time, part-time or not at all ... READ a)–d) BELOW AND CODE ONE FOR EACH						
	a) ... after marrying and before you had children?	1	2	3	8		1474
	b) ... and what about when a child was under school age?	1	2	3	8		1475
	c) ... after the youngest child started school?	1	2	3	8		1476
	d) ... and how about after the children left home?	1	2	3	8		1477
						1478-80	SPACE
						1506-07	CARD 15

– 7 –

OFFICE USE ONLY

2.16 Have you ever been divorced?
PLEASE TICK ONE BOX ONLY

Yes (✓) ⎫ PLEASE ANSWER Q.17 BELOW
No   2   ⎬ → GO TO Q.20, PAGE 8
Never married

1860

2.17 Are you married or living as married now?
PLEASE TICK ONE BOX ONLY

Yes (✓) → PLEASE ANSWER Q.18-19 BELOW
No   2   → GO TO Q.20, PAGE 8

1861

2.18a Has your husband or wife or partner ever been divorced?
PLEASE TICK ONE BOX ONLY

Yes (✓)
No   2
Not married

1862

b) Did you live with your husband or wife or partner before you got married?
PLEASE TICK ONE BOX

Yes (✓)
No   2
Not married 3

1863

2.19a Do you and your husband or wife or partner both have paid work at the moment?
PLEASE TICK ONE BOX

Yes (✓) → ANSWER b), BELOW
No   2   → GO TO Q.20, PAGE 8

1864

b) Who earns more money?
PLEASE TICK ONE BOX ONLY

Husband earns much more 1
Husband earns a bit more 2
We earn about the same amount 3
Wife earns a bit more 4
Wife earns much more 5

1865

Please continue ...

INTERNATIONAL SOCIAL SURVEY PROGRAMME

1989 MODULE

WORK ORIENTATIONS

(ENGLISH LANGUAGE VERSION)

- 1 -

B

2.01 Suppose you could change the way you spend your time, spending more time on some things and less time on others.

Which of the things on the following list would you like to spend more time on, which would you like to spend less time on and which would you like to spend the same amount of time on as now?

PLEASE TICK ONE BOX ON EACH LINE

	Much more time	A bit more time	Same time as now	A bit less time	Much less time	Can't choose/ Doesn't apply	OFFICE USE ONLY
							CARD 19
a. Time in a paid job?							1908
b. Time doing household work?							1909
c. Time with your family?							1910
d. Time with your friends?							1911
e. Time in leisure activities?							1912
f. Time to relax?							1913

2.02 Please tick one box for each statement below to show how much you agree or disagree with it, thinking of work in general.

PLEASE TICK ONE BOX ON EACH LINE

	Strongly agree	Agree	Neither Agree nor disagree	Disagree	Strongly Disagree	Can't choose	
a. A job is just a way of earning money - no more.							1914
b. I would enjoy having a paid job even if I did not need the money.							1915
c. Work is a person's most important activity.							1916

Please continue ...

- 2 -

B

2.03 Are you the person responsible for doing the general domestic duties - like cleaning, cooking, washing and so on - in your household?

PLEASE TICK ONE BOX ONLY

Yes, I am mainly responsible

Yes, I am equally responsible with someone else

No, someone else is mainly responsible

OFFICE USE ONLY 1917

2.04 Think of two people doing the same kind of work. What do you personally think should be important in deciding how much to pay them?

Looking at the things below, please write '1' in the box next to the thing you think should be most important.

Then write '2' next to the thing you think should be next most important. And '3' next to the thing you think should be third most important. Leave the other boxes blank.

Write 1,2 and 3 in THREE boxes; leave the other boxes blank

In deciding on pay for two people doing the same kind of work how important should be ...

... how long the employee has been with the firm? 1918

... how well the employee does the job? 1919

... the experience of the employee in doing the work? 1920

... the standard rate - giving both employees the same pay? 1921

... the age of the employee? 1922

... the sex of the employee? 1923

... the employee's family responsibilities? 1924

... the employee's education and formal qualifications? 1925

OR TICK:

Can't choose 1926

Please continue ...

- 3 -

2.05 How much do you agree or disagree with these two statements?

PLEASE TICK ONE BOX ON EACH LINE

	Strongly agree	Agree	Neither agree nor disagree	Disagree	Strongly disagree	Can't choose	OFFICE USE ONLY
a. There will always be conflict between management and workers because they are really on opposite sides.							1927
b. Workers need strong trade unions to protect their interests.							1928

2.06 From the following list, please tick one box for each item to show how important you personally think it is in a job.

PLEASE TICK ONE BOX ON EACH LINE

How important is ...	Very important	Important	Neither important nor unimportant	Not important	Not important at all	Can't choose	OFFICE USE ONLY
a. ... job security?							1929
b. ... high income?							1930
c. ... good opportunities for advancement?							1931
d. ... a job that leaves a lot of leisure time?							1932
e. ... an interesting job?							1933
f. ... a job that allows someone to work independently?							1934
g. ... a job that allows someone to help other people?							1935
h. ... a job that is useful to society?							1936
i. ... a job with flexible working hours?							1937

Please continue ...   1938-40

- 4 -

2.07 Suppose you were unemployed and couldn't find a job. Which of the following problems do you think would be the worst?

Please write '1' in the box next to the worst thing.
Then write '2' beside the next worst thing.
And '3' beside the third worst thing.
Leave the other boxes blank.

Write 1,2 and 3 in THREE boxes: leave the other boxes blank

	OFFICE USE ONLY
Lack of contact with people at work	1941
Not enough money	1942
Loss of self-confidence	1943
Loss of respect from friends and acquaintances	1944
Family tensions	1945
Loss of job experience	1946
Not knowing how to fill one's time	1947
OR TICK: Can't choose	1948

2.08 Suppose you were working and could choose between different kinds of jobs. Which of the following would you personally choose?

PLEASE TICK ONE BOX ONLY

a. I would choose ...

... being an employee

... being self-employed   1949

Can't choose

PLEASE TICK ONE BOX ONLY

b. I would choose ...

... working in a small firm

... working in a large firm   1950

Can't choose

Please continue ...

B

- 5 -

2.08 (cont'd)

And which of the following would you personally choose?

PLEASE TICK ONE BOX ONLY

I would choose ...

c.   ... working in a manufacturing industry [1]

    ... working in an office, in sales or in service [2]

    Can't choose [8]

1951

PLEASE TICK ONE BOX ONLY

I would choose ...

d.   ... working in a private business [1]

    ... working for the government or civil service [2]

    Can't choose [8]

1952

2.09 On the whole, do you think it should be or should not be the government's responsibility to ...

PLEASE TICK ONE BOX ON EACH LINE

	Definitely should be	Probably should be	Probably should not be	Definitely should not be	Can't choose	
a. ... provide a job for everyone who wants one?	[1]	[2]	[3]	[4]	[5]	1953
b. ... provide a decent standard of living for the unemployed?	[1]	[2]	[3]	[4]	[5]	1954

2.10 Do you usually work 10 hours or more a week for pay in your (main) job?

PLEASE TICK ONE BOX ONLY

Yes, I usually work 10 hours or more a week in my (main) job [1] → GO TO Q.13, PAGE 7

No, I usually work less than 10 hours a week in my (main) job [2] } PLEASE ANSWER Q.11, PAGE 6

No, I don't work for pay at the moment [3]

1955

Please continue ...

B

- 6 -

2.11 Would you like to have a paid job now?

PLEASE TICK ONE BOX ONLY

Yes, I would like a full-time job now (30 hours or more per week) [1] } PLEASE ANSWER Q.12 BELOW

Yes, I would like a part-time job now (10-29 hours per week) [2]

Yes, I would like a job with less than 10 hours a week now [3]

No, I would not like to have a paid job now [4] → GO TO Q.22 PAGE 12

1956

2.12 If you were looking actively, how easy or difficult do you think it would be for you to find an acceptable job?

PLEASE TICK ONE BOX ONLY

Very easy [1]

Fairly easy [2]

Neither easy nor difficult [3]

Fairly difficult [4]

Very difficult [5]

Can't choose [8]

1957

Please continue ...

- 7 -

	OFFICE USE ONLY

PLEASE ANSWER Q.13 - Q.21 ABOUT YOUR MAIN JOB.

2.13 Which of the following statements best describes your feelings about your job?

PLEASE TICK ONE BOX ONLY

In my job ...

... I only work as hard as I have to 〔 〕1

... I work hard, but not so that it interferes with the rest of my life 〔 〕2   1958

... I make a point of doing the best work I can, even if it sometimes does interfere with the rest of my life 〔 〕3

Can't choose 〔 〕8

2.14 Think of the number of hours you work, and the money you earn in your main job, including any regular overtime.

If you had only one of these three choices which of the following would you prefer?

PLEASE TICK ONE BOX ONLY

Work longer hours and earn **more money** 〔 〕1

Work the **same** number of hours and earn the **same money** 〔 〕2   1959

Work fewer hours and earn **less money** 〔 〕3

Can't choose 〔 〕8

Please continue ...

- 8 -

	OFFICE USE ONLY

2.15 Think of two people doing the same kind of work in your place of work. What do you personally think is important in deciding how much to pay them?

Looking at the things below, please write '1' in the box next to the thing you think is most important at your place of work.

Then write '2' next to the thing you think is next most important. And '3' next to the thing you think is third most important. Leave the other boxes blank.

Write 1, 2 and 3 in THREE boxes. Leave the other boxes blank

At your workplace, in deciding on pay for two people doing the same kind of work, how important is ....

... how long the employee has been with the firm? 〔 〕 1960

... how well the employee does the job? 〔 〕 1961

... the experience of the employee in doing the work? 〔 〕 1962

... the standard rate - giving both employees the same pay? 〔 〕 1963

... the age of the employee? 〔 〕 1964

... the sex of the employee? 〔 〕 1965

... the employee's family responsibilities? 〔 〕 1966

... the employer's education and formal qualifications? 〔 〕 1967

OR TICK: Can't choose 〔 〕8 1968

1969-70

Please continue ...

B

- 9 -

2.16 For each of these statements about your (main) job, please tick one box to show how much you agree or disagree that it applies to your job.

PLEASE TICK ONE BOX ON EACH LINE

	Strongly agree	Agree	Neither agree nor disagree	Disagree	Strongly disagree	Can't choose	OFFICE USE ONLY
a. My job is secure	☐	☐	☐	☐	☐	☐	1971
b. My income is high	☐	☐	☐	☐	☐	☐	1972
c. My opportunities for advancement are high	☐	☐	☐	☐	☐	☐	1973
d. My job leaves a lot of leisure time	☐	☐	☐	☐	☐	☐	1974
e. My job is interesting	☐	☐	☐	☐	☐	☐	1975
f. I can work independently	☐	☐	☐	☐	☐	☐	1976
g. In my job I can help other people	☐	☐	☐	☐	☐	☐	1977
h. My job is useful to society	☐	☐	☐	☐	☐	☐	1978
i. My job has flexible working hours	☐	☐	☐	☐	☐	☐	1979

Please continue ...   1980

B

- 10 -

2.17 Now some more questions about your working conditions.
Please tick one box for each item below to show how often it applies to your work.

PLEASE TICK ONE BOX ON EACH LINE

How often ...	Always	Often	Sometimes	Hardly ever	Never	Can't choose	OFFICE USE ONLY CARD 20
a. ... do you come home from work exhausted?	☐	☐	☐	☐	☐	☐	2008
b. ... do you have to do hard physical work?	☐	☐	☐	☐	☐	☐	2009
c. ... do you find your work stressful?	☐	☐	☐	☐	☐	☐	2010
d. ... are you bored at work?	☐	☐	☐	☐	☐	☐	2011
e. ... do you work in dangerous conditions?	☐	☐	☐	☐	☐	☐	2012
f. ... do you work in unhealthy conditions?	☐	☐	☐	☐	☐	☐	2013
g. ... do you work in physically unpleasant conditions?	☐	☐	☐	☐	☐	☐	2014

2.18 And which of the following statements about your work is *most* true?

PLEASE TICK ONE BOX ONLY

My job allows me to design or plan *most* of my daily work   ☐ (✓)

My job allows me to design or plan *parts* of my daily work   ☐

My job *does not really* allow me to design or plan my daily work   ☐

2015

Please continue ...

B

- 11 -

2.19 If you lost your job for any reason, and were looking actively for another one, how easy or difficult do you think it would be for you to find an acceptable job?

PLEASE TICK ONE BOX ONLY

	(✓)
Very easy	☐ 1
Fairly easy	☐ 2
Neither easy nor difficult	☐ 3
Fairly difficult	☐ 4
Very difficult	☐ 5
Can't choose	☐ 6

OFFICE USE ONLY

2016

2.20 In general, how would you describe relations at your workplace ...

PLEASE TICK ONE BOX ON EACH LINE

	Very good	Quite good	Neither good nor bad	Quite bad	Very bad	Can't choose
a. ... between management and employees?	☐ 1	☐ 2	☐ 3	☐ 4	☐ 5	☐ 8
b. ... between workmates/ colleagues?	☐ 1	☐ 2	☐ 3	☐ 4	☐ 5	☐ 8

2017

2018

2.21 How satisfied are you in your (main) job?

PLEASE TICK ONE BOX ONLY

	(✓)
Completely satisfied	☐ 1
Very satisfied	☐ 2
Fairly satisfied	☐ 3
Neither satisfied nor dissatisfied	☐ 4
Fairly dissatisfied	☐ 5
Very dissatisfied	☐ 6
Completely dissatisfied	☐ 7
Can't choose	☐ 8

2019

Please continue ...

2020

INTERNATIONAL SOCIAL SURVEY PROGRAMME

1990 MODULE

ROLE OF GOVERNMENT II (part replication)

(ENGLISH LANGUAGE VERSION)

- 1 -

L.

20.1 In general, would you say that people should obey the law without exception, or are there exceptional occasions on which people should follow their consciences even if it means breaking the law?

PLEASE TICK ONE BOX

	(✓)	
Obey the law without exception	[ ]	1
Follow conscience on occasions	[ ]	2
Can't choose	[ ]	8

(Office use only: 2121)

20.2 There are many ways people or organisations can protest against a government action they strongly oppose.

Please show which you think should be allowed and which should not be allowed by ticking a box on each line.

PLEASE TICK ONE BOX ON EACH LINE

	Should it be allowed?					Office use only
	Defin-itely	Prob-ably	Probably not	Definitely not	Can't choose	
Organising public meetings to protest against the government	[1]	[2]	[3]	[4]	[8]	2122
Publishing pamphlets to protest against the government	[1]	[2]	[3]	[4]	[8]	2123
Organising protest marches and demonstrations	[1]	[2]	[3]	[4]	[8]	2124
Occupying a government office and stopping work there for several days	[1]	[2]	[3]	[4]	[8]	2125
Seriously damaging government buildings	[1]	[2]	[3]	[4]	[8]	2126
Organising a nationwide strike of all workers against the government	[1]	[2]	[3]	[4]	[8]	2127

- 2 -

L.

20.3 There are some people whose views are considered extreme by the majority.

First, consider people who want to overthrow the government by revolution. Do you think such people should be allowed to ...

PLEASE TICK ONE BOX ON EACH LINE

	Defin-itely	Prob-ably	Probably not	Definitely not	Can't choose	Office use only
i) ... hold public meetings to express their views?	[1]	[2]	[3]	[4]	[8]	2128
ii) ... publish books expressing their views?	[1]	[2]	[3]	[4]	[8]	2129

20.4 Second, consider people who believe that whites are racially superior to all other races. Do you think such people should be allowed to ...

PLEASE TICK ONE BOX ON EACH LINE

	Defin-itely	Prob-ably	Probably not	Definitely not	Can't choose	Office use only
i) ... hold public meetings to express their views?	[1]	[2]	[3]	[4]	[8]	2130
ii) ... publish books expressing their views?	[1]	[2]	[3]	[4]	[8]	2131

20.5 Suppose the police get an anonymous tip that a man with a long criminal record is planning to break into a warehouse.

Do you think the police should be allowed, without a Court Order ...

PLEASE TICK ONE BOX ON EACH LINE

	Defin-itely	Prob-ably	Probably not	Definitely not	Can't choose	Office use only
i) ... to keep the man under surveillance?	[1]	[2]	[3]	[4]	[8]	2132
ii) ... to tap his telephone?	[1]	[2]	[3]	[4]	[8]	2133
iii) ... to open his mail?	[1]	[2]	[3]	[4]	[8]	2134
iv) ... to detain the man over-night for questioning?	[1]	[2]	[3]	[4]	[8]	2135

Please continue ......

- 3 -

L.

20. 6 All systems of justice make mistakes, but which do you think is worse:

PLEASE TICK ONE BOX

	(✓)	
to convict an innocent person,	☐	1
OR		
to let a guilty person go free?	☐	2
Can't choose	☐	8

OFFICE USE ONLY 2136

20. 7 What are **your personal feelings** about ...

A. People who organise protests against a government action they strongly oppose?

PLEASE TICK ONE BOX

	(✓)	
Extremely favourable	☐	1
Favourable	☐	2
Neither favourable or unfavourable	☐	3
Unfavourable	☐	4
Extremely unfavourable	☐	5
Can't choose	☐	8

OFFICE USE ONLY 2137

B. People who want to overthrow the government by revolution?

PLEASE TICK ONE BOX

	(✓)	
Extremely favourable	☐	1
Favourable	☐	2
Neither favourable or unfavourable	☐	3
Unfavourable	☐	4
Extremely unfavourable	☐	5
Can't choose	☐	8

OFFICE USE ONLY 2138

C. People who believe whites are racially superior to all other races?

PLEASE TICK ONE BOX

	(✓)	
Extremely favourable	☐	1
Favourable	☐	2
Neither favourable or unfavourable	☐	3
Unfavourable	☐	4
Extremely unfavourable	☐	5
Can't choose	☐	8

OFFICE USE ONLY 2139

Please continue .....

- 4 -

L.

20. 8 Some people think those with high incomes should pay a larger proportion (percentage) of their earnings in taxes than those who earn low incomes. Other people think that those with high incomes and those with low incomes should pay the same proportion (percentage) of their earnings in taxes.

Do you think those with **high** incomes should ...

PLEASE TICK ONE BOX.

	(✓)	
... pay a **much larger** proportion,	☐	1
pay a **larger** proportion,	☐	2
pay the **same** proportion as those who earn low incomes,	☐	3
pay a **smaller** proportion,	☐	4
or - pay a **much smaller** proportion?	☐	5
Can't choose	☐	8

OFFICE USE ONLY 2140

20. 9 What is your opinion of the following statement: It is the responsibility of the government to reduce the differences in income between people with high incomes and those with low incomes.

PLEASE TICK ONE BOX

	(✓)	
Agree strongly	☐	1
Agree	☐	2
Neither agree nor disagree	☐	3
Disagree	☐	4
Disagree strongly	☐	5

OFFICE USE ONLY 2141

- 5 -

2.10 Here are some things the government might do for the economy. Please show which actions you are in favour of and which you are against.

PLEASE TICK ONE BOX ON EACH LINE

	Strongly in favour of	In favour of	Neither in favour of nor against	Against	Strongly against	OFFICE USE ONLY
A. Control of wages by law						2142
B. Control of prices by law						2143
C. Cuts in government spending						2144
D. Government financing of projects to create new jobs						2145
E. Less government regulation of business						2146
F. Support for industry to develop new products and technology						2147
G. Support for declining industries to protect jobs						2148
H. Reducing the working week to create more jobs						2149

2.11 Listed below are various areas of government spending. Please show whether you would like to see more or less government spending in each area.

Remember that if you say "much more", it might require a tax increase to pay for it.

PLEASE TICK ONE BOX ON EACH LINE

	Spend much more	Spend more	Spend the same as now	Spend less	Spend much less	Can't choose	OFFICE USE ONLY
A. The environment							2150
B. Health							2151
C. The police and law enforcement							2152
D. Education							2153
E. The military and defence							2154
F. Old age pensions							2155
G. Unemployment benefits							2156
H. Culture and the arts							2157

Please continue ......

- 6 -

L.

2.12 If the government had to choose between keeping down inflation or keeping down unemployment, to which do you think it should give highest priority?

PLEASE TICK ONE BOX

Keeping down inflation ☐ 1

Keeping down unemployment ☐ 2

Can't choose ☐ 8

OFFICE USE ONLY — 2158

2.13 Do you think that trade unions in this country have too much power or too little power?

PLEASE TICK ONE BOX

Far too much power ☐ 1

Too much power ☐ 2

About the right amount of power ☐ 3

Too little power ☐ 4

Far too little power ☐ 5

Can't choose ☐ 8

OFFICE USE ONLY — 2159

2.14 How about business and industry? Do they have too much power or too little power?

PLEASE TICK ONE BOX

Far too much power ☐ 1

Too much power ☐ 2

About the right amount of power ☐ 3

Too little power ☐ 4

Far too little power ☐ 5

Can't choose ☐ 8

OFFICE USE ONLY — 2160

- 7 -

2.15 And what about the government, does it have too much power or too little power?

PLEASE TICK ONE BOX

Far too much power	1
Too much power	2
About the right amount of power	3
Too little power	4
Far too little power	5
Can't choose	8

OFFICE USE ONLY: 2161

2.16 In general, how good would you say trade unions are for the country as a whole?

PLEASE TICK ONE BOX

Excellent	1
Very good	2
Fairly good	3
Not very good	4
Not good at all	5
Can't choose	8

OFFICE USE ONLY: 2162

2.17 What do you think the government's role in each of these industries and services should be?

The government should:

PLEASE TICK ONE BOX ON EACH LINE

	Own it	Control prices and profits but not own it	Neither own it nor control its prices & profits	Can't choose	OFFICE USE ONLY
A. Electricity	1	2	3	8	2163
B. The steel industry	1	2	3	8	2164
C. Banking and insurance	1	2	3	8	2165

Please continue ......

- 8 -

2.18 On the whole, do you think it should or should not be the government's responsibility to ...

PLEASE TICK ONE BOX ON EACH LINE

	Definitely should be	Probably should be	Probably should not be	Definitely should not be	Can't choose	OFFICE USE ONLY
A. ... provide a job for everyone who wants one	1	2	3	4	8	2166
B. ... keep prices under control	1	2	3	4	8	2167
C. ... provide health care for the sick	1	2	3	4	8	2168
D. ... provide a decent standard of living for the old	1	2	3	4	8	2169
E. ... provide industry with the help it needs to grow	1	2	3	4	8	2170
F. ... provide a decent standard of living for the unemployed	1	2	3	4	8	2171
G. ... reduce income differences between the rich and poor	1	2	3	4	8	2172
H. ... give financial help to university students from low-income families	1	2	3	4	8	2173
I. ... provide decent housing for those who can't afford it	1	2	3	4	8	2174

2.19 How interested would you say you personally are in politics?

PLEASE TICK ONE BOX

Very interested	1
Fairly interested	2
Somewhat interested	3
Not very interested	4
Not at all interested	5
Can't choose	8

OFFICE USE ONLY: 2175

2176-80

INTERNATIONAL SOCIAL SURVEY PROGRAMME

1991 MODULE

RELIGION

(ENGLISH LANGUAGE VERSION)

1

A 2.01 If you were to consider your life in general these days, how happy or unhappy would you say you are, on the whole?

PLEASE TICK ONE BOX ONLY

	(✓)
Very happy	1
Fairly happy	2
Not very happy	3
Not at all happy	4
Can't choose	8

A 2.02 On the whole, do you think it should or should not be the government's responsibility to ...

PLEASE TICK ONE BOX ON EACH LINE

	Definitely should be	Probably should be	Probably should not be	Definitely should not be	Can't choose
	1	2	3	4	8
a. Provide a job for everyone who wants one?					
b. Reduce income differences between the rich and poor?					

A 2.03 Here are some measures to deal with crime. Some people are in favour of them while others are against them. Do you agree or disagree that ...

PLEASE TICK ONE BOX ON EACH LINE

	Strongly agree	Agree	Neither agree nor disagree	Disagree	Strongly disagree	Can't choose
	1	2	3	4	5	8
a. People who break the law should be given stiffer sentences?						
b. People convicted of murder should be subject to the death penalty?						

OFFICE USE ONLY: CARD 19, 1921, 1922, 1923, 1924, 1925

2

A 2.04 Do you think it is **wrong** or not wrong if a man and a woman have sexual relations **before marriage**?

PLEASE TICK ONE BOX ONLY

	(✓)
Always wrong	1
Almost always wrong	2
Wrong only sometimes	3
Not wrong at all	4
Can't choose	8

A 2.05 What about a **married** person having sexual relations with someone other than his or her husband or wife, is it ...

PLEASE TICK ONE BOX ONLY

	(✓)
Always wrong	1
Almost always wrong	2
Wrong only sometimes	3
Not wrong at all	4
Can't choose	8

A 2.06 And what about sexual relations between two adults of the same sex, is it ...

PLEASE TICK ONE BOX ONLY

	(✓)
Always wrong	1
Almost always wrong	2
Wrong only sometimes	3
Not wrong at all	4
Can't choose	8

OFFICE USE ONLY: 1926, 1927, 1928

Please continue ...

3

A 2.07 Do you think the law should or should not allow a woman to obtain a legal abortion ...

PLEASE TICK ONE BOX ON EACH LINE

	Definitely should allow it	Probably should allow it	Probably should not allow it	Definitely should not allow it	Can't choose	OFFICE USE ONLY
a. If there is a strong chance of a serious defect in the baby?	1	2	3	4	8	1929
b. If the family has a very low income and cannot afford any more children?	1	2	3	4	8	1930

A 2.08 Do you personally think it is wrong or not wrong for a woman to have an abortion ...

PLEASE TICK ONE BOX ON EACH LINE

	Always wrong	Almost always wrong	Wrong only sometimes	Not wrong at all	Can't choose	OFFICE USE ONLY
a. If there is a strong chance of a serious defect in the baby?	1	2	3	4	8	1931
b. If the family has a very low income and cannot afford any more children?	1	2	3	4	8	1932

A 2.09 How much do you agree or disagree ...

PLEASE TICK ONE BOX ON EACH LINE

	Strongly agree	Agree	Neither agree nor disagree	Disagree	Strongly disagree	Can't choose	OFFICE USE ONLY
a. A husband's job is to earn the money; a wife's job is to look after the home and family	1	2	3	4	5	8	1933
b. All in all, family life suffers when the woman has a full-time job	1	2	3	4	5	8	1934

4

A 2.10 Consider the situations listed below. Do you feel it is wrong or not wrong if ...

PLEASE TICK ONE BOX ON EACH LINE

	Not wrong	A bit wrong	Wrong	Seriously wrong	Can't choose	OFFICE USE ONLY
a. A taxpayer does not report all of his income in order to pay less income tax?	1	2	3	4	8	1935
b. A person gives the government incorrect information about himself to get government benefits that he is not entitled to?	1	2	3	4	8	1936

A 2.11 How much confidence do you have in ...

PLEASE TICK ONE BOX ON EACH LINE

	Complete confidence	A great deal of confidence	Some confidence	Very little confidence	No confidence at all	Can't choose	OFFICE USE ONLY
a. The British parliament?	1	2	3	4	5	8	1937
b. Business and industry?	1	2	3	4	5	8	1938
c. The Civil Service?	1	2	3	4	5	8	1939
d. Churches and religious organisations?	1	2	3	4	5	8	1940
e. Courts and the legal system?	1	2	3	4	5	8	1941
f. Schools and the educational system?	1	2	3	4	5	8	1942

Please continue ...

5

A 2.12 How much do you agree or disagree with each of the following?

PLEASE TICK ONE BOX ON EACH LINE

	Strongly agree	Agree	Neither agree nor disagree	Disagree	Strongly disagree	Can't choose	OFFICE USE ONLY
a. Politicians who do not believe in God are unfit for public office	1	2	3	4	5	8	1943
b. Religious leaders should not try to influence how people vote in elections	1	2	3	4	5	8	1944
c. It would be better for Britain if more people with strong religious beliefs held public office	1	2	3	4	5	8	1945
d. Religious leaders should not try to influence government decisions	1	2	3	4	5	8	1946

A 2.13 Do you think that churches and religious organisations in this country have too much power or too little power?

PLEASE TICK ONE BOX ONLY

Far too much power	1	
Too much power	2	
About the right amount of power	3	
Too little power	4	
Far too little power	5	
Can't choose	8	1947

Please continue ...

6

A 2.14 Please tick one box below to show which statement comes closest to expressing what you believe about God.

PLEASE TICK ONE BOX ONLY

		OFFICE USE ONLY
I don't believe in God	1	1948
I don't know whether there is a God and I don't believe there is any way to find out	2	
I don't believe in a personal God, but I do believe in a Higher Power of some kind	3	
I find myself believing in God some of the time, but not at others	4	
While I have doubts, I feel that I do believe in God	5	
I know God really exists and I have no doubts about it	6	

A 2.15 How close do you feel to God most of the time?

PLEASE TICK ONE BOX ONLY

Don't believe in God	1	1949
Not close at all	2	
Not very close	3	
Somewhat close	4	
Extremely close	5	
Can't choose	8	

A 2.16 Which best describes your beliefs about God?

PLEASE TICK ONE BOX ONLY

I don't believe in God now and I never have	1	1950
I don't believe in God now, but I used to	2	
I believe in God now, but I didn't used to	3	
I believe in God now and I always have	4	
Can't choose	8	

8

A 2.19 How much do you agree or disagree with each of the following?
PLEASE TICK ONE BOX ON EACH LINE

	Strongly agree	Agree	Neither agree nor disagree	Disagree	Strongly disagree	Can't choose	
a. There is a God who concerns Himself with every human being personally	1	2	3	4	5	8	1957
b. There is little that people can do to change the course of their lives	1	2	3	4	5	8	1958
c. To me, life is meaningful only because God exists	1	2	3	4	5	8	1959
d. In my opinion, life does not serve any purpose	1	2	3	4	5	8	1960
e. The course of our lives is decided by God	1	2	3	4	5	8	1961
f. Life is only meaningful if you provide the meaning yourself	1	2	3	4	5	8	1962
g. We each make our own fate	1	2	3	4	5	8	1963

A 2.20 How often have you felt as though you were ...
PLEASE TICK ONE BOX ON EACH LINE

	Never in my life	Once or twice	Several times	Often	Can't say	
a. Really in touch with someone who had died?	1	2	3	4	8	1964
b. Close to a powerful, spiritual force that seemed to lift you out of yourself?	1	2	3	4	8	1965

7

A 2.17 Do you believe in ...
PLEASE TICK ONE BOX ON EACH LINE

	Yes, definitely	Yes, probably	No, probably not	No, definitely not	Can't choose	
a. Life after death?	1	2	3	4	8	1951
b. The Devil?	1	2	3	4	8	1952
c. Heaven?	1	2	3	4	8	1953
d. Hell?	1	2	3	4	8	1954
e. Religious miracles?	1	2	3	4	8	1955

A 2.18 Which one of these statements comes closest to describing your feelings about the Bible?
PLEASE TICK ONE BOX ONLY

The Bible is the actual word of God and it is to be taken literally, word for word	(✓) 1	1956
The Bible is the inspired word of God but not everything should be taken literally, word for word	2	
The Bible is an ancient book of fables, legends, history and moral teachings recorded by man	3	
This does not apply to me	4	
Can't choose	8	

Please continue ...

9

A 2.21 Has there ever been a turning point in your life when you made a new and personal commitment to religion?

PLEASE TICK ONE BOX ONLY

Yes	[ ] 1
No	[ ] 2

Office use only: 1966

A 2.22 What was your mother's religion, if any, when you were a child?

PLEASE TICK ONE BOX ONLY

Office use only: 1967-8

No religion	[ ] 01
Christian – no denomination	[ ] 02
Roman Catholic	[ ] 03
Church of England/Anglican	[ ] 04
Baptist	[ ] 05
Methodist	[ ] 06
Presbyterian/Church of Scotland	[ ] 07
Free Presbyterian	[ ] 21
Brethren	[ ] 22
United Reform Church (URC)/Congregational	[ ] 23
Other Protestant *(PLEASE WRITE IN WHICH)* _____	[ ] 27
Other Christian *(PLEASE WRITE IN WHICH)* _____	[ ] 08
Hindu	[ ] 09
Jewish	[ ] 10
Islam/Muslim	[ ] 11
Sikh	[ ] 12
Buddhist	[ ] 13
Other non-Christian *(PLEASE WRITE IN WHICH)* _____	[ ] 14
Never knew mother/does not apply	[ ] 15
Can't say/can't remember	[ ] 98

10

A 2.23 What was your father's religion, if any, when you were a child?

PLEASE TICK ONE BOX ONLY

Office use only: 1969-1970

No religion	[ ] 01
Christian – no denomination	[ ] 02
Roman Catholic	[ ] 03
Church of England/Anglican	[ ] 04
Baptist	[ ] 05
Methodist	[ ] 06
Presbyterian/Church of Scotland	[ ] 07
Free Presbyterian	[ ] 21
Brethren	[ ] 22
United Reform Church (URC)/Congregational	[ ] 23
Other Protestant *(PLEASE WRITE IN WHICH)* _____	[ ] 27
Other Christian *(PLEASE WRITE IN WHICH)* _____	[ ] 08
Hindu	[ ] 09
Jewish	[ ] 10
Islam/Muslim	[ ] 11
Sikh	[ ] 12
Buddhist	[ ] 13
Other non-Christian *(PLEASE WRITE IN WHICH)* _____	[ ] 14
Never knew father/does not apply	[ ] 15
Can't say/can't remember	[ ] 98

Please continue ...

11

IF YOU ARE CURRENTLY MARRIED OR LIVING AS MARRIED, PLEASE ANSWER Q2·24

IF YOU ARE NOT CURRENTLY MARRIED OR LIVING AS MARRIED, PLEASE GO TO Q2·25

A 2.24 What is your husband's/wife's/partner's religion, if any?

PLEASE TICK ONE BOX ONLY

	(✓)	
No religion		01
Christian – no denomination		02
Roman Catholic		03
Church of England/Anglican		04
Baptist		05
Methodist		06
Presbyterian/Church of Scotland		07
Free Presbyterian		21
Brethren		22
United Reform Church (URC) Congregational		23
Other Protestant (*PLEASE WRITE IN WHICH*) _____		27
Other Christian (*PLEASE WRITE IN WHICH*) _____		08
Hindu		09
Jewish		10
Islam/Muslim		11
Sikh		12
Buddhist		13
Other non-Christian (*PLEASE WRITE IN WHICH*) _____		14
Can't say		98

Please continue ...

12

EVERYONE PLEASE ANSWER REST OF QUESTIONNAIRE

A 2.25 When you were a child, how often did your mother attend religious services?

PLEASE TICK ONE BOX ONLY

	(✓)	
Never		01
Less than once a year		02
About once or twice a year		03
Several times a year		04
About once a month		05
2–3 times a month		06
Nearly every week		07
Every week		08
Several times a week		09
Never knew mother/does not apply		10
Can't say/can't remember		98

A 2.26 When you were a child, how often did your father attend religious services?

PLEASE TICK ONE BOX ONLY

	(✓)	
Never		01
Less than once a year		02
About once or twice a year		03
Several times a year		04
About once a month		05
2–3 times a month		06
Nearly every week		07
Every week		08
Several times a week		09
Never knew father/does not apply		10
Can't say/can't remember		98

13

A 2.27 And what about when you were around 11 or 12, how often did you attend religious services then?

PLEASE TICK ONE BOX ONLY

Never	01
Less than once a year	02
About once or twice a year	03
Several times a year	04
About once a month	05
2-3 times a month	06
Nearly every week	07
Every week	08
Several times a week	09
Can't say/can't remember	98

Now thinking about the present ...

A 2.28 About how often do you pray?

PLEASE TICK ONE BOX ONLY

Never	01
Less than once a year	02
About once or twice a year	03
Several times a year	04
About once a month	05
2-3 times a month	06
Nearly every week	07
Every week	08
Several times a week	09
Once a day	10
Several times a day	11

Please continue ...

14

A 2.29 How often do you take part in the activities or organisations of a church or place of worship, other than attending services?

PLEASE TICK ONE BOX ONLY

Never	01
Less than once a year	02
About once or twice a year	03
Several times a year	04
About once a month	05
2-3 times a month	06
Nearly every week	07
Every week	08
Several times a week	09

A 2.30 Would you describe yourself as ...

PLEASE TICK ONE BOX ONLY

Extremely religious	1
Very religious	2
Somewhat religious	3
Neither religious nor non-religious	4
Somewhat non-religious	5
Very non-religious	6
Extremely non-religious	7
Can't choose	8

A 2.31 In your opinion, should there be daily prayers in all state schools?

PLEASE TICK ONE BOX ONLY

Yes, definitely	1
Yes, probably	2
No, probably not	3
No, definitely not	4
Can't choose	8

15

A 2.32 How much do you agree or disagree with each of the following statements?

PLEASE TICK ONE BOX ON EACH LINE

	Strongly agree	Agree	Neither agree nor disagree	Disagree	Strongly disagree	Can't choose	OFFICE USE ONLY
a. Right and wrong should be based on God's laws	1	2	3	4	5	8	2012
b. Right and wrong should be decided by society	1	2	3	4	5	8	2013
c. Right and wrong should be a matter of personal conscience	1	2	3	4	5	8	2014

A 2.33 Some books or films offend people who have strong religious beliefs. Should books and films that attack religions be prohibited by law or should they be allowed?

PLEASE TICK ONE BOX ONLY

Definitely should be prohibited — 1
Probably should be prohibited — 2
Probably should be allowed — 3
Definitely should be allowed — 4
Can't choose — 8

2015

2016 SPARE

Please continue ...

16

A 2.34 Now thinking about the present. How often do you attend religious services?

PLEASE TICK ONE BOX

Never — 1
Less than once a year — 2
About once or twice a year — 3
Several times a year — 4
About once a month — 5
2-3 times a month — 6
Nearly every week — 7
Every week — 8
Several times a week — 9

2017

A 2.35 Now please think about something different. Please tick one box on each line below to show whether you think each statement is true or false.

PLEASE TICK ONE BOX ON EACH LINE

	Definitely true	Probably true	Probably not true	Definitely not true	Can't choose	OFFICE USE ONLY
a. Good luck charms sometimes do bring good luck	1	2	3	4	8	2018
b. Some fortune tellers really can foresee the future	1	2	3	4	8	2019
c. Some faith healers really do have God-given healing powers	1	2	3	4	8	2020
d. A person's star sign at birth, or horoscope, can affect the course of their future	1	2	3	4	8	2021

2022-2030 SPARE

Subject Index